SHADOWS OF CONSPIRACY

The Untold Story of the OKLAHOMA CITY BOMBING

KATHY SANDERS

A POST HILL PRESS BOOK
ISBN: 979-8-89565-096-7
ISBN (eBook): 979-8-89565-097-4

Shadows of Conspiracy:
The Untold Story of the Oklahoma City Bombing

Cover design by Conroy Accord

Post Hill Press
New York • Nashville
posthillpress.com

Published in the United States of America
1 2 3 4 5 6 7 8 9 10

To Tom,

For standing beside me through my heartbreaking loss and years of investigation. Your unwavering strength and quiet support have been my anchor, guiding me through the darkest days and giving me courage to keep seeking the truth. This journey would not have been possible without you.

With all my love and gratitude,
Kathy

AUTHOR'S NOTE

This book is based on my personal experiences during the Oklahoma City Bombing and nearly thirty years of subsequent research. While much of the content reflects actual events as I remember them, I have incorporated speculative and interpretive elements to provide a fuller narrative. These interpretations are based on available evidence and my own investigation, but they should not be considered as verified facts. Creative license has been taken to craft conversations and statements between certain parties that I believe occurred, though I was not present, nor a party to all conversations.

Wherever I have speculated on events or motives, these interpretations are my own and are not intended to assert absolute truth, nor to assert absolute fact. Readers are encouraged to consider this story as a combination of personal experience and creative interpretation of the facts and information as I encountered them on my journey.

While I believe strongly that Timothy McVeigh was not the sole individual involved in the bombing, this remains my personal view based on research and available evidence, not an established legal or historical fact.

PROLOGUE

I felt compelled to write this book following the release of two previous works: *After Oklahoma City*, which chronicled my unwavering quest for deeper insights into the bombing investigation, and *Now You See Me*, a heartfelt account of my emotional journey from overwhelming grief and anger to eventual forgiveness for those responsible for my grandsons' tragic deaths.

Throughout my nationwide book signings and presentations, one question echoed persistently from audiences: "Kathy, what do you believe is the untold truth behind the bombing?" While my prior books were anchored in factual evidence, this question compelled me to delve into my own interpretations through the realm of fiction.

The narrative within these pages is grounded in truth, meticulously pieced together from extensive interviews with key figures, 302 witness statements submitted to the FBI, and confidential government documents. My relentless pursuit of understanding led me into the intricate and mysterious heart of this story.

My journey took me to the Aryan Nations, where I met Pastor Richard Butler face-to-face. His reverence for Timothy McVeigh was palpable, portraying him as a martyr for their cause. His tears were genuine as he expressed remorse for the loss of my "Aryan" grandsons.

At Elohim City, I was greeted by armed men and escorted into their church, where Reverend Robert Millar delivered a sermon detailing the raid on the CSA Compound in 1985, offering a chilling glimpse into their world.

Carol Howe, an ATF informant, shared alarming warnings about individuals plotting to target buildings for destruction during our three meetings. Her insights were eerily prescient.

In Junction City, Kansas, I interviewed Eldon Elliott, the man who rented the bomb truck to McVeigh. He refuted claims of mistaken identity between Todd Bunting and John Doe 2, asserting his absence from work on the day Bunting rented the vehicle.

At the Dreamland Motel, I gathered testimonies from various individuals, including the owner, her son, the maid who serviced McVeigh's room, a guest, and even the Chinese food delivery man. They all reported sightings of unidentified men frequenting McVeigh's room, casting doubt on the FBI's findings.

My correspondence with Pete Langan, known as "Commander Pedro" in the menacing Aryan Republican Army recruitment video, shed light on the Midwest Bank Robbers' involvement, further deepening the enigma.

In Kingman, Arizona, I met Lori Fortier at the Dam Bar. While her husband served a decade in prison, she evaded jail time through a plea bargain. They now reside in witness protection, prompting me to question who, precisely, is being shielded and from whom.

The sealing of security camera tapes from the Murrah Building by Judge Matsch remains a contentious issue. Transparency should prevail if McVeigh acted alone. Despite Jessie Trentadue's persistent efforts, a court order, and claims of their loss, these tapes remain elusive.

Lastly, the discovery of an unidentified leg at the bombing site raises unsettling questions. DNA testing was delayed for over a decade, with no efforts made to match it against existing databases.

As you contemplate these revelations, I leave you with the same haunting questions that have consumed me: Who orchestrated this devastating act? And what secrets remain buried beneath the rubble of the Oklahoma City bombing?

The Oklahoma City bombing was a harrowing milestone, marking the first significant act of domestic terrorism on American soil. As I embarked on my investigative journey, I often found myself telling others that a time would come when mentioning the loss of my grandchildren in the bombing would prompt the question, "Which bombing?"

Fueled by this profound sense of duty, I spent two years collaborating with Blowback Productions on *An American Bombing—The Road to April 19th*, a documentary now available on HBO. This project aimed to illuminate the complexities surrounding this tragic event and its enduring impact on our nation.

Our country stands at a critical crossroads, grappling with insurmountable challenges. While political debates may dominate our public discourse, the core of our nation's struggles transcends mere politics. The root of our challenges lies deep within the spiritual and moral fabric of our society.

Furthermore, the violence must stop. As Timothy McVeigh infamously stated, it was "168 to one." This tragic reality underscores the urgent need for unity, understanding, and a collective commitment to peace. Only by confronting the darkness of our past and present can we hope to build a brighter, more harmonious future for all.

In this pivotal moment, it is imperative that we rekindle and uphold the foundational principles that have long guided our nation—principles anchored in faith, morality, and decency. By embracing these enduring values, we can aspire to heal, unite, and fortify the essence of our beloved country.

PART ONE

Hell in the Heartland

1

LETTING GO OF MCVEIGH

June 11, 2001
Six years, one month, and twenty-three days after the bombing

In the six years between judgment and execution, I ate, breathed, and dreamed Timothy James McVeigh. I retraced his steps and slept in his motel room. I shook hands with his father and imagined what he would tell me.

Then at seven o'clock, on the morning of the eleventh day of June, 2001, the executioner rolls him into the death chamber.

I would have paid for the privilege of strapping Timothy James McVeigh into the electric chair and throwing the switch. No one, however, offered me the opportunity; justice didn't need my assistance. I have to be satisfied just watching, as the federal government's executioner slips the IV lines into the arms of Timothy James McVeigh.

It is too easy for Timothy McVeigh. What he deserves is a firing squad, a hanging, the guillotine—something that he can see coming. Something that will make him really shake, tremble, urinate in his pants. Something to make him scream before his lights go out. Something terrifying, like the electric chair.

Timothy McVeigh never once apologized. He never faked it or pretended that he was sorry. He never named names—

just basked in the glare of publicity, proud to hold the title of "Lone Bomber."

But Timothy McVeigh isn't the only one who should be stoking Lucifer's fires for these murders. There are plenty of others who should be shoveling coal alongside him. Tim McVeigh and Terry Nichols did not act alone when they killed and maimed hundreds of innocent victims at the Alfred P. Murrah Building. These two men are the only ones the federal government chose to catch, accuse, put on trial, and convict. Timothy James McVeigh was the only one they put on the train out of town. Many conspired, mapped, and packed the truck with fertilizer, but Tim McVeigh is the only one who will pay with his eye for an eye. To be exact, he will pay for those three hundred thirty-six eyes with his two. That is one hundred sixty-eight per eye; he is getting off cheap. When he does pay, they will make the transaction quick. Timothy McVeigh will slip away in luxury, sent off with state-prescribed, Supreme-Court-approved, recommended-by-nine-out-of-ten-executioners, permanent-sleep-inducing drugs. We should all launch into eternity in such comfort and be informed of the time and date we will die.

As I watch Tim McVeigh on the executioner's table, his backside is down, his arms strapped to the table, a camera above him for closed-circuit television. The federal government's executioner's assistant gently slips the IV needles into his arms. Only one set of arms! Timothy McVeigh is the only one paying for this murderous crime.

The IV tube in McVeigh's arm runs through a port in the wall where, on the other side, doctors are inspecting the three drugs in three separate syringes, which when combined will kill him. The person who pushes the plunger will never see what happens. I wish Glenn had lived to see this: He would stand here in front of McVeigh and slam the poison cocktail into the arm himself.

Timothy McVeigh's life ends painlessly and quickly. He takes a deep breath; his eyes stare up at us. He lies dead on the gurney before me with two pints of mint ice cream souring in his belly.

Meanwhile, 168 men, women, and children sleep in their graves, having suffered unmercifully all alone, scared, and with a painful death when it came. Crushed by debris, slowly suffocating under the rubble, all alone and terrified in their last seconds of life, bleeding out in excruciating pain. Six hundred and eighty more suffer from injuries, many left maimed for life. Where is their justice?

To the end, McVeigh tries to convince us that he is a hero, giving his life for the cause, a martyr protecting and willing to lay down his life for his friends. On the giant closed-circuit screen, I gaze upon his lifeless body, his steel-cold eyes frozen upon us. I am curious: Are there more McVeighs among us? If so, is anyone safe?

I'm no psychologist, but I now wonder why McVeigh didn't kill himself before giving himself up. Was it because he was willing to give his life later for a slice of fame, the fame that he so craved all his life but was unable to obtain?

After being stopped ninety minutes after the bombing for having no license plate, Timothy McVeigh simply steps out of that eighteen-year-old Mercury Marquis and walks halfway to the trooper's car before the officer even asks him to get out of the car. He gives up his gun and tells Trooper Charlie Hanger he is carrying a knife on his belt. He doesn't pull the .45 from the shoulder holster under his jacket. He doesn't wait for

Trooper Hangar to show his face in his car window. He could have stuck his gun to the trooper's forehead and fired a Black Talon slug between the trooper's eyes. He could have emptied the clip, except for one bullet. The bullet that he should have saved for himself.

Instead of going down in a blaze of glory, McVeigh surrenders peacefully and allows Hangar to drive him to Perry, blue lights blazing, and is left at the Noble County jail. Soon he will be a true celebrity, one of the most infamous of all time. Lee Harvey Oswald, eat your heart out.

When Timothy McVeigh turned his head toward the witness gallery, I stared through the windows of his black soul. In the fifteen minutes between the lethal injection and his eternity, I felt nothing, my heart as dead as he was.

As for me, no closure, no relief, no sadness, no happiness, nothing at all. My belief about his destination brought no closure, because it brought nothing back. The one hundred sixty-eight he sent on ahead of him, including the two boys that were my breath and light—those innocents were—are—still out of reach.

2

THE DAY BEGINS

April 19, 1995, 8:45 a.m.
Seventeen minutes before the bomb explodes

DON BROWNING

Sergeant Don Browning is filling his gas tank at the Oklahoma City Police's substation, eight miles north of downtown Oklahoma City. The deputy sheriff is fueling up for another day of patrol in the northeast corner of Oklahoma County. A lone white puff of a cloud floats on the north horizon. Channel Nine has nailed the forecast for April 19: cool temperature, clear skies in the morning, rain in the afternoon.

The petrol gurgles inside the tank as Don Browning leans back against the rear of the Crown Victoria next to the pump handle. He smooths his thick, black mustache with his finger, then chuckles as he recalls the previous late-afternoon conversation with his five-year-old neighbor, Mikey....

"My papa told me that's a caterpillar under your nose," Mikey said to Don.

"Your papa is right," he replied, as Mikey's papa followed them into Don's front yard.

"How long have you had a caterpillar?" Mikey asked.

"How old are you?" Don asked in return.

"Five years old."

"Isn't that something? I've had this caterpillar since I was five years old," Don replied, winking at Mike senior, who preferred the nickname Don gave him—John Wayne.

"Where'd you get him?" Mikey asked.

"He crawled onto my lip one day while I was taking a nap."

Mikey looked concerned. "Will he come off?"

"If you pull him."

"Can I pull him?"

Browning squatted so that he was face-to-face with the little boy. "Sure."

Mikey reached toward the walrus mustache, but before he can latch on, Don growled and yelled, "Boo!" clamping vise-grip hands on each side of Mikey's belly. The boy squealed, laughed, and wiggled free. He hid behind John Wayne's legs.

"How long *have* you had your mustache?" Mike senior asked.

"Since Vietnam…my wife's never seen me without it," Don Browning answered.

KATHY WILBURN—8:50 A.M.

I am sitting at my IRS desk, talking to Toni Gable by telephone.

"Edye and the boys will be moving out," I'm telling her. "I guess it's time for them to leave."

Edye is my second child and only daughter. She and her sons, Chase and Colton, have lived with my husband Glenn and me for nearly two years since her divorce. Edye was ready to move out, but she didn't warn us. She had found a house two blocks away and had broken the news to us the previous evening.

"Mom, I know you don't want to hear this," she had said as I pulled a heavy stainless-steel skillet from a cabinet, "but we can't live with you forever. I bought a house, Mom. I wasn't really sick today; I was closing on the loan."

I couldn't say anything.

"You'll like the house, Mom, and it's only two blocks over."

I banged the skillet on the countertop. Then, getting a grip, I knelt to talk to my grandsons, the babies.

"You'll still have your room at my house," I managed. Words that I, not the boys, needed to hear.

"Can I take my Easter bunny to school tomorrow, Nana?" Chase asked.

"We're not going to school tomorrow, sweetie," Edye said. "Remember, we're going to the park after Mama finishes her errands."

"Am I the last one to hear your news?" I asked.

"No, Mom," Edye replied.

"What did you tell your boss?"

"I told Alyson I was having eye trouble…told her I couldn't see myself coming in to work," she quipped.

"Real funny.… I'll take the boys if you want," I said.

"No, I promised to take them to the park."

The telephone interrupted us, and Edye answered.

"Hey Julie."

I could hear the voice on the other end. "You're coming to work tomorrow, right, Edye?"

"I'm still sick," Edye said, forcing a cough. "Don't think I can make it."

"You *have* to come to work tomorrow—it's the April birthdays," Julie told her. "Your cake's in my oven."

Julie won. "Okay," Edye laughed, "I can't miss my own party. I'll be there."

"Can I take my Easter bunny?" Chase said, standing up on the stool by the bar. He lost his balance and fell to the floor. He lay still for a minute then giggled, rolled onto his side, and stood. "My Easter bunny gets to go to school."

At 9:00 a.m. on April 19, 1995, the Wednesday after Easter, and two minutes before the bomb went off, Chase was lining up with the older children in the daycare center, grabbing the safety rope and preparing for the walk downtown to the library, while Colton was sitting down for breakfast with the other two-year-olds.

At 9:01 a.m., one minute before the bomb went off, I was saying to Toni Gable over the phone:

"Edye and the boys will be moving out. I guess it's time for them to leave."

3

FIRST BLOOD

August 18, 1969
Twenty-five years, eight months,
and one day before the bombing

DON BROWNING

Army Sergeant Don Browning first smells death in the blood at a Viet Cong graveyard at twelve hundred hours, Vietnam time.

Browning's platoon had missed the wide-open cemetery on the map, and without warning, they were in the wide open in a storm of lead. The VC has penned him, and what is left of his platoon, in the graveyard almost ten thousand miles from home. Red-hot AK-47 rounds with his name engraved on each one were kicking up dirt around him.

Sergeant Browning falls forward into the dirt; his green steel helmet has fallen off and rolled into a creek, his head is now unprotected. His forehead grazes the corner of a headstone as he drops, and he puts his right hand to the cut and pulls back bloody fingers. As his finger crosses over his face, he smells the blood, which has a metallic odor like a handful of pennies.

He pulls his arms tight to his side and begins to grind his way into the dirt. He tries to move forward to check on his men; it feels like he is digging his own grave. He is a cadaver in waiting.

Three feet to Browning's right, Private Harvey Yancy howls and falls backwards. He lies directly in Browning's line of sight as blood bubbles and oozes through the green camouflage pants on his left thigh. Sergeant Browning smells the pennies.

Another scream to his left. The boy from Breaux Bridge, whom they call Breaux, falls face down and lands perpendicular across the back of Browning's knees. Browning bends sideways at the waist, twisting his head and turning his face to see. The left side of Breaux's face is flat in the dirt, his back arching over Browning's legs, his helmet is shoved back on his head, with the chin strap tight against the GI's neck. Breaux's right eye gapes in surprise. "Breaux!" Browning shouts. He reaches back with his left hand, tries to slide his index finger underneath the chin strap, and pulls back bloody fingers, and then blood gushes from the clean bore at the base of Breaux's neck between the clavicles. As he draws his hand back, he runs his blood-slathered fingers beneath his nose. The smell is not pennies, the smell is pungent. Tears pour from his eyes as he gags, then gives up the Army-issued military rations that were curdling in his belly. He smelled the death in Breaux's blood before death claimed him.

Bursts of dirt erupt in all directions, blocking Don Browning's vision. The odor of Breaux's blood is suffocating. Time slows, and the bullet whistles, the screams, and the jabber threats from the Viet Cong fade to silence. What he is certain of would be the end in slow motion.

His tears and sweat run down his face and cut streams in the graveyard dirt. He inhales, opens his mouth, and gulps air. He blows it out, closes his mouth, and sucks the air in through his nose, trying to clear the smell of Breaux's blood. In the instant before he loses consciousness, he knows with certainty that he is smelling Breaux's death in that blood. Before he passes out, he knows they will soon be dragging Breaux to the chopper for his last trip home. The blood tells him that....

Browning awakes slowly, with the weight of Breaux heavy on his legs. The light, which had dimmed as consciousness drained from him, has returned. The shooting has stopped.

"Yancey!" he shouts. "You still there?"

Yancey replies, "Not for long and Breaux didn't make it."

"Hell," Browning says as he pulls his legs from beneath Breaux. "Let's move out," he orders.

Browning walks among the dying and the dead; he knows the difference because the blood tells him which is which.

The smell of death would be with him for life....

For the twenty-five years since, it has always been the same. When he comes up on a wreck, when he walks into a crime scene, he knows what he is about to find. If blood has spilled, he knows.

At 9:30 a.m. on April 19, 1995, while driving at fifty-two miles per hour, Police Sergeant Don Browning knew.

⌘

The gas gurgles as it nears the top of the patrol car's tank. A wisp of a breeze whisks the woodsy smell of gasoline past Browning's woolly caterpillar. He smiles to himself, recalling his exchange with little Mikey.

As he stops and starts the lever to pump the final half gallon of gas into the tank, the concrete beneath his feet vibrates and a distinct, audible rumble startles the deputy sheriff..

"What the hell was that, Sarge?" a mechanic hollers from across the parking lot.

"I don't know, but whatever it is, it's bad, really bad." He removes the nozzle, twists the gas cap back on, and hangs the handle back on the pump.

Then the radio dispatcher's voice crackles out of Don Browning's patrol car speakers: "All units, 10-39, 200 North West Fifth Street, 10-39, 200 North West Fifth Street."

Don Browning sucks hard on the half-smoked Marlboro between his lips, then tosses the butt onto the concrete. He jumps into his car, jerks the shifter into drive, and yells to his German shepherd sidekick in the back seat, "Hang on, Gunny!"

Blue lights pulsating, sirens wailing, Browning and a hundred other police officers from points all over Oklahoma County push their gas pedals flat to the floorboards and zip through stop lights, ignoring speed limits and pedestrian crossings, speeding as fast as the streets and nerves allow.

Browning instinctively notes his speed at fifty-two miles per hour when he smells death for the first time that day.

A mile away from the Alfred P. Murrah Building, the smell comes in waves. He catches a whiff of the ammonia. He smells burning gasoline, burning rubber, scorched auto body paint, and cordite. Over it all, he smells burnt flesh and the odor of blood, the tainted spilled blood that reeks of death.

The stench swirls in through the four open windows of his patrol car, as he powers through stop lights and swerves like Mario Andretti around drivers who are obeying the speed limit. In the back seat, Gunny lays back his ears and sniffs. He stabs at the air with his snout and barks twice, whimpers, then whines.

4

HELL DESCENDS

April 19, 1995, 9:02 a.m.

KATHY WILBURN

The moment I say to Toni, "I guess it's time for them to leave," the windows in the IRS building rattle and all the floors shake. I lay down the receiver without a word to Toni and run to the north-facing window that overlooks downtown. Nothing different, but the phones on my floor are ringing all at once.

As I am laying down the receiver, Edye is on the third floor, drawing a deep breath to blow out the twenty-three candles on her cake. A moment later, I rush up the stairwell and burst into the third-floor office, while wisps of birthday candle smoke spiral toward the ceiling. Before I can speak, a woman with a phone receiver in her hand announces in a panic, "Somebody blew up the bank!"

"Edye! Let's go see!" I say, grabbing my daughter by the arm.

She and I run down the three flights of stairs. We step out the front doors of the IRS lobby and onto the street and notice flecks of white and specks of silver raining from the sky to the north. I looked north at the bank, which appears intact. Then I look at the Murrah.

My mouth gapes involuntarily as I cover it with my hand.

"My God! Edye! The babies!" Pointing toward the federal building, I cry, "It's the Murrah Building!"

Three-year-old Chase and two-year-old Colton are in the daycare there.

We start running toward the Murrah while large sheets of glass are falling around us. Glass mist stings our faces, hangs in our hair, cutting our sinuses and throats. I chase the white blur of Edye's Nikes as we close the distance to the Murrah Building. I don't know what we are running into and wonder if we are running to our own deaths.

The next day, I would wish that we had.

DON BROWNING

Sergeant Don Browning is running fifty-two miles per hour when the odor of death rushes into his patrol car. He immediately pushes the needle to sixty-three on the twenty-five mile per hour streets of downtown Oklahoma City.

From five blocks away, Browning sees the smoke, and as he closes the distance, the smell of death thickens. "They can't all be dead," he says aloud. "We'll get the ones who aren't." He rides hell-for-leather because the wounded can't wait forever.

The call had sounded over the police frequencies at 9:05 a.m., three minutes after the bomb went off. Sergeant Don Browning is nineteen minutes away from the Alfred P. Murrah Building, but he drives it in nine.

Up ahead two police cars sit sideways, blocking Fifth Street. An Oklahoma City police officer waves him off and he cuts the wheel, shoving the brake pedal to the floorboard. He tightens his fingers at ten and two on the Crown Vic's steering wheel, bouncing over the curb and onto the sidewalk. Browning stops the patrol car halfway onto the concrete, the front chrome inches from an aluminum streetlight pole while the rear half of the car remains in the street.

His wristwatch shows 9:14 when he jumps the curb, jams the shifter into park, twists the key to kill the engine, yanks the door handle with his left hand, and shoves the door open with his shoulder.

Then he sees the entire front of the Murrah is gone.

"Holy crap!" he shouts at the police officer who was waving him off and now is standing next to him. "What is it?"

The cop shrugs. "Some kind of explosion, just happened."

Browning sees his brown hat lying upside down in the passenger seat but leaves it. "Gunny!" He jerks on the back-door handle, and his German shepherd partner is all paws on the street before the door fully opens. The dog's leather leash drags the concrete behind him as he instinctively scampers in the direction of the chaos. Browning steps on the leash. "Gunny! Heel!" he shouts. Gunny obeys, flinching and whining and straining at the leather leash. Browning bends, grabs the loop, then lifts his foot. "Gunny! Go!"

Sergeant Don Browning and Gunny run south against a northbound tide of humanity, dirty faces with bloody clothes, some screaming, many crying. The smell of death draws close.

In five minutes, they have dashed as far as they can go. Browning stops twenty feet from the mountain of debris. It's an ascending pile of crushed steel filing cabinets, smashed Southwestern Bell telephones, powdered mortar, pretzeled rebar, sun-glittered shards of safety windows, shredded vacation requests and sick-leave approvals, toddlers' shoes, credit-union account balances, and chunks of concrete hanging by threads of steel, dangling as if they would fall.

The chunks are as big as the Volkswagen Beetle that exploded while they were ten feet in front of Browning as he and Gunny peer into the gates of hell.

KATHY WILBURN

I see the first blood two blocks from the Murrah Building as Edye and I run toward the smoke in downtown Oklahoma City.

Hundreds of people are running toward us, running south, screaming, rivulets of blood streaking their faces, tracing over their eyes to their chins. We pass a thin, pale man in a pin-striped white shirt, standing with his eyes fixed south. His blue tie hangs straight down from his Adam's apple, a wide band of blood saturating the front of his shirt from the knot in his tie to his belt. A single red thread runs from the bridge of his nose to the tip, perfectly splitting his face.

I chase the blur of Edye's white Nike soles, confused about the vision of hell I was running into. "Off the sidewalk!" someone yells. "Get in the street! *In the street!*" We jump off the curb. An Oklahoma City fire truck drives up from behind, the driver steering with cautious urgency, siren wailing and horn blowing.

"Wait! Wait! Edye! Wait!" I cry as Edye reaches the south face of the Murrah. The burning in my lungs and throat intensifies as smoke rises from the building. The south side appears intact until we move closer, then we see the windows are blown out. Mini blinds hang out the windows.

As we stand and look, I drape my right arm across Edye's shoulders and our chests heave. I close my eyes and pray that this might all be a bad dream and I will wake up. Another explosion brings me back. Edye is bent, her hands on her knees, face to the ground, sides heaving like a bellow—a posture I will see yet again, when we bury Edye's sons.

"My babies!" Edye cries. "They must…"

But I can't hear her clearly for the cars exploding in the parking lot and catching fire. We resume our run, heading to the other side of the building, and stop.

The north face of the building is obliterated. The explosion has decimated the front of the building. Wires and cables hang from the nine floors like veins and muscles, tendons and ligaments. There is nothing left but a pancake pile of steel and rubble at the foot of the Murrah.

Nothing is left of the second floor, where twenty minutes earlier Chase and Colton had been waiting to walk to the library.

Edye falls in slow motion to her knees, her eyes never leaving the front of the building. "My babies!" she screams. "My babies!"

I kneel beside her, wrap my arm around her neck, and cradle her head to the curve of my neck.

"It will be all right," I tell her. "It has to be all right."

"It will not be all right!" Edye screams, and she jerks her head free from my embrace. "Momma, it's never going to be all right. Look at that building!"

She stands suddenly, and I stand, too, and we run toward the building, through thick smoke and dust. We stumble over chunks of debris, twisted aluminum window frames, glass, and concrete powder, which crunch beneath our feet. We are going to climb this rockslide, never thinking that we are climbing over those who had perished.

A man steps into our path, his arms extended, his palms open toward us. I push his arms away and Edye runs around him. The man catches me from behind, a hand on each of my shoulders. He pulls me backwards.

"My grandsons are in there!"

"Ma'am, we'll get 'em," he yells into my ear.

"Stop it. Leave me alone!" I shout and shake loose of his grip, then trip and fall to my right knee. He catches me before I can stand, bear hugs me, helps me to my feet, and steers me away from the building. Out of the corner of my eye, I see Edye prone in the debris; a woman is bending next to her, a hand on her back.

An Oklahoma City police sergeant appears from behind me. A black German shepherd strains at the leash in the deputy's hand.

"What gives?" asks the deputy, stepping between me and the man who is trying to stop me.

"ATF, pal," he says.

"Oklahoma City police," says the other man, pointing to his badge. A brown patch on the other side of his shirt bore the name *Sgt. Browning.*

"Our jurisdiction," says the ATF agent.

"We'll figure that out later," Sergeant Browning says. "You got a problem with this woman?"

"She was trying to enter the building; she needs to leave the area. No one is allowed in here," the ATF agent says. "No civilians, no police officers, I'm following orders. We've got to get all these people out of here. There's been a bomb."

"How do you know it wasn't a gas leak?"

The ATF agent doesn't answer and says, "Get this woman out of here."

Sergeant Browning takes the ATF agent by the forearm and removes the agent's hand from my arm. "You okay, ma'am?" he asks.

"No. I am not. My grandbabies are in there," I tell him.

When Sergeant Browning reunites me with my daughter, we hug like we had never hugged before, Edye's arms encircling my neck, my arms tight around her waist. Her tears run down my right shoulder and my back.

I didn't take my eyes off the rubble. I scream and Edye breaks from our embrace. We watch in horror as a football-size chunk of concrete falls from above and strikes a blonde woman wearing a white sweatshirt and blue jeans. The woman wobbles, then blood streaks through her hair. "Somebody help her!" I scream. "Somebody!"

A man standing next to the injured woman steadies her with a hand and points with his other, as if to direct her away from the building. The woman shakes her head and steps toward the spot where she had been digging. She bends as if to continue, then collapses face down onto the rubble. Several others quickly kneel beside her. A woman from the group runs toward the phalanx of first responders that stand ready with gurneys and stretchers, gauze, and body bags. The woman speaks to a man who is standing on the leading edge of the group and points toward the fallen rescuer. Two medics grab a stretcher and run.

Sergeant Browning gives Gunny the command, "Stay!" He steps through the debris to help lift the injured rescuer onto the stretcher. He bends and holds her head as four others lift her from the ground and place her on the stretcher. He eases her head to the canvas. When he removes his hands from the back of her head, they are stained with her blood.

He walks back to his German shepherd and rubs between the dog's ears.

The woman is talking, but he smells it in her blood and knows she wouldn't be talking for long.

I ask Browning, "Is she okay?"

Browning doesn't answer my question; all he says is, "They said her name is Rebecca. She's a nurse." Then he asks me my name. I tell him. He hands me his card and asks, "How old are your boys? Do you remember what they were wearing today?"

Edye had dressed Colton that morning and answers, "Colton has on little green shorts and a white T-shirt."

I chime in, "Chase is wearing plaid shorts and a yellow tank top." Then I remember his shoes. "And blue sandals," I say. "Chase was wearing his blue sandals."

5

WE'VE GOT A VICTIM

10:34 a.m.
Ninety-two minutes after the bomb explodes

DON BROWNING

Sergeant Don Browning leaves Edye and me at the sidewalk and returns to join a hundred other deputies, firefighters, paramedics, and nurses on the south side of the Murrah. Several people are standing around a black man who is lying on his back, facing the building. He apparently landed there when the explosion blew him through a third-floor window. Nothing is left of his legs below the knees.

"He's gone," Browning says as he and a fellow officer, Lieutenant Busby, watch from five feet away. "It's over for him. I can smell it."

Lieutenant Busby looks at Browning without speaking.

Static from his Motorola radio draws Busby's attention. The voice from the radio is deep. "Go to the elevator shaft. They've got a victim."

"*We've got a victim,*" Lieutenant Busby says to Browning, "C'mon."

Sergeant Browning, Lieutenant Busby, and seven others step toward a gash in the wall that opens into the elevator shaft. Captain Mark Comstock, chief of Oklahoma County sheriff's patrol, is leading the line. He is the first to step off into the dark chasm.

"Careful guys!" Comstock hollers. "Water!"

The water is ankle deep in the underground parking garage and rising. Clear water is pouring into the garage from the freshwater pipes that supply the sinks, water fountains, and toilets in the Murrah. Rank gray water pours in from twisted and burst pipes that drain wastewater from the Murrah's sinks, water fountains, and toilets. The clear and the rank blend into a putrid brown.

"Water!" Comstock yells back at the eight men behind him.

The men, some in daisy-yellow bunker Goodyear rubber boots, three in street shoes, are silent. Their breath comes in staccato bursts, the way breath always comes as you approach danger, so loud in your ears you're sure your breathing will give you away. With each sloshing stride through the rising tide of nasty water, their hearts quicken, their stomachs sicken, and their blood pressure rises. They tingle at the back of their necks and behind their knees. The water sloshes quietly around their legs with the silence agonizing. They listen, hoping to hear the voices of the living as they step over the dead. That eerie silence will haunt their dreams. It is a soundtrack of sadness. This dirge of death will forever play in an endless loop as they try to sleep.

A sticky liquid drips from above and plinks quietly into the rising water. It spots their shirts and drips onto their cheeks.

"Guys, it's bad, really bad!" Comstock says. "Blood!"

Browning can smell it.

At 10:37 a.m., three minutes in, Bradford Holderfield, second in line, stops and holds his arm straight in the air. "On the right," he says.

The lead rescuer, Comstock, points his three-cell Maglite to the east. The cone of light catches the back of a head, and Comstock follows the shape of a body.

"It's a woman," he says. "She's trapped."

Five or six more flashlights illuminate the woman who is lying at a slant, her head slightly higher than her feet. A cement beam pinned her, and the beam lies across her right leg between her ankle and knee.

"Helllp meee! Pleeeease!" she cries. "Where are my babies?"

Bradford Holderfield reaches over her shoulder with his left arm and grasps the woman's left hand, which lies palm down on her abdomen; he can't see her face.

"My name's Brad," he says. "What's yours?"

The woman tilts her head as far back as she can in a futile effort to see him. "Don't let me die."

"We're going to get you out."

"Have you seen my children?" she asks.

"No, ma'am. Can you tell me your name?"

"What happened?" she asks.

"We're not sure, an explosion."

"My name is Daina. Daina Bradley."

"Okay, Daina. Take a deep breath through your nose as deep as you can and hold it. Now blow out your mouth. Can you tell me what today is?"

Daina Bradley's lips quiver and her arms shake. "I'm freezing," she says. "Please help me."

"Who is president of the United States?"

"President Clinton."

"What is today's date?"

"April 19."

"Where were you in the building?"

"I'm soooo cold."

"We'll get you out," says Holderfield, whose hand has never left hers since he grabbed it. He wants to say, "I promise," but he didn't. "Where were you when the building blew up?"

"Social Security office."

"What floor is that on?"

"First floor. Did you find my children?"

"We haven't, but we're looking."

The water rises three inches in the hour after they find Daina Bradley. While they wait, a Salvation Army officer shows up unannounced with two blankets. The Army officer talked her way past an FBI agent, climbed in through the gash in the wall, and waded bare-calved through the water, with her long skirt skimming the surface. Holderfield rolls up one blanket and wedges it beneath Daina's neck, spreading the other one over her upper body and arms and tucking it beneath her chin.

At 12:03, fifteen minutes after the blankets arrive, an Oklahoma City police officer trudges in, followed by two men in surgical scrubs. "These doctors volunteered," the officer says.

Holderfield steps away from Daina Bradley, turns his back to her. "I'm no doctor," he whispers to the doctors, "but I think we're losing her."

DAVID TUGGLE

David Tuggle is one of the doctors.

Ninety minutes earlier, he was leaning in over a five-year-old patient, his scalpel in his right hand, which hovered over the patch of orange belly the surgical nurse scrubbed with antiseptic. Dr. Tuggle pulled at the boy's skin as if to smooth it, then held it tight. A second before he cut a hand touched his left arm. Dr. Tuggle pulled the scalpel back from the boy's abdomen.

"Emergency management has put out a call for surgeons," said Dr. Jerry Breland, chief of pediatric surgery at Children's Hospital. "Something downtown at the federal building."

"Right now?"

"It's urgent. I'll take this—just a hernia, right?"

"I can do this, forty-five minutes."

"They need people now; they're talking dozens of victims."

"Children?" Dr. Tuggle asked, his eyebrows arching above his mask.

"Don't know. Broward called and asked that we send you."

"Where?"

"Saint Joseph's Cathedral downtown. He says you'd know when you see it."

Dr. Tuggle returned the scalpel to the surgical tray and rolled the cart away from the table. "Hernia's right on top," he said. "Two-inch incision at the most."

Dr. Breland clasped the back of Dr. Tuggle's left bicep. "Grab the bag phone off my desk. Thank you."

By 12:13 p.m., less than ten minutes later, Dr. Tuggle is striding out of the sliding double glass doors of the emergency room, the bag phone in his left hand. He steps out of the path of Andrew Sullivan, the orthopedic surgeon, who is arriving.

"You hear?" Dr. Tuggle asks. "Something downtown, they're calling for surgeons."

Dr. Sullivan, the smaller of the two, turns and follows. Dr. Tuggle hails a police officer who is walking toward his patrol car.

"Officer, we're doctors. We're supposed to go downtown, but we don't know why."

"Explosion," the officer says. "The Murrah Building. I just came from there and you won't believe your eyes. I escorted the first ambulance with three kids."

"Bad?"

"One kid was missing the top of his skull. Boy or girl, couldn't tell."

"Can you take us?"

"Climb in."

The doctors tumble through the driver's side door and into the back seat. The officer slams it behind them, then jumps behind the wheel of the car, which he had left running. The officer switches on the lights and siren as he jerks the car into drive in one motion.

"Car 72—dispatch. Car 72—dispatch. Over."

"This is dispatch. Over."

"Dispatch, this is Officer Jim Pickens. En route to Murrah with two doctors. Over."

The siren of a west-bound ambulance obliterates the radio conversation momentarily. Officer Pickens turns his head toward the back seat. His mouth is moving but the doctors can't hear his words. Dr. Sullivan cups his right hand behind his ear.

"Dispatcher wants to know what kind of doctors you are."

"Surgeons," Dr. Sullivan says.

"Dispatch, Officer Pickens. Surgeons. Over."

"Car 72. Go to south courtyard."

By 12:28 p.m., fifteen minutes after leaving Children's Hospital, the doctors are in the bowels of the creaking building and talking to Daina Bradley.

"I'm a doctor," Dr. Tuggle tells her, his mouth at her left ear, his arm on her shoulder. "We're going to figure out how to get you out. We'll give you something for the pain, I have a bottle of water I'm going to put it to your mouth."

Daina Bradley sips at the water. Most of it dribbles out down her cheeks and chin. While Dr. Tuggle holds the bottle to her lips, Andy Sullivan studies the situation. The concrete beam clearly has broken her left shin.

"Put someone on this beam, lay a hand on it," Dr. Tuggle says to Bradford Holderfield. "I want to know every time it vibrates. This building could fall some more."

"I'll monitor," Holderfield says.

"Can we lift the beam off her leg?" Dr. Tuggle asks.

"Not without equipment, sir."

"What about a cement cutter?"

"Too risky. Can't control it down here."

"We've got only one option, David," Dr. Sullivan says to Tuggle.

Dr. Tuggle nods, casting his eyes from Dr. Sullivan's to the water rising up his legs. "Stay with her, Andy. I'll back out of here and call for the equipment."

"Morphine, too," Dr. Sullivan says. "We got to get her some relief...."

A male voice over a bullhorn interrupts him. "All personnel clear the building," the man says. "All personnel must clear the building immediately."

"The hell, you say," Dr. Sullivan shouts in the direction of the voice.

"David, hurry. Help me slide in here. I'm going to tie off her leg."

The space between Daina's body and the collapsed building is less than two feet. There is no room on either side of her body. The only way for Sullivan to reach her knee is to go in headfirst and belly-to-belly with Daina.

"Give me some light," he says. "A lot of light."

He creeps to the gap, bends slightly at the waist, puts his mouth to Daina's left ear, and whispers. "I am going to slide in on top of you," he says. "Holler if I'm hurting you. I am going to tie a cord around your leg to keep it from bleeding."

Sullivan bends lower. He inserts his arms into the gap and then, his face to the left, he eases in over her left shoulder. He holds the ligature in his right hand. David Tuggle picks up Sullivan's left leg, and Holderfield picks up the right. Each man places Sullivan's foot against his stomach. Sullivan locks his knees, and they push him into the coffin-size crevice. Sullivan's face moves across Daina's chest and then her belly, and when he is at her waist, he can reach her knee.

"Stop!"

From this position, with his belly flat against hers, Sullivan cannot see the bottom half of Daina's leg behind the beam. The pressure of his belly against hers complicates their efforts to breathe. He raises his head to better see her knee and smacks his crown against the cement above him.

In the gauzy light behind him, the assistant fire chief emerges from the smoke and dust like an apparition, with a bullhorn in his left hand. His voice is rising from his measured command on the bullhorn to banshee screams.

"Did you not hear my order?" he shrieks without amplification. "Everyone out!"

The assistant chief is standing next to Don Browning. Browning has his hands placed on Dr. Tuggle's lower back.

The chief puts his mouth next to Sergeant Browning's ear and screams. "Out! There's another bomb."

Browning turns to the man with the bullhorn. "Another bomb? Who says? How do we know it was a bomb? Dr. Tuggle, the FBI is ordering us out."

"Tell them we haven't pulled the woman out of the rocks."

"Did. Deaf ears."

"She'll die," Dr. Tuggle says. Then he lowers his head so that he can talk to Sullivan. "David? Is her leg tied off?"

"Yes."

"We'll pull you out."

"I'm staying until I'm done. Bring me the tools."

"We're going to pull you out." Dr. Tuggle grabs one foot, and Sergeant Browning the other, and they pull. When Dr. Sullivan's head is on Daina Bradley's chest, he kicks his feet free.

"Stop! Stop, damn you! Stop!" Dr. Sullivan's face is at her chin. "Daina, I've got to leave for a few minutes."

"Don't leave me!" she screams. "Do not leave me. I'll die. Where are my children?"

"Daina! Breathe," Dr. Sullivan says. "Deep, steady."

David Tuggle regains his hold on Sullivan's feet and is pulling. "Give me a second!" Sullivan yells. "This woman's in distress!"

Dr. Tuggle loses his grip of Sullivan's feet and places a palm on either side of Daina's head above her ears and presses firmly starting at the top, rubs down, and repeats. Her entire body shivers from shock and the chilly water that is rising slowly beneath her. She quiets enough to hear Dr. Sullivan.

"Daina. I'm going for some surgical instruments. I'm going to have to amputate your leg."

She screams again. "No! No! No! No!"

"Daina, listen, we have to remove your left leg to save your life."

"Just pull me out of here!" she screams.

"We can't."

Daina's screams diminish and she breathes deeply. Then the sobs take her, her body shakes. Dr. Sullivan twists his neck so that he can see Daina's face. Dr. Tuggle continues to stroke Daina's hair.

"Let me die then. I don't want to be a cripple."

"I can't do that, your children would rather have you with one leg than not at all," Sullivan says.

She pauses. "Please don't leave me," Daina cries.

"I have to go just long enough to get my tools and pain killers," he says.

"How long will you be gone?"

"Not long," he says as he begins to push against the concrete beam with his hands until he is clear of Daina and the concrete crypt. "I will be back."

He turns and finds Tuggle. "What the hell is going on? We don't leave people to die."

"FBI says there's another bomb. We're the last three out," he says, indicating Sergeant Browning, who is standing three feet away.

How could they know it was a bomb?

6

THE SEARCH CONTINUES

April 19, 1995, 12:28 p.m.
Three hours and twenty-seven minutes after the bomb explodes

Daina Bradley's rescuers reluctantly crawl out of the Alfred Murrah into a crowd of other first responders clad in blue and khaki and medical scrubs. The sun, just past high noon, glints off badges of silver and gold.

Mist from fire hoses rains on them. It collects into drops on the rims of their helmets and the bills of their hats. The mist hangs in the air like fog. The slight breeze mixes the smoke, the soot, and the silt of concrete and sheetrock into the mist and seems to turn the air into mud. Many cough and spit. A few heave and throw up.

Some in the south courtyard stand apart from the crowd. Some sit cross-legged on the concrete, others in the grass. Others lean on the chain-link fence that surrounds the America's Kids playground. They watch in horror as medics line the dead children in the shadow of swings and an aluminum slide and cover them the best they can. The playground that once rang with the sounds of children's laughter has become the children's morgue.

Sergeant Browning stands outside the Murrah Building, near the gash in the wall where he and the others entered and exited the Murrah. He leans against an aluminum extension ladder that stands at an angle against the south wall. He hangs the heel of his left boot over the bottom rung. Holderfield sits on the concrete six feet in front of him. Busby lies next to Holderfield, eyes closed. Dr. Sullivan is traveling to his clinic in the front seat of a squad car.

Dr. Tuggle stands to Sergeant Browning's right, the latter talking to a woman in an FBI raid jacket, who has introduced herself as Special Agent Feldman.

"Sergeant, could I ask you to move into the courtyard?" she asks.

"When are we going back in?"

"Soon as we get the all clear."

"Who authorized us to abandon those people in there?"

"Nobody authorized you to leave anybody. The FBI ordered you to leave for your own safety." Agent Feldman steps back.

Browning waits a second, then moves away from the ladder. He and Tuggle cut their way through the first responders and walk to the edge of the courtyard. Browning turns back toward the building and sees that the agent who had earlier ordered him into the courtyard was lifting the ladder and moving it to the west. He leans it against the wall. Then the Agent Feldman female FBI agent walks to the ladder.

"Now why would they be climbing a ladder that's leaning against the one wall with no doors or windows?" Browning says.

He and Tuggle watch Agent Feldman climb and then stop near the top of the ladder, about twenty feet off the ground. They realize she is going after the tape in the security camera positioned up there. Agent Feldman holds tight to the ladder rail with her right hand. With her left, she snaps the camera out of the bracket and drops it into a canvas bag that dangles at her waist.

"Good move, securing the tape," Browning says to Tuggle. "They've got cameras on all the doors. The film will show everything that happened."

Agent Feldman pulls a small tool from her back pants pocket and snips the wire that carries the images from the camera to the transmitter, which beams it to the nerve center in the federal Protective Services building across town. Then the agent reaches into the canvas bag and pulls out a small cordless drill. One by one, she backs out the four bolts that hold the camera bracket to the wall. She removes the bracket and puts it into the bag. She looks at an agent at the foot of the ladder and gives him the thumbs up. He walks to the wall and tugs at the wire, which falls to the ground. He picks it up and coils it.

"You'd never know a camera was ever there," Browning says. "I've watched a lot of technicians grab film from security cameras. I've never seen them take the whole camera."

The two agents move the ladder to the other side of the doors, and in less than ten minutes, the second camera is gone.

"Let's go to the front," Browning says to the doctor. "I want to see about those cameras."

They head around the building.

"Holy shit!" Doctor Tuggle says when he sees the north side. "How did anyone survive?"

They push through the crowd of restless rescuers chomping to get back to their work.

"There's a camera," Browning says. The section of wall where this camera is attached is leaning in at a forty-five-degree angle. "That camera's going to show everything," he continues. "It was pointed right at the front door. I'm guessing that'll be the best film they've got."

7

THE SAVE

April 19, 1995, 1:37 p.m.
Four hours and thirty-six minutes after the bomb explodes

While Browning waits for the all clear, he walks to his squad car to get a pack of smokes and to check on Gunny. "Hey ol' boy," he says as he opens the door for Gunny to jump down. The dog sits at Browning's feet, face up, his eyes on the water bottle in Browning's right hand. Browning unscrews the cap and tilts the bottle a couple of inches from Gunny's mouth so that a wobbly stream dribbles in.

"Something's not right," Browning says to Gunny. "Why is the FBI holding up rescue efforts to take down cameras? They're working some other angle, and they aren't letting us in on the secret."

Then a voice rises above the others on the scanner. "All units. All clear. All units that were inside the building cleared to return. Repeat. All units cleared to return to the building."

"That's me, Gunny."

Entering the building, Browning asks a couple of firefighters, "What's the word?"

"Bomb squad tells us it was a false alarm," the younger one replies. "Just a training device used by the ATF. Wasn't real."

"Is it official that it was a bomb that blew up the place?"

"That's the word," the older firefighter says. "Middle Eastern terrorists. They're putting out a five-state 'be on the lookout.'"

When Browning finds Tuggle and Sullivan, the trio joins the surge of others who are shoving their way to the building to resume the search. Browning steps back through the gash in the wall and into the elevator shaft. He reaches up and grips Dr. Sullivan's leather surgical kit by the handle, then assists Sullivan as he step down into the water, which is a foot deep at the bottom of the shaft. He reaches up once more to assist Dr. Tuggle.

"I'll go first," Browning says, and splashes ahead of the doctors through the water. "False alarm!" he mutters under his breath. "Unbelievable. If she's dead…"

Six firefighters trail Browning and the doctors. Holderfield and Comstock, the firefighters who led them to Daina Bradley, bring up the rear. Eleven rescuers are returning for Daina Bradley.

The beam of Browning's flashlight flashes on a small object afloat. "Oh God," he says. "A kid's shoe?" He stops, turns, and hands the surgical kit to Sullivan. Then he picks up the small shoe and stuffs it into his left rear pants pocket.

Daina's moans echo off the fallen beams and the walls and the water, coming at them from five directions. "My children, my children. Don't let me die. Don't let me die. Oh Jesus! Please save us."

Tuggle rushes ahead so that he is at Daina's head moments before the others. He palms her head as he had earlier. He strokes her hair. "Body temp's falling," he says. "She's shivering like a leaf. Officer Comstock. Come over here to my right. I need you to help give her the amnesiac."

"Why no anesthesia, doc?" Holderfield asks.

"You don't put someone to sleep if you aren't sure of their injuries. We can't stop her from hurting, but we can fix it so she won't remember it."

"You're going to feel a stick in your neck," Tuggle warns Daina, and he immediately recognizes the absurdity of warning a woman who is dying beneath a hundred tons of rubble to brace for a needle. She doesn't flinch.

Tuggle turns and moves to the side so that Sullivan can work. Sullivan slides in over Daina, his hands first, and then his chest against hers. Holderfield and Jeff Wesley, a lieutenant in the police department, each take one of Sullivan's feet and place them flat against their abdomens. Sullivan pushes against their stomachs, pushes himself across Daina and deeper into the cavity. Two officers each take a position on either side of Daina and point the beams from their police-issue Rayovac spotlights at her leg.

The tourniquet above Daina's knee has loosened in the hour since Sullivan had tied it. He unties it, pulls it tight, and reties it. He slides his hand around her surprisingly knobby knee, which feels like all bone. Then he finds the spot. He centers the eighteen-inch blade of his amputation knife at the spot. He stares at the teeth on the blade, then at the smooth brown skin that covers the boney knee.

Guide my hands, Sullivan prays silently.

Before he makes the first cut, he realizes the knife is too long. He can't go full stroke, so he lays the blade in the rubble and pulls one of the disposable scalpels from the top pocket of his scrubs. Water splashes into his rubber boots, and a chill sets in, the way it did before dawn in the duck blind when water splashed into his waders.

Sullivan draws in a deep breath, and at the same moment slices Daina's leg. She jumps and screams. Her left knee comes up and smacks him in the jaw. Blood runs down her leg and over his hands and arms. He shifts his weight onto the top of her leg. With his left hand, as best he can, he pins her calf to the rubble beneath her leg. He saws for two minutes, until the scalpel will cut no more. He tosses it and pulls a second one from his pocket. The blade cuts through the tendon. He tosses it.

"Done!" he shouts. "Pull me out."

In less than a minute, Sullivan is on his feet in the water looking back in. "Pull her out quick," he says. "The tourniquet's not holding, and she'll bleed out."

Comstock and Tuggle each put a hand under an armpit. "One. Two. Gently. Three," Comstock says. As they pull, Daina screams.

"She's not coming," Tuggle says.

"She's not coming!" Sullivan swears. "Load her up with cephalosporin," he says. "This water is nasty and it's already in the wound."

He dives back in and ties a second tourniquet above the first one. He lies on her left leg. Comstock holds Daina's head in both heads. "Cutting!" Sullivan shouts before he cuts, and she screams. Instead of throwing her head forward, she bows up her spine and throws Sullivan farther to her left. "Cutting!" The third scalpel dulls so he tosses it. He pulls out the last one and cuts. Daina screams without breathing.

God! Knock her out! Sullivan pleads. *Don't let her feel anything.* He yells, without words, a scream that burns his vocal cords. Then he weeps. His shoulders flex up and down with the sobs as he cuts. With all the force left in his right hand, he saws and rips. The dulling blade snags on the top of the shin. The plastic handle snaps.

"Pull me out!"

Holderfield and Comstock pull.

"Pull her!"

Holderfield and Tuggle pull and Daina screams.

Sullivan's eyes widen and he swears. "I'll make the surgical blade work," he says and goes back in on top of Daina. When he is in place, he can't see the eighteen-inch blade. "Light!" he shouts and points to his left. Tuggle scans the debris to his left, and the light glints off the stainless-steel blade far to the left.

But Daina, twisting and writhing in agony, kicks the blade out of reach.

Sullivan rolls to his right. A hard object in his back pocket presses against his buttock, and he remembers. He rolls back flat on his belly, reaches into his back pocket, and retrieves the folding knife his father-in-law had made and gave him when he finished med school. His name is engraved on the blade. He keeps it razor-sharp with a whetstone. He opens the knife, repositions himself on Daina's left leg.

"Light." Sullivan looks. "Shine it up her leg." Then he sees the problem: one strap of tendon that is tying Daina to the Murrah. "There, keep the light there." He closes his eyes. *Please, God, save her.* He opens his eyes and slides the blade beneath the tendon. The light angles in so that for a second, he can read his name etched on the blade.

God! Please…

He pulls up on the blade and saws, and Daina screams, and the steel cuts through.

"Pull me out!" the doctor shouts.

When he is on his feet, he hands the knife to Holderfield, bloody and flecked with Daina's tissue. Then he and Tuggle put their hands under her shoulders, and this time she comes. When they pull Daina's body free, her left leg drops, dead weight and rag-doll-like—along the top of the debris pile, bumping with the rise and fall of concrete, phones, and shredded paper that two hours earlier had been confidential ATF documents.

Her right leg, with nothing below the knee, dangles, and bleeds. They all see it at the same time, Daina too—the empty space where, five minutes earlier, her leg had been.

Daina's scream fills the cavernous hole beneath the Murrah.

8

THE SANDAL

April 19, 1995, 8:17 p.m.
Eleven hours and forty-one minutes after the bombing

After they pull Daina Bradley from the Murrah Building, Sergeant Don Browning goes back into the underground parking. For four more hours, he joins a hundred others poking into the darkness of the Murrah parking lot with beams of light. At a briefing before he leaves, the FBI confirms what the reporters have been saying all day: Someone has bombed the Murrah Building.

The sun is setting fast when Browning returns to his house.

He pulls off his boots at the garage door and walks inside. He stops in the laundry room and removes his soaked socks, stinking with the putrid brown water from the parking lot. Then he peels off his khaki Oklahoma City police pants, and as his pants slide off, a lump travels down the back of his left thigh. Stepping out of the pants he stands straight shaking out the legs. He reaches into the left rear pocket and finds the child's shoe he had picked up in the rubble near Daina Bradley.

He walks into the den and sets the shoe on the fireplace mantle. He turns on the television, then sits in the rocking chair near the fireplace, wearing only boxers, with Gunny flopping at his feet. After a moment he stands again, walks to the fireplace, and picks up the shoe. He shows it to Gunny.

"Wish we could've found the little boy who belongs to this shoe."

The shoe is wet. He holds his right palm out flat and sets the shoe on it, then raises it to eye level, moving it away from his face until every detail is sharply focused.

How did this shoe separate from the foot of its owner? Less than twelve hours before, it had been snug on a little boy's foot, a living little boy who now probably wasn't. He rubs the shoe beneath his nose and smells death. He looks closer, and there it is, on the inside sole—a smear of darkened blood. He knows the young owner of the shoe is dead.

The shoe leads his thoughts to the pile of shoes in the Holocaust Museum in Washington, which mesmerized him for hours when he was there with his wife years ago. The shoes were piled behind plate glass, a diorama of mass murder that had stopped him cold. Hundreds of shoes piled high and strewn about. Hundreds of shoes that had protected human feet on their way to the showers. Fifty years before, these shoes had covered the feet of tens of thousands of humans who had died merciless deaths. He had stood at the glass and counted shoes: boots, slippers, dress shoes, and a pink pair with a buckle just above a tiny patent-leather pink bow. All shoes belonging to Jewish feet.

Now here was this small shoe from Oklahoma City that only hours before had covered the foot of a child who had died simultaneously with a hundred other people. The hate was the same, only the shoes had changed. He will save the shoe, and someday he will add it to a pile of other Oklahoma City shoes. Someday he will stare at the pile of shoes and count. But for now, he will leave it on the mantle.

He leans over and rubs Gunny's head between the ears. The images on the television screen catch his eye. The face of Kelly Ogle, Channel Nine's star anchor, morphs into the face of President Clinton, who is standing at the lectern in the White House briefing room. Browning walks to the TV, which is inside a six-foot-tall armoire, and turns up the volume. The digital clock in the top right corner of the screen shows 7:31 p.m. when the president's voice comes through the speaker.

"...an act of cowardice, and it was evil," the president says. "Let there be no room for doubt. We will find the people who did this. When we do, justice will be swift, certain, and severe. These people are killers, and they must be treated like killers."

Browning increases the volume, then walks into the bedroom. He sits on the edge of the bed and lies back without slipping under the sheets. Gunny leaps from the side and over him. He chases his tail for a moment, softening his spot in the mattress, and lies down.

Browning hears Janet Reno's voice coming from the TV, and her words piss him off.

"The FBI and the law enforcement community will pursue every lead and use every possible resource to bring the people responsible to justice," she drones as he tries to drift into unconsciousness. "The FBI has established a command post in Oklahoma City, and it is in twenty-four-hour contact, four special FBI agents in charge have been dispatched, four evidence response teams, and five of the best FBI agents experienced in this type of investigation are arriving from Boston, Chicago, Miami, San Francisco, and Los Angeles. The rapid-start team will be entering data as it is collected. Superb cooperation from local authorities, ATF, US Army, Secret

Service, Tulsa, and FEMA. We cannot tell how long this will take but we will find the perpetrators, and we will bring them to justice."

As he walks back into the living room the scene on the television screen returns to coverage from the Murrah. Reporters stick microphones into the faces of anyone within striking distance. Two faces emerge from the crowd, two female faces framed with fiery red hair, and he instantly recognizes one woman's face and voice as that of the woman he had rescued from the ATF agent that morning...Kathy something.

"We just want our babies back," Kathy tells the reporter. As she talks, Browning recalls that she had told him about one of her grandsons. *Chase was wearing plaid shorts, a yellow tank top. and blue sandals.*

He sits upright on his bed. Then stands, then walks back to the mantle above the fireplace, where he had left the child's shoe that he had stuffed in his back pants pocket that morning.

Sergeant Don Browning picks it up again and stares at it by the last light of April 19, 1995.

It is a blue sandal.

9

EASTER SUNDAY

April 16, 1995
Three days (4,320 minutes) before the bombing

Chase is keenly aware of his "big brother" responsibility to Colton: He refers to him as "Little Buddy." There is no jealousy between the boys; they are truly buddies. Sometimes on the weekends, when Edye goes out, I let the boys snuggle together under the blankets on their mother's bed and watch cartoons wearing their mother's baggy T-shirts, something they loved to do. Their giggles would filter down the hall and into the night.

When Colton got sleepy, Chase would pat him lovingly on the back and whisper, "It's okay, Little Buddy." Then he would stroke Colton's head until he drifted off to sleep. Once Colton was asleep, Chase would run down the hall into my room and say, "Nana, come looky." We'd tiptoe ever so quietly into their mommy's room. Chase would put his finger to his lips: "Shhh! Don't wake him up." Bursting with pride, Chase would ask, "Isn't he precious? Isn't he sweet?" Grabbing his big fluffy pillow, Chase would place it right next to his little brother and nuzzle up as close as humanly possible. Stretching his little arm over his brother's back, Chase would continue to watch cartoons until he too fell fast asleep. Everything the boys did, they did together.

Easter Sunday is no different. They sleepily open their eyes at the sound of their mother's voice. "Get up boys, look what the Easter bunny brought," she calls, pointing to the two large Easter baskets sitting on their dresser. Each basket has a giant bow—one is brilliant purple, the other is royal blue.

As their eyes focus on the baskets, they spring from the bed. "Looky, Colty, looky, the Easter Bunny came!" Chase exclaims, clapping his hands. Colton's face beams as he hops out of bed. Colton does not talk much; he is only two. He does not need to because his older brother Chase, who will be four in three weeks, does all the talking for him.

Colton reaches for the basket with the purple bow, grabs the handle with both hands and says, "My batket."

"Okay Little Buddy, you can have that one," Chase answers.

They begin pulling out handfuls of plastic pink Easter grass, tossing it everywhere. It is like just last Christmas morning when they discovered Santa had come. There are electrifying squeals with each new find.

Glenn comes inside from the backyard, where he has been preparing for the Easter egg hunt that would soon take place. He hears their squeals and walks down the hall into their room.

"What do you boys have there?"

The boys pick up the baskets and begin to show Papa the Easter eggs they had colored the day before with their mom and me, along with chocolate bunnies, marshmallow peeps, plastic eggs filled with Easter candy, coins, and Colton's personal favorite, Hershey Kisses. There is a stuffed bunny in each basket that looks like he has been taken from the pages of Beatrice Potter's book *Peter Rabbit.*

Chase announces, "Looky, Crayolas! I'm a good drawer. I'm going to color you a picture," he says to his mother. No longer satisfied to just look at the tempting sweets, Chase asks, "Can we eat some candy? Pwease?"

Edye teases, "No, you guys don't like candy."

"Yes we do!" he says gruffly, folding his arms and turning to me standing in the doorway.

Papa chimes in, "Give me that candy," and reaches for a chocolate bunny.

"Nana, Papa's being mean. He's taking our candy."

"Papa, put that back, the Easter bunny brought that for the boys," Nana scolds.

Glenn puts the candy back in the basket and pretends to cry. The boys know he is teasing and begin to giggle.

Edye steps into the boys' walk-in closet and shuts the door behind her. Chase gets down on the floor and listens underneath the door. Colton bends down beside him with his elbows on the floor and his bottom is sticking up in the air.

"What's she doing in there, Nana?"

"I don't know," I answer.

Then out jumps Edye with a loud "Boo!" It startles the boys, and they jump up giggling and run from the room. Edye and I start laughing. Edye calls out, "Come back, there's more!"

Chase tiptoes back to the door and sticks his head inside the room, Colton is close behind. "What you got?"

"Easter clothes," Edye tells him.

"Bunny suits?" Chase asks.

"No, some dress-up clothes, so you'll look nice today!"

"Just plain clothes?" he says, disappointed.

"Yes, would you like to see them?"

"Nope, not weally." He thinks about it for a few seconds and says, "We'll look at the clothes if we can eat some candy."

"Okay grab them, grab a couple of pieces, but not too much because we're going to be eating dinner soon."

Unimpressed with the new clothes, they stood eating their candy. Edye pulls a sack down from the top of the closet, and again their interest is piqued.

"What's that?" Chase asks.

"Something special," she says as she pulls two boxes from the bag.

"Is that shoes?" Chase sighs.

"Not just any shoes. These are magic shoes," Edye says.

"Magic? What they do?" Chase asks.

"They light up when you run," she tells him. That is all it takes, and the boys are all in.

"We wanna try them on, we wanna try them on," Chase says, jumping in place.

"Okay, then sit down." Edye helps Chase put on his shoes first. You can see the growing excitement in Colton's face as he watches. He isn't sure what is going on, but he knows if his brother likes it, he will, too.

Chase bounds from the floor. "Looky Colton, looky!" he says as he runs circles around the room. His shoes are flashing red lights. The faster he runs, the faster the lights blink.

Colton stands in awe at such a mystical sight. He grabs his shoes and brings them to me. "My shoes," he says, wanting me to put them on his feet. I pull a pair of Lion King socks from the dresser drawer. I put them on Colton, and he squeezes his chubby feet into his new shoes. Colton begins to run. There is no stopping the boys now.

"Looky how fast we can run, Papa," Chase says as they zoom through the house with their flashing red shoes.

When they stop to catch their breath, Chase looks at his mother with his big blue eyes and says, "Mommy, these shoes are way cool!"

"Good, I'm glad you like them."

I respond, "What do you say?"

"Thank you, Mommy."

Edye bends down and gives both boys a kiss on the top of their heads. I return to the kitchen. All the family is coming for lunch.

The first guests to arrive are my brother Bobby and his daughters, Jennifer and Lisa, who are about Edye's age. The cousins are close. Edye, Glenn, and I go out the front door to greet Bobby and the girls. As we are hugging, my son Danny pulls in behind Uncle Bobby's Mustang convertible. We're so excited to see them. The last time we saw our granddaughter Caitlin, who would turn two in three weeks, was at Colton's second birthday a month ago.

Chase comes out the front door into the yard where the family is standing. Edye tells him to go find his brother. Chase goes inside and when he comes back, he shrugs his shoulders and says, "Mommy, I can't find him."

"What do you mean you can't find him? Did you look in your room?"

"Yep."

"Did you look in the back yard?"

"Yep, I'm a big boy, I know how to look."

Edye goes back inside and starts calling Colton's name. When there's no answer, she comes to the door and announces, "Mom. I can't find Colton."

The adults join in the search. Glenn and I go through the house and into the backyard while my brother and his daughters go door-to-door, searching between the houses. Edye's running down the street calling Colton's name. The neighbors hear the calls and join the search. Colton's name echoes through the neighborhood.

Panic sets in and I suggest calling the police. Edye says, "Let's look through the house one more time, Mom, before we call." We go back into the house and methodically go through one room at a time, looking behind doors, drapes, furniture, and anyplace else a child could hide. When we get to the boys' room I get down on my knees and check under Colton's bed. No Colton.

"Mom, did you check the closet?"

"No, but I'm going to."

Before I can get up, Edye opens the closet door and calls Colton's name. Still no answer. Then she sees something—little fat toes sticking out from under the hanging clothes. She pulls the clothes back, and there sits Colton with his face covered. He takes his chocolate-covered fingers and pulls his Easter basket close to his chest.

"No. *My* canny," he whines, as he sticks his tongue out blowing air through his lips.

Relieved, Edye begins to laugh. Chase comes in the room and says, "Little Buddy, I thought a stranger got you." When I see Colton, I fall to my knees and hug him while fighting back tears.

"Why you cryin', Nana?" Chase asks.

"Because I love you boys so much. I don't ever want to lose you."

"Nana, you're silly. You can't lose us."

With the crisis averted, Glenn and I go back to the kitchen and resume the preparation of the meal. Glazed ham, deviled eggs, sweet potato soufflé, and "mean beans," which is the name given by Chase for green beans.

The adults eat at the formal table in the dining room and the children sit at a child-sized table in the kitchen. The grownups watch as Chase hovers over Caitlin and Colton. When Caitlin starts to sit in Colton's chair, Chase herds her to the other side of the table. "No, no, you can't sit there, that's my brother's seat. You sit here," he says, pointing to the chair next to him.

When the carrot cake is served, Chase asks in his sweetest childlike voice, "Mommy, can we have eyescream?" Caitlin and Colton squeal with excitement and grab their spoons, tapping them on the table, waiting to be served.

The children eat their dessert while Danny goes outside to hide their eggs in the backyard, which is terraced like an English tea garden. It has a pond with a Grecian statue in the middle. Water flows from the maiden's vase.

Danny hides the eggs among the rows of lovely flowers which are in full bloom, their stalks reaching to the heavens. With the eggs hidden Danny asks the children, "Who wants to hunt Easter eggs?"

Chase starts jumping up and down, waving his hands over his head. "I do, I do!" Colton and Caitlin mimic him. Easter baskets are handed out and the boys begin racing around the yard, their shoes flashing and Caitlin toddling close behind.

"I found one, I found one!" Chase shouts. "Come on, guys," he yells to Colton and Caitlin. They have trouble understanding and aren't finding many eggs, so Danny and Chase begin to help them.

The children run around the yard happily as they filling their baskets. With the baskets loaded, Chase begins to count his eggs: "One, two, three, seven, nine, fourteen…."

Bobby pulls a penny out of his pocket and asks, "Do you guys want to see some magic?" Chase, jumping excitedly once again, yelps, "I do, I do!"

Colton and Caitlin are interested but unsure about what is happening. When Bobby pulls a penny out of Caitlin's ear, all the children squeal and giggle.

"How you do that?" Chase asks quizzically.

"I can't tell you," Bobby responds and grins.

"Sure, you can, I'm a big boy," Chase insists.

"No, I can't, it's my secret."

"I'm not going to be your friend, then."

"That's okay, I'll be your friend," Uncle Bobby says and smiles.

"Nope, you can't be my friend anymore if you don't tell me."

10

AMERICA'S KIDS

April 19, 1995
122 minutes before the bombing

The day starts normally enough. A laser sunlight beam pierces the slightly open drapes, waking me like a soundless alarm. I hear songbirds and look at the clock beside the bed. It is 7:00 a.m. I recall a list of a dozen things I need to do. I hop from bed and slip into the flamingo-print robe Edye gave me for Christmas. The first and happiest thing on my list is waking my grandsons.

The boys' room is next to mine, and as I step inside, I'm surprised when I look at their twin beds. The beds that boast my garage-sale-find white sheets with black spots, which Chase calls "Dalmatian sheets," are empty. The blankets are thrown back and the boys aren't there.

I walk down the hallway toward Edye's room, where I find them. Sometime during the night both boys had climbed out of their own beds and sneaked down the long hallway to get into bed with their mother. I enter the room and start to sing:

"Good morning to you, good morning to you.

"We're all in our places,

"With sunshiny faces.

"What a nice way to start a new Wednesday!"

Chase giggles and pulls the covers over his head. "Turn off that light, Nana," he says gruffly. Colton squirms up next to his mom as Edye blinks, trying to wake up.

"Nope, it's time to get up, sleepy head," I tell him.

Glenn comes in and says, "Chaser, you and Butterbean need to get up, it's almost time for school."

Chase snaps to attention, sitting sleepily on his mother's king-size bed. Glenn helps him get dressed while Edye puts gel on his hair and begins to style it. Meanwhile I talk "Butterbean" into brushing his teeth, which is something he hates.

Glenn and I sometimes make a game out of getting ready. I wink at him and say, teasing: "You know, I've always wanted a couple of little girls. Let's change Chase and Colton's names to Shirley and Suzy. We'll buy them some little dresses, and they'll be really cute."

Chase is appalled. "I'm not going to be a dumb-head girl. I hate girls," he protests. "And I'm not going to wear a stupid old dress. I'm a boy and I'm cool!"

Gleeful, teasing chatter fills the room as they finish getting ready. Then they all move to the big ranch-style kitchen. They eat breakfast at home every morning and then again at the childcare center. They are good eaters, especially Colton, which is why we call him Butterbean.

Colton sits at the kiddie table drinking a glass of milk, while Chase sits at the breakfast bar on a high stool. Glenn buckles Chase's loose blue sandals, then picks him up and hugs him. "Paw Paw loves you, Chaser," he says and kisses him on top of the head.

As Edye, the boys and I arrive at the Murrah Building around 8:00 a.m., we pull under the overhang into the loading zone. Colton is asleep in the backseat holding his Easter bunny. Edye begins to wake Colton while I lift Chase from his car seat and sit him on the sidewalk. A car pulls in behind us. It's Chase's friend Christopher Nguyen. When Chase sees him, he begins to jump up and down and clap his hands. Mr. Nguyen gets his son out of the car and Chase runs to open the door of the Murrah Building.

Mr. Nguyen, a Vietnam War refugee, tells me, "Your grandson is exceptional. You do a good job with him, and he has impeccable manners."

"Thank you," I reply as Chase and Christopher bounce up the stairs, holding hands.

Inside the daycare, Denice Bell holds her two-year-old daughter, Danielle, who is clinging to her mommy. She begins to cry when Denise, who is stooped over, tries to unwrap her daughter's hands from around her neck.

Colton sees his crying friend and puts his hand on her back and begins to pat it. Danielle lifts her head and sees Colton; her face brightens and her tears stop.

At 8:30 a.m., Jannie Coverdale enters the daycare with her two grandsons. When Chase sees Aaron, he gives him a big hug. She takes her younger grandson, Elijah, to Colton's classroom. She passes the babies whose beds are lined up in front of the windows. Baylee Almon, who just turned one yesterday, is standing in her crib, reaching for the light beams that are flickering across her face like dancing butterflies. Miss Brenda, who lovingly looks over the babies, sits rocking six-month-old Antonio Cooper as he holds his bottle.

At 8:45 a.m., the two-year-olds are preparing for breakfast in Ms. Wanda's classroom. They can't read, but recognize their own name tags on the tiny table. Colton sits with his friends, Dominique, Elijah, and Anthony, whose mother Dana is the director of the daycare as well as his teacher. Danielle, Jaci Rae, and Rebecca are sitting across from the boys, and they are all smiling and happy. Colton is looking at the girls like he can understand every word they are jabbering.

Ms. Wanda walks in with a pan full of tater tots and begins to serve the children. When she comes to Elijah, he quickly tosses one of his tots across the table and all the children begin to laugh. Ms. Wanda does not laugh, and Elijah quickly retrieves the tot as the little ones go silent.

At 9:00 a.m., the Murrah Building stands proudly on its firm foundation in the beauty of early spring, its windows clean, its hallways freshly waxed, its landscaping displaying careful maintenance. Inside, the occupants go about the government's business. The Social Security office on the main floor is full of people waiting for appointments. In the Credit Union, tellers are conducting business with customers standing in line. Military families and service men and women are in the US Army and US Marine Corps recruitment offices. Other agencies in the building include the Veterans Administrations, the General Services Accounting Office, the Department of Health and Human Services, the Department of Transportation, as well as high-risks offices of the Department of Defense, the US Customs Service, the Bureau of Alcohol, Tobacco, and Firearms, the Drug Enforcement Administration, and the Secret Service.

Finally, there are the precious little ones; twenty-three children who are being looked after in the America's Kids Day Care Center.

Altogether, there are 640 souls doing what they do in the heart of America, at what most would consider to be the safest place in the heart of America.

The four-year-olds are preparing to go to the library for their weekly visit. They are lined up by the front door, waiting for Christopher, who has gone to the bathroom. The boys are waving the rope used to keep them in single file as they walk to the library, which is a little too much for the girls, who back away.

"Miss Dana, will the lady at the book place read *Peter Rabbit* to us today?" asks Aaron.

"I don't know what story she is going to read this morning, but we can sure ask if that is the story that everyone wants," Dana replies.

All the hands go up and the kids say, "Yes! Yes! Yes!"

The clock on the wall reads 9:01 a.m.

"Where is Christopher?" asks Chase, obviously annoyed that Christopher is taking so long.

"Let's give him one more minute; then, if he doesn't come back, I will let you go see about him," Dana says.

In the nursery, background music plays softly, and the babies are mostly asleep. Down the hall, the two-year-olds play with blocks, dolls, and toy trucks. A few, including Colton, are looking at picture books.

The adult employees in the soon-to-be-famous building might be thinking about a promotion or summer vacation or going to a movie later while going about their daily tasks. The children, still in complete innocence, with limitless futures not yet dreamed about, live solely in the present, enjoying every moment of their little lives.

On the second floor, a truck can be heard swinging into the area below where the children were dropped off one hour ago. The sleeping babies stir; no one else reacts. Miss Dana says to Chase, "Okay Chase, it's been a minute. Go get Christo—"

The clock clicks to 9:02.

The power of evil descends on the building like a giant mallet, deafening the ears and ravaging the bodies of its occupants. Scores of voices go silent immediately, while hundreds scream and moan as they lay dying and maimed in the crumbling edifice.

Of the twenty-three children in the daycare, nineteen are dead or soon will be. Colton will be found under the rubble with only his small hand reaching out of the debris in hopeless desperation. Chase receives a mortal wound from a large chunk of concrete smashing the back of his head. Ms. Wanda will be found lifeless, holding one of the motionless babies in her motionless arms. Miss Dana will breathe her last breath lying in the huge crater next to Anthony, the boy she loved so much.

Innocence in the heartland is lost forever.

PART TWO

Questions in the Ruins

11

PREPARING FOR THE DINNER

May 11, 1995
Twenty-two days after the bombing

Nineteen children and three teachers died in America's Kids daycare that day. The nineteen were eight percent of Tim McVeigh's victims.

I memorized the names of the seventeen children who died with Chase and Colton. I spoke to them in my mind, over and over. And I spoke to them aloud. *The Oklahoman* published photographs of all the victims, arranged alphabetically. I cut out the photos of America's kids and taped them to a single sheet of paper and hung their pictures on my refrigerator.

In the days after the murders, I alternated between numb, when I wouldn't have noticed if Timothy McVeigh walked right up to me and stabbed me in both eyes, and grief that broke my bones and wrung crannies deep inside me, forcing sounds that weren't human.

Eventually, I knew I'd have to sleep, and I would have to eat. I slept the way I used to snack—a bite here, a bite there. Now I slept, a bit here, a bit there, and rarely after dark. Usually, I wasn't aware when I did sleep. I remained conscious, it seemed, even in my deepest sleep. More than once, I would wake up in a different room than the one I had fallen to sleep in.

Shortly after the memorial service, as I looked at the pictures of the children hanging on my refrigerator, I hit upon the idea of supper at my house. I sat down at my computer and composed an invitation to all the families who had lost children in the bombing, and every family accepted.

I have set the date for May 14, a Sunday, three weeks after the bombing. On the Friday before, I dress for a trip to the grocery. Glenn would smoke a ham. I would stir up potato salad and bake peach cobbler. I walk into the garage, step into my Jeep, back out, and drive, fighting back tears on the way.

The sadness that has consumed me since the babies died is growing. As I think about all the children that perished alongside Chase and Colton, I want to scream. I often feel this way, but this time is even worse. I should have gone back inside my house, but did not.

In the Safeway parking lot, I step out of the Jeep and walk across the parking lot, yanking a cart from the line in front of the store. The electronic door slides open before me, and I walk through, aware that the boys aren't riding in the cart. My cart is empty—like the car seats, like their beds. They should be in this cart.

At the meat counter, I pick through the hams to find one big enough to feed a crowd. Then I struggle to pick it up and drop it into the buggy. I turn down the breakfast aisle. Cap'n Crunch, Fruit Loops, Cocoa Puffs, and I want to shut my eyes. I cannot bear looking at the cereals I fed my grandsons. I still cannot believe I will never see them again. They had been my life, and now they are gone. At the produce section, I grab a plastic sack and fill it with peaches for the cobbler, stuffing the bag, which tears. Peaches tumble to the floor, rolling in all directions.

An elderly man bends to pick up the fruit as a flood of tears fall from my eyes. I kick a peach and leave the cart in the middle of the aisle as I head for the door. I hear a woman's voice, "Ma'am, Ma'am, Ma'am? Ma'am!" A hand grips the back of my left arm between my shoulder and elbow. "Ma'am, are you okay?" the woman asks as she hands me a tissue from her purse.

"No, I am not," I answer.

The manager of the store who knows me, and knew my grandsons, offered us the break room.

I choke back tears as I try to explain to the kind woman that I lost my grandsons in the bombing. Before I knew it, she was crying with me as I reminisced about my grandsons.

"The daycare was on the second floor of the Murrah Building. The cribs were always lined up next to the windows. The babies used to try to grab the sunlight. I didn't mind because the sunlight was good for them. The babies loved to watch the clouds, to watch the cars, to watch the people pass by. I used to watch them reach out for the rays of sunlight, they thought they could touch them, and make little shadows with their hands. I thought they were safe."

The kind woman held me as I cried uncontrollably while we sit in the grocery store break room.

"It's not your fault," she says as she tries to console me.

When my sobbing begins to let up, I tell her, "All the families who lost children are coming to my house for supper. I'm trying to buy the groceries." The woman hugs me, and we sit quietly. After a few minutes we pull ourselves together. "Honey, don't worry about the groceries. I have friends that will be happy to help me make this dinner happen."

12

THE FAMILIES ARRIVE

Sunday, May 14, 1995
Twenty-five days after the bombing

On the day that the survivors are coming for supper, I pull the copy of the *Oklahoman* in which the editors have printed the photograph of each child who died. I snip each picture from the page and glue each in the middle of a three-by-five index card. I punch two holes in the top edge of each card and string ribbon through the holes, pink or blue, to create a necklace to loop around the neck of each mother or grandmother as she arrives. Jannie Coverdale and I were the only grandmothers with two photographs on a card.

Helena Garrett is the first to arrive. When I open the door to her at 5:17 p.m., she is moaning as if she hadn't stopped since April 19. She falls into me, throws her arms around me and sobs. I hug her tightly for a few minutes, my arms around her waist, her arms around my neck. She gulps for air, and as she tries to speak the sobs intensify, and she resumes the moans that only God can understand.

"I didn't leave him, Kathy," she says between stuttered breaths, her chin resting on my right shoulder and her warm breath tickling my ear. "I didn't leave Colton. They laid him beside me, and I didn't leave him."

I pull my head back and look at her. "You saw Colton?"

She nods without lifting her head, and with each nod, her chin digs into the meat behind my collarbone. "I came early so I could tell you."

This news cut deep. She saw Colton after he died, and I didn't. When I had the chance, the funeral director told me I would regret looking. My regret is that I didn't.

"Tell me about it, Helena."

Helena cups her face in her hands and waits until Glenn is standing beside us. My arms are still around Helena's waist. "It's okay, sweetie, tell me."

"He was bleeding from the mouth," Helena says and stops. "His stomach, Kathy, my goodness, it looked like it had been busted open. I didn't leave him, Kathy. My Tevin was missing, but I didn't leave Colton. I stayed with him until they carried him away."

She buries her face in my shoulder again and shivers, then lifts her head and steps away. Glenn drags a padded chair over, and she sits down.

"Rebecca Denny was the first baby they brought out," she continues. "I was screaming, 'My baby's in there!' Then I saw Rebecca—she looked like she was dipped in blood, her eyes were open, and I screamed her name, she looked at me and I knew she was alive. That's when they brought out Colton, they laid him on the bench by my knees and the doctor said, 'There's nothing I could do.'

"There was this black glass everywhere, like it had snowed glass. Then they were laying the other babies in a line on the ground. I screamed at them to please don't lay our babies on the glass. This man came over with a big push broom and didn't say anything, just swept away the glass. Then this lady came, she put paper labels on the babies. That's when I realized our babies were dead…I didn't see Tevin until Monday. Said his head was busted, so I was only able to see my baby's feet and hands. I kissed his feet, and I kissed his legs. That's as high as they would let me see."

I walk to Helena and hang Tevin's card around her neck.

By 6:30, more than thirty people have gathered in our backyard, some standing in quiet conversation while others sit at folding tables borrowed from the Catholic church. The air is rich with the comforting aroma of smoke brisket and crispy fried chicken, while an array of homemade sides and desserts cover the tables. The women who prepared the meal not only delivered it with warm smiles but also stayed behind and served the grieving families, ensuring that every plate was full, and every need met. Later, as the evening winds down, they quietly clean up—one final act of kindness for grieving hearts.

Renee Cooper, who lost her son Antonio in the bombing, begins to tell us a disturbing story. "I'm so sorry about all the babies, but I've got to tell you what happened to me," she says.

As she begins to speak, we all grow quiet.

"I seen something no one else is mentioning. When I dropped off my son at daycare a few minutes before 9:00 a.m. on April 19, I seen the bomb squad downtown."

We can't believe what we are hearing. Glenn excuses himself and goes inside the house, gets from his desk the cassette recorder he uses for audits, and slips it into his pocket. With the recorder running, Glenn asks Renee to repeat her story.

"How do you know for sure it was the bomb squad?" Glenn asks.

"Because they had big blue letters on their jackets that said, 'Bomb Squad,'" Renee answers a bit indignantly and begins to wipe tears that are forming from the corners of her eyes.

Ernestine Looney, whose grandson, Dominique London, was killed, chimes in. "A friend of mine, who is a nurse at Mercy Hospital, told me she overheard an interview of a man whose wife had worked in the credit union and been injured. She said the husband told how he came immediately to the Murrah Building to look for his wife, and an ATF agent informed him that ATF agents were not in the building."

The night ends early. As soon as our guests leave, Glenn goes to his office and starts searching the internet. He finds a newspaper article from the *Panola Watchman* out of Carthage, Texas. The article was about Norma Joslin, a woman who worked downtown in Oklahoma City. Norma was walking through her building's parking lot about 7:45 a.m. when she too saw the bomb squad. There was some talk among the employees in her office, wondering what the bomb squad was doing there. "Well, I guess we'll find out soon enough," Norma had joked. Shortly after her statement, the Alfred P. Murrah Building exploded.

We could not believe our eyes. Had the bomb squad really been downtown? Did they know? Could there have been prior knowledge? Was there prior warning?

We do not know but intend to find out.

13

CHIEF REILLY

May 15, 1995
Twenty-six days after the bombing

Glenn and I arrive at the fire department headquarters the next morning at 7:50. Chief Charlie Reilly, who is surprised to see us when he finally does show up for work, didn't arrive until almost nine. His dark brown hair was cut close on the sides and flat on the top. I remember him from the memorial service.

"Kathy, Glenn," he says and motions us to follow him into his office. We take two of the six straight-back wooden chairs with thin-cushioned seats that are positioned around a conference table. A woman follows us through the door and sets an aluminum carafe on the table nearest Chief Reilly. She leaves and then returns with three white ceramic cups emblazoned with the red insignia of the Oklahoma City Fire Department, founded 1899.

We small talk our way through the past two weeks, then Glenn steers straight into the fast lane.

"Chief, we think somebody's lying about what happened on April 19. We had about thirty-five people at our house last night, and some of them, including me, think someone is lying. Every one of them lost someone at the Murrah Building—listen to this."

Glenn was holding the recorder with which he had recorded the stories the previous night. He has it queued to Renee's story. He sets the recorder on the table and switches it on. Chief Reilly locks his eyes on the recorder.

"I saw something no one else has mentioned," said the voice coming from the recorder. "When I walked into the Murrah, I saw the bomb squad outside the building." "Bomb squad?" Glenn's voice was louder on the tape than Renee's. "How do you know it was the bomb squad?"

At that point, Glenn snaps off the recorder and looks at the chief, who is still looking at the recorder. "Chief, your bomb squad was at the Murrah Building before eight in the morning?"

"That's not true."

"More than an hour before the explosion, Renee Cooper saw a member of your bomb squad and a truck."

"I assure you, Glenn, the city's bomb squad was not downtown before the bombing."

"Listen to this, Chief."

Glenn fast-forwards the player to the number on the tape counter where Ernestine Looney's story begins and snaps it on.

"The agent told her husband that no one from ATF was in the building when it blew up. Not one single ATF agent was at work by nine o'clock that morning. What are the chances of that?"

Chief Reilly looks at Glenn. "What are you saying?"

Glenn says, "I'm not saying a thing. But by what these women are saying, I believe there's a whole lot you're not telling us. Your bomb squad was there an hour before, and if the ATF didn't get a warning, how do you explain it? That they all had the flu and called in sick? Could it be that you guys had prior warning?"

"We did not have prior warning. Somebody needs to prove otherwise," Chief Reilly says. "That's the first I've heard that ATF wasn't in the office, but I don't believe that's true."

"You can put that story to rest right now. Just call the ATF and ask them."

"You are making a serious allegation. Why don't you just relax and let the authorities do their job."

Glenn stands and slams the ball of his right fist on the tabletop as he leans across the table into the chief's face. "My grandsons were killed, and I need some answers."

"The bomb squad was not at the Murrah Building before—"

"That's not true!" Glenn yells.

"—the bombing," Chief Reilly continues. "No one had prior—"

"Shut! Up!" Glenn is screaming now, and his face is flushing red. The color has started at his chest, visible through the unbuttoned collar of his shirt, and now rises to his hairline. "Look at this," he yells, a little less hysterically. He pulls out the article from the *Panola Watchman* and begins to read it aloud. When he gets to the part that says, "They had to have known there was a bomb," Chief Reilly interrupts.

"I'm sorry, Mr. Wilburn, this meeting is over."

Glenn grabs the recorder and his sunglasses off the tabletop and Chief Reilly stands staring. Glenn reaches into his shirt pocket and pulls out a second pocket-size recorder, which has been recording their conversation. "Not that you said anything worth hearing," Glenn says and holds the second recorder in the space between their faces, "but this conversation is on the record."

He walks out of the room in a huff as I hurry to catch up. He is striding by the dispatcher's desk when Rudy Whitmore, the dispatcher, calls Glenn over and whispers, "I'm not going to lie for anyone. We got a memo this week warning us to be on high alert for terrorist activity."

Glenn is seething. His face is crimson red as he pushes his way through the left side of the double glass doors to exit the fire department.

On the way home, Glenn stops and buys a carton of Marlboros, a habit he had given up twenty years ago but has resumed since the bombing. "We're calling Lou Kilzer."

Lou is an old college friend of Glenn's who is working as a journalist for the *Denver Post.* After we got home, his conversation with Lou that day reduced Glenn's anger greatly. By the evening, he was calm, though still butt-lighting his Marlboros.

"Kilzer may not write the story, but at least he's listening."

14

PROBLEMS FOR THE ATF

May 23, 1995
Thirty-four days after the bombing

Glenn and I are beginning to believe that some people inside the government had prior warning. Even so, we are not overly suspicious when investigators announce May 23 as the date they would demolish what is left of the Murrah Building. When you've been taught all your life that the government is here to help, it's hard not to believe them.

Experts explain that the risk was that the Murrah Building could fall and leaving it standing could be dangerous. Other experts disagree, but they never make it onto the network news.

On the morning of May 23, CNN has reserved a prime spot from which Glenn, Edye, and I can see the implosion. Although, truth be told, CNN picked the spot, so their cameras have an unobstructed view of our three faces as the building falls. The noise of the crowd is so loud that we did not hear the siren, warning the observers that the demolitionists were about to detonate the explosives. So, when the TNT roars, the surprise is devastating-sounding, just like the morning of the bombing. I gasp, cover my face, and sob at this graphic replay of the worst moment of my life.

I imagine what Chase and Colton were doing when the bomb went off. I think about the innocents airborne, scattering in all directions, legs, arms, blood, people lying near death, alone, scared, then lifeless in the rubble.

The building falls in on itself, and the dust settles as the investigators—in broad daylight in front of God and everyone watching television—cover up the largest crime scene in American history.

Suddenly, we are surrounded by reporters with notepads, with microphones, with camera lights shining in our faces.

"Mrs. Wilburn, do you see any closure for you now?"

I stare at the reporter, and those around them go quiet awaiting my answer. Glenn jumps in and yells, "That's a stupid question. Watching a building implode will not bring our boys back. There is no closure for us. You clearly never have had a child murdered."

The reporter doesn't flinch. He holds the microphone steady near my mouth. "How do you feel about the decision to implode the Murrah Building?"

"What was the hurry?" I ask.

"You're not happy about the decision to take down the building?"

"I'm more concerned about getting some questions answered," I tell him.

"What are the questions?" the reporter asks.

"Who warned the ATF?" I say. "They were the target of this bombing, and no one died in their office. Did they have a warning, and that's why nobody was in the office that morning?"

I look over and see CNN reporter Gary Tuchman talking to my daughter Edye. The wind is blowing her long red hair up in the air. She wipes the hair from her face, and I hear her say, "Where was the ATF? Seventeen employees work on the ninth floor, and not one of them was injured? Who warned them not to go to work that day? Why didn't they warn my kids to stay away from school that day?"

"You're suggesting someone in the government—"

"I'm telling you straight up someone in the government warned them!" Edye is screaming. "I want the ATF to look me in the eye and tell me I'm wrong."

15

May 24
Thirty-five days after the bombing and the day after the implosion

Half the newspapers in the United States print the picture that the Associated Press photographer snapped of our family at the moment the dynamite brought down the Murrah Building. CNN starts every broadcast with a replay of the interview.

Sometime after nine o'clock that morning, our doorbell rang.

"Sorry to bother you, Mr. Wilburn," the lead man says when Glenn opens the door. "May we have a word?"

The man speaking is US Attorney Pat Ryan, whom Glenn recognizes. He introduces the two standing behind him, ATF agents Luke Franey and Alex McCauley.

"I see you brought your posse with you," Glenn says, when he sees the media pack on the curb in front of our house.

"Didn't invite them," Ryan says, "but can't stop 'em... Mr. Wilburn. if you'll just invite us in, we'll be gone in five minutes."

Glenn glares at the reporters and says to the three men, "C'mon in."

I grab Glenn's arm and caution him to be nice. Glenn motions to the chairs and sofa, then takes a cigarette from his shirt pocket and puts a match to it and I sit down beside him.

"You told the TV reporters you wished the ATF would look you in the eye," Mr. Ryan says. "We're here now."

"My daughter said that," I answer, "but I'm glad you are here."

"I want to assure you that the ATF had no warning. We are here to answer any questions you might have."

Sporting long, scraggly hair and a ring in one ear, undercover agent Luke Franey, with his hands still bandaged from injuries he tells us he received in the bombing, proceeds to give us his emotional account of what happened on April 19. He told us he was sitting at his desk in the Murrah Building when the floor beneath him began to rumble and he immediately jumped under his desk for cover. The ceiling and walls started coming down around him, and he was trapped on the ninth floor. He says he injured his hands while karate-chopping through the walls to get out of the building.

We are stunned by his story! We have a copy of the sheriff's video from the day of the bombing, and agent Luke Franey is on it, heartily shaking hands with law-enforcement officials. Now here he is, almost a month later, sitting in our home with his hands still wrapped from the reported injuries.

"We were there," claims Agent McCauley. "I was in an elevator in the Murrah Building when the bomb went off. I was trapped inside and was lucky to survive a free fall from the eighth floor to the third."

What they don't know is Glenn had worked as an auditor for the Mid-Western Elevator Company, the firm that actually searched the elevators for survivors. Glenn's friend, Duane James, who worked there as an engineer, told Glenn that the first thing they did was split up and check, then double-check, each elevator for occupants. They found that five of the six elevators were frozen between floors, and a sixth had stopped near floor level. They had to go in through the ceilings of the elevators to check for people, and all the elevators were empty. Glenn had even seen the extensive photographs taken to document Mid-Western's inspection, and the pictures confirmed that all safety cables were intact.

Glenn knows Agent McCauley could not possibly have broken out before the elevator company team arrived—not unless he had a blowtorch with him—and, according to Duane, all the doors were frozen shut. So, Glenn challenges McCauley's story and shares the information he had learned from Duane. As the ATF's story unravels, McCauley begins to back away from his account. He suggests that the blast might have created the "sensation" of a falling elevator.

As a certified public accountant, Glenn is always meticulous when it comes to details. As he investigates the bombing, he gathers a tremendous amount of information. He tediously sifts through each and every piece of evidence, letting the facts develop the theory, not the other way around. Day and night he searches for the truth. It is unnerving for him.

Just hours after the US Attorney and ATF agents leave our home, Glenn calls ADT Security Systems and makes arrangements for a high-tech security system to be installed in our home. He spares no expense, even having glass-break detectors installed on every window of our 3,800-square-foot home.

We no longer know who to trust. Glenn is concerned that McVeigh's accomplices will try to stop us from identifying them, but he is even more afraid of the people inside the government who seem to be working to hide the truth about what really happened. We are not sure where to turn.

16

GARY LEWIS AND JOHN DOE 2

Saturday, May 27
Thirty-eight days after the bombing

Three days after meeting with the ATF, the headline on Lou Kilzer's front-page story in the *Denver Post* reads:

22 witnesses saw bomb squad hour before blast
The subhead reads:

Revelations raise suspicions that government had warning

But at seven o'clock that morning, we are not aware of that. All we know is that we need to talk to Gary Lewis. He is a printer at the *Journal Record*, a business newspaper in Oklahoma City. The *Journal Record* is across the street from the Murrah Building.

We were told by Lou that Gary saw McVeigh seconds before the bomb went off, but had refused to talk.

A little past seven that morning, Glenn and I park in Gary's driveway.

"The recorder's on," Glenn informs me as he hands it to me, and I slip it into the outside pocket of my purse.

We exit the car and walk through the dewy grass to the front door. Glenn pushes the doorbell button, and it begins to chime. From inside comes a deep gruff bark that sounds like a hunting dog. We can hear footsteps, but the door doesn't open. Glenn pushes the button again. We stand looking at each other. After a couple of minutes, the door wedges open and a man is standing there.

"Good morning. I'm Kathy Wilburn."

"I know who you are. I'm Gary Lewis, but I guess you already know that."

"We'd like to ask you some questions," Glenn says.

"The FBI told me not to talk to anybody."

"Why? They can't arrest you for saying what you saw," Glenn tells him.

"Sorry, the agent told me not talk. I'm pretty scared," he tells us.

"This guy's a chicken," Glenn says indignantly. "Come on, Kathy, let's leave."

"Stop it, Glenn," I scold.

Glenn returns to the car, but I remain on the porch. Gary is still standing on the threshold, with the door open slightly wider.

"What are you afraid of Gary?" I ask.

"I'm afraid of the FBI. They told me in no uncertain terms not to tell anyone what I saw."

"Please, our grandchildren were killed," I plead.

His eyes tear up. "I'm sorry about your grandchildren, ma'am. I'll talk to you, but if anyone asks me about it, I'll deny it. The morning of the bombing I was on break and standing outside the door, smoking my pipe, a little before nine. I watched a man, who I now know was McVeigh. I watched this man get out of the truck and strut across the street into the alleyway, to the Mercury Marquis. The one he was driving when he got stopped.

"Another man got in the passenger's side, and McVeigh was in the driver's seat. I heard the engine start, and he took off with the tires squealing. He nearly hit a dumpster, jumped a concrete barricade, and turned east down the alley. I clearly saw the man in the passenger seat; he was so close, I could've punched him. That's the one I'm scared of because he's still on the run.... I don't understand why the FBI doesn't believe me. I saw John Doe 2, but the FBI tells me I was mistaken. They say no one else was in the Marquis with McVeigh, and that I need to keep my mouth shut."

"You saw John Doe 2?"

"I picked him out of a lineup of drawings. Yeah, I'm sure."

The interview with Gary lasts slightly less than ten minutes. We walk into our house at 7:50 a.m. Glenn drinks five cups of coffee and smokes three Marlboros with each cup. Then he goes into his office.

At ten past ten that morning, Lou Kilzer faxes his story to our house. Then he telephones, and we tell him about our meeting with Gary Lewis.

17

THE FENCE

Tuesday, May 30, 1995
Forty-one days after the bombing

I cross off each day after April 19 on Guarantee Bank's 1995 calendar and number it. April 20 is Day One, April 26 is Day Seven. On Day Thirty-Four, the Murrah Building is imploded. A week later, on May 30, which was Day Forty-One, Glenn and I eat lunch at Ted's Café Escondido on Northwest Sixty-eighth and drive the seven miles for another look at the Alfred P. Murrah Federal Rubbish Heap. We are among a couple of dozen people there this day. Some walk the perimeter, as Glenn and I stand at the chain-link security fence and watch two people dig where the daycare had been.

I hook my fingers onto the links, on either side of my face. Before the bombing, this is the spot I would stand during my lunch break and look for the boys through the plate-glass windows of the daycare. On this day, Day Forty-One, it has been 987 hours since the boys died. I stand staring and recall Edye with Chase and Colton feeding the geese by the playground on Lake Hefner. When the geese snap up the pieces of bread, the boys scream in delight, the kind of delight granted only to small children. When they see me, they jump up and down and the little voices cry out, "Nana, Nana," and with open arms I run to them. Glenn taps my shoulder, and my sweet memory is replaced with reality. In front of me are the tumbled walls of the Murrah Building. My spine tingles with the chill of death that fills the air.

The wind that blows from the west rattles a torn-out piece of spiral-notebook paper attached to the fence with two bread-wrapper twist ties. "We Will Always Remember," the author has written by hand in red crayon.

A man is walking in our direction and slows his pace as he nears us, stopping three feet away. He is close enough that I can see that the middle finger of each of his blue-gray gloves are worn through to his fingerprints. He's wearing a khaki shirt with the sleeves rolled up neatly above his elbows. He stands looking at us through the fences. Sweat cuts shiny wet trails through the dirt that bronzes his face.

"Good afternoon," he says as he wipes his forehead with a blue shop rag which he pulls from his back pocket.

"Who you working with?" Glenn asks when he sees the plastic ID badge clipped to the left front of the man's pocket.

"FEMA," he answers, flipping his badge so that we can read it. "I'm Robert Warren."

Glenn takes a long draw from his cigarette and exhales smoke that momentarily obscures his face. He pinches the butt between his thumb and middle finger and flicks it to sail over the fence. Awkward silence follows.

While they chat, I stare at the ground with tears flowing as I think about the boys. Mr. Warren sees my tears, and he turns away and starts to move back toward the digging area. Then he stops and comes back to the fence.

"Y'all know someone in the building?" he asks.

I tighten my lips and look away. I know Glenn will answer, and he nods, yes.

"I'm so sorry," Mr. Warren says, "I should have known you weren't sightseers."

"We lost both our grandsons," Glenn says, fumbling, as if this is the first time he ever answered the question. "They were in the daycare."

Mr. Warren shakes his head, stuffs his gloves back into his pants pocket, and walks through the north gate, where US Marshals stand sentry round the clock. He walks quickly to us, extends his right arm to Glenn. Then he takes mine, and he holds it softly for a moment.

"I'm so sorry, folks. I don't know what to say. I wish there was something I could do."

"Things aren't adding up around here," Glenn tells him. "Did you see the AP photographer's picture of the ATF agent who was stranded on the ninth floor after the bombing? The north wall of his office had been blown away, he was standing on the ledge, holding a silver lock box into the air like it was real important. It must have been, because he was trapped in the building with all those dead people below him. When we ask him what was in the lockbox, he says he isn't allowed to discuss. A few days later a reporter friend of ours takes him to lunch, and he tells him that the box had one hundred and fifty dollars' worth of his children's savings bonds. Just doesn't add up."

"Looks like he could have told that?" Warren says.

"Excuse me."

Until she speaks, I did not notice the woman standing on the other side of the fence with a golden lab standing by her side. She is slender, wearing a pullover blue shirt. She has on high-top field boots that are tucked into her khaki pants.

"I need my associate. Warren, we're burning daylight! Let's finish that section before sundown."

"This is Kathy and Glenn, they lost their grandsons in the building."

"I'm sorry to hear that," she says.

"This is Sheila, she's with the FBI."

Her dog is standing by her side. As I admire her dog, she tells me his name is Silverheels, and that he is a search-and-rescue dog. Warren excuses himself and goes back to work.

An hour later, I am still at the fence, watching, mourning, when Mr. Warren returns.

"I've been thinking about what Glenn said and I sure hope you get your answers. I'm sorry, but I'm going to ask you to leave; they are ordering everyone to clear the area."

I turn to walk to the car, where Glenn sits smoking. He sees me talking to Warren and gets out of the car.

Warren pauses a second and says, "We found a leg."

He pauses again before continuing. "I can tell this is a big deal because of the way they're handling it. For a couple of weeks, they've been telling everyone all the bodies are accounted for, but that's not so. This leg is cut off in the middle of the thigh. And wearing a combat boot. I start digging after Silverheels finds it. When we realize what it is, forensics takes photos and finishes digging. They tag it and bag it, and ask me some questions.

"The FBI told all of us 'No one is to talk about what we found today until we can identify it.' If I hear about this on the ten o'clock news, we'll all be in trouble."

"Obviously, somebody doesn't want this story leaked," Glenn says.

"Don't tell anyone yet, let's just wait and see what they do. You could get me in some big trouble."

18

THE FINAL CALL

THURSDAY, JUNE 1, FORTY-THREE DAYS AFTER THE BOMBING

We are excited after talking to Mr. Warren yesterday. I snatch the *Daily Oklahoman* from the driveway and scan the front page expecting to see something about the leg—but nothing.

FRIDAY, JUNE 2, FORTY-FOUR DAYS AFTER THE BOMBING

Nothing on the TV news about the leg found.

SATURDAY, JUNE 3, FORTY-FIVE DAYS AFTER THE BOMBING

Glenn and I drive by the Murrah site at a quarter past two for a glimpse of Warren. We know it has been a long time since the weekend, but we are desperate to hear something. We didn't see him.

JUNE 4, FORTY-SIX DAYS AFTER THE BOMBING

No word from Warren, and still nothing reported on the leg.

THURSDAY, JUNE 8, 1995, FIFTY DAYS AFTER THE BOMBING

Four days have passed, and there are no reports about the leg. Today at daybreak the *Oklahoman*, as usual, is on the driveway. The headline on the day's top bombing story says that McVeigh's lawyer, Stephen Jones, plans to ask the judge to move McVeigh's trial to another jurisdiction. In all its hundreds of words, however, the story doesn't mention the leg. Another bombing story reports that doctors have moved one of Chase's and Colton's playmates from the daycare out of ICU. The headline: "Toddler's smile brightens doctors' day as he moves to children's unit." There are two bombing stories on the front page, and neither mention the leg, and we can't find Warren. Looks like the leg he dug up might be a problem for someone. But for whom?

19

ONE LEG TOO MANY

On May 30, the leg Warren recovered makes the news. Authorities have one leg too many, and as legs go, this is an important one. It is a left leg that a cadaver dog found in the rubble of the Alfred P. Murrah Building forty-one days after the Timothy McVeigh massacre. Whoever lost the leg was in the vicinity when Tim McVeigh blew up the Ryder truck.

Authorities can't find the person missing this leg. Of the scores of people Tim McVeigh murdered, eight were missing a left leg. No match, so they bury those victims without a left leg. Now they have this left leg they don't know what to do with. Are the authorities missing a body? Do they have one leg too many? Either way, it's a big problem for investigators for months.

They didn't disclose the leg publicly when they unearthed it. They finally admit they found an extra leg after we leak the story to *The New York Times*. The one leg too many raises several questions. To whom does this extra leg belong? Was the owner a victim of the bombers, or a bomber who became his own victim? If it is a victim of the bombing, then why has this person not been identified as missing? If it belongs to a bomber, then this investigation is far from over.

The FBI's reports from over twenty eyewitnesses who saw McVeigh the day of the bombing all report seeing him with other men, yet they continue to insist that McVeigh was alone. If the witnesses are correct, they have seen John Doe 2 and possibly 3, but the FBI refuses to admit these men exist. Could it be that one of the John Does does not exist anymore because he was unable to make his escape after the fuse was activated? No one has come forth about a missing victim, so I believe the leg must belong to a perpetrator.

When authorities finally admit they have Specimen P-71, the name they have given the leg, they are 75 percent certain that Specimen P-71 is a male leg. They dissect P-71 like a biology-class frog and analyze it anthropologically. However, they do not run DNA on the leg. They report that P-71 has been "traumatically amputated," and their "anthropological analysis" reveals that P-71's owner is younger than thirty, light of skin, not white, but light, and dark of hair. He was short, five-foot-five-ish, give or take.

The left leg that investigators leave with the medical examiner has been separated from its owner for several weeks, and so it is ripe and well on its way back to dust, but its parts are still easily recognizable as a thigh, a knee, a shin, an ankle, and a foot, with all five toes intact. Oh, and there is this: P-71 is wearing a black combat boot and two socks.

As it turns out, authorities say they are mistaken after they apply science to the leg and do DNA testing. They learn that the he-leg is, in fact, a she-leg. The leg's DNA matches that of a twenty-one-year-old woman, an enlisted airman assigned to Tinker Air Force Base, who now is at rest in a mausoleum in New Orleans.

Airman First Class Lakesha Levy had been applying for a new Social Security card when the bomb exploded. They interred Lakesha without a left leg or with someone else's leg. Two forensic investigators fly P-71 to New Orleans. The FBI meets them at the airport, and they drive straight to the cemetery. They roll Lakesha Levy's coffin out of its crypt and crack open the lid. Lakesha has two legs, but the left one isn't attached and is noticeably longer than her right leg. They remove the wrong left leg and replace it with her own leg.

But there is still one leg too many.

Who killed my grandsons? My only two grandsons? Was the owner of that leg one of the perpetrators? I know there is more than just McVeigh and Nichols. I don't have an exact number yet. May never, but the number is more than two. Way more.

If the leg's owner is identified and turns out to be an accomplice, how will the FBI explain it? They have staunchly proclaimed that only McVeigh and Nichols were involved in the bombing. If we don't know about the leg, what else don't we know?

PART THREE

The Hunt for Answers

20

GLENN WILBURN

June 1996

Glenn Wilburn is a quiet gentleman who loves his family. At the time of the bombing, he is forty-four, and he has a successful accounting practice. His tastes are quite simple. In the evenings he takes his grandsons out for a walk. On the weekends he works in the yard. Yet this "ordinary man" is led to do extraordinary things. After the bombing, he becomes a major figure in the largest manhunt in America: searching for John Doe 2. *The New York Times* refers to Glenn as the "Unlikely Lone Ranger."

All the media attention means nothing to him. The only reason this modest man ever allows his name to be used is to further the cause. He really doesn't want credit for his work. He uses every ounce of energy to search for the truth behind the bombing. Glenn is convinced that the entire American public has been lied to and deceived by the government, and that fills him with anger. He also hates Timothy McVeigh and can't wait for McVeigh to be executed. Glenn says, "On the day they execute Timothy McVeigh, I'm going to toast his death with a bottle of the best champagne money can buy, smoke a fine cigar, and spit on his grave."

Glenn is furious with God for not saving Chase and Colton. If God loves us so much, why would he let the boys die? And why would he spare some of the children, but not Chase and Colton? My feelings are very different. I am in so much pain from the loss that I can't find any anger. Although my faith is badly shaken, I am trying desperately to hang on.

Little do we know that Glenn's anger is destroying him. One Friday evening in June 1996, Glenn comes home looking distressed. I can tell something is terribly wrong.

"What's the matter?" I ask.

Glenn paces silently up and down the kitchen, reluctant to answer me. I press rather anxiously once again. "Glenn, what is it?"

"I'm passing blood in my urine," he says, looking at me with a somber expression.

For the previous several weeks, Glenn has not been feeling well. He thought it was an old ulcer flaring up, so he's been popping antacids by the handful. I know we need to get him to the doctor right away, so I make arrangements to take him the next morning. That night is sleepless for both of us. It is as if we already know another catastrophic event is about to befall our family, with Glenn the target this time.

Early the next morning, Glenn and I arrive at the doctor's office and are led into an examination room. I can tell Glenn is apprehensive. The tall, distinguished doctor enters the room slowly reading Glenn's chart. He carefully looks Glenn over, then asks, "How long have you been yellow?"

I study Glenn; he *is* a funny color. To my horror, I realize I hadn't noticed. Someone had commented earlier about how pale Glenn was, and we'd just assumed it was because we were rarely out in the sunshine anymore. Then the doctor points out that the whites of Glenn's eyes are yellow as well. Once again, I missed it. For the previous fourteen months, Glenn and I have cried ourselves to sleep. I was used to his eyes being bloodshot and swollen. Perhaps that's why I missed the signs of his illness.

An internist is called in, and the appropriate tests are ordered. Glenn is paralyzed with fear. When the test results are in, Glenn refuses to go back to discuss them. He seems to know it is bad news. I phone Edye and ask her to go with me.

As soon as I see the internist's face, I know something is dreadfully wrong. She asks me where Glenn is. I tell her he refused to come. There is a long pause, then she asks, "Why did he refuse?"

"He is afraid that the news is bad," I tell her.

"I know your family has been through a lot," the doctor begins, "and I wish there was some way I could offer you hope."

Our worst fears are confirmed. Glenn is dying of pancreatic cancer.

I am crushed. I leave the doctor's office with Edye by my side and an unbearable weight on my shoulders. Edye weeps in disbelief. How can I go home and face Glenn? There is no good way to tell him.

Edye and I stall for time by going by her house. As soon as I am inside, I break down and Edye goes outside to cry. Finally, we are home. Glenn is sitting in the dark on a stool in the kitchen. He can tell by our faces that the news is not good. When our eyes meet, no words come. Finally, he says, "Go ahead, tell me."

I'm not sure that I actually told him. I just remember him saying, "All I need is a little more time."

At that moment, I must confess, I think about myself; I just don't think I can handle this. Glenn enters the hospital within two weeks of his diagnosis. Doctors remove his pancreas, gallbladder, duodenum, and one third of his stomach. He is never able to eat again, and I become his nurse, feeding him intravenously through a triple lumen in his chest.

The first time, Glenn is in the hospital for over a month. He is in agony and has already begun to deteriorate, and there is nothing I can do. Yet even as Glenn fights for his life, he continues his quest for the truth, as long as he is physically able.

Over time, Glenn becomes too weak for even the simplest of tasks. Edye and I struggle to lift him out of bed. Then, with his dead weight propped safely between us, we endeavor to carry him, his feet dragging the floor, down the narrow hallway from the bedroom to the den. It is a pathetic sight. Edye and I look at what is left of Glenn hanging there between us, and our eyes meet. We often must fight back the tears; we know he will soon be leaving us.

No one could have guessed that a mild-mannered CPA would become a driven criminal investigator, or that his research would be used and respected by top journalists across the country. Nor could we have dreamed that, because of the bombing, Glenn himself would pay the ultimate price.

Glenn Wilburn had been my port from the storm for over eleven years, my shoulder to cry on. He'd been a wonderful stepfather to Edye. What will we do now?

21

STEPHEN JONES

November 1996

It's been four months since Glenn was diagnosed with pancreatic cancer. It's been eighteen months since the babies died. I am driven to continue to investigate the bombing and feel like I owe it to Glenn, since he is no longer able, and to the boys, and to myself.

I turn right off the highway onto Stephen Jones's asphalt driveway and brake at the wrought-iron bars. I roll down the driver's window, thrust my left arm out, and aim my index finger at the white button beneath the intercom speaker. For a moment, my courage wanes as I wonder about the wisdom of visiting the lawyer of Timothy McVeigh, the most hated man in America. I hesitate and want to slam the Jeep into reverse and pull backwards, but can't. A black Mercedes pulled in behind me. I stretch my arm as far out the window as I can and press the buzzer.

"Kathy Wilburn," I say when the voice answers. "Mr. Jones is expecting me."

Mr. Jones is expecting me because I phoned him after watching an interview he had with Connie Chung on national television yesterday.

"You don't need a criminal justice degree to figure out that Timothy McVeigh and Terry Nichols did not do this alone," is what Mr. Jones had told Connie Chung and six million television viewers. "As part of my defense of Mr. McVeigh, I intend to find the others who helped. I am going to prove that McVeigh did not act alone. I am going to prove that in fact, there was a web of really bad people involved. I'm going to show that the federal government doesn't want to find the others."

"That's a rather bold assertion, Mr. Jones," Connie Chung had said, "that sounds like you're peddling a conspiracy theory."

"It is a conspiracy; it's not a theory, it's fact that I'm going to prove."

"By definition," Connie Chung said, "until you prove a fact, your fact remains a theory."

"Don't doubt me, Connie. There's a growing population of disenchanted white men that believe the federal government eventually will tax the oxygen we breathe. These are the heirs of the men who dumped the tea into Boston Harbor, they believe the federal government is overstepping its bounds."

"With all due respect, Mr. Jones," Connie Chung said, "you sound like a conspiracy kook with a law degree."

"They want revenge."

"Revenge for what, Mr. Jones?"

"Revenge for the Covenant, The Sword—"

"I'm sorry, Mr. Jones, that was ten years ago. We're out of time."

"I've all the time in the world, Connie, I'm trying to save a man from execution. They want revenge for—"

"Mr. Jones—"

"You asked the question, Connie. Let me answer. They want revenge for the Covenant, the Sword and the Arm of the Lord (CSA). They want revenge for the execution of Randy

Weaver's wife and son at Ruby Ridge. They want revenge for the execution of David Koresh and seventy-five of the men, women, and children who lived with him at the Branch Davidian compound in Waco. Now they want revenge for the execution of CSA leader Richard Snell. Do you think it was a coincidence that Arkansas executed Mr. Snell on the tenth anniversary of the raid of the CSA? April 19 is Patriots Day, and the second anniversary of Waco. They want revenge, and Oklahoma City was their first shot."

When the interview ends at 6:45 p.m., I dial 4-1-1 to get Stephen Jones's telephone number. I phone his office, expecting to leave a message. "Stephen Jones," he says after the fourth ring.

My mouth and tongue go dry, but I manage to say, "I'm Kathy Wilburn."

"Mother of Colton and Chase?" he asks.

"Grandmother."

"What can I do for you?"

"I need to talk to you about an unconventional idea I have."

"Don't say another word," Jones says, "the FBI probably has my phones tapped. Come to Enid; we can talk at my home."

At ten the next morning, I am at the gate to the estate of the second most hated man in the United States, who is defending the most hated man in the United States. The intercom pops when I release the button. The voice of the woman on the other end replies, "Follow the drive to the front of the house, park in the shade if you'd like."

The wrought-iron gate swings open. I take my foot off the brake and the Jeep rolls slowly past the rock columns. The driver of the black Mercedes behind me is tight on my bumper and slips in without stopping. I follow the curve of the drive, which loops into a circle at the front of the palatial three-story house, and park under a stand of oaks. Men in long-sleeved white shirts and white pants are trimming the trees and mowing grass. The driver of the Mercedes, instead of taking the circle, has followed the straight section of drive to an apron of concrete that spreads out in front of a five-car garage and disappears into one of the garages.

I step out of the Jeep and walk one hundred feet to the front door. The chill in the fall air is blowing through me, and I can't wait for someone to open the door. I look for a doorbell, but instead I find a door knocker, a massive brass fist, hinged at the wrist and hanging upside down so that the knuckles will rap the brass plate, I grab the fist and rap three times.

An Asian woman, at least six inches shorter than I am, answers the door. Her uniform is a white cotton dress and she is wearing a sky-blue apron that ties at the waist.

"I'm Kathy Wilburn," I repeat. "Mr. Jones is expecting me."

"Yes, ma'am, I'm the one you spoke to at the gate."

The woman bows slightly and walks away from the door. I follow her up the curved stairs to the second floor. A second woman appears on the second-floor landing; her hair is dark, looking almost black against her white blouse. She approaches me.

"I'm so sorry for your loss, Mrs. Wilburn," the woman says and extends her right hand. "I'm Savannah, Mr. Jones assistant. He is eager for this visit. Please follow me."

We continue the walk up the stairs, which are lined with hundreds of books. She opens a door at the top of the third flight of stairs, leads me into an office, and motions to a Victorian parlor chair that is centered on a window. A mahogany desk sits empty across from the chair, with the sun from the window reflecting on the wall behind it.

After a few minutes, Stephen Jones enters and walks toward me, extending his right arm. I stand and give him my hand.

"I'm having iced tea; will you join me?" he says.

"Of course."

He looks toward the Asian woman, who is standing behind him. "Suzi, tea please." He motions for me to sit as he takes a seat at his desk.

"Ma'am, first of all I would like to tell you how sorry I am about your husband and grandsons."

I nod. "Thank you."

"I have to tell you that I'm puzzled by your visit. What can I do for you?"

I wait while Suzi drops ice cubes into the glasses and pours the tea to within half an inch of the rim in each glass.

"I'm not here to ask you for anything, I want to help you."

"Why would you want to do that?" Jones asks.

"Glenn and I don't believe we were given the truth about the bombing. I also believe the stress of the bombing is killing him, so I owe it to him and the babies to keep searching. If you're looking for the other people involved in this crime, I'd like to help you find them."

"If the people of Oklahoma find out you're offering to help me, they won't be too happy."

"A lot of people are already upset with me because I've been very verbal. They think I'm going to screw up the case and possibly get McVeigh off by asking questions."

Jones sips his tea; then he stands and walks from behind the desk.

"If you're sure you're up to this, I could use your help. Most people don't want to help McVeigh and won't talk with my investigators. I don't see how they can turn you down, a victim of the bombing. This is brilliant."

22

CALL TO JESSE TRENTADUE

Thursday, August 10
113 days since the bombing

I learned about Kenneth Trentadue from Stephen Jones. It seems that after his arrest, he was flown to Oklahoma and held in a federal holding facility where he died a mysterious death. I agree to call Trentadue's family. Jones is finding me to be quite an asset with his investigative work. People will talk to me that refuse to talk to McVeigh's defense team: no one in America wants to help Timothy McVeigh.

On June 10, 1995, Kenneth Trentadue, a construction worker and convicted bank robber, was driving a 1986 Chevy pickup when he was pulled over at the Mexican border on his way home to San Diego. He was dark-haired, five feet eight inches, and well-muscled—a former athlete who did construction work when he wasn't robbing banks—and his left forearm bore a dragon tattoo. Highway patrol officers ran his license, found that it had been suspended, and that he was wanted for parole violations. On August 18, after two months in jail in San Diego, Trentadue was shipped to a prison in Oklahoma City for a hearing on the parole violations. The move placed him in close proximity to the most famous federal prisoner in America—and it also sealed his fate.

Four months earlier, Timothy McVeigh and Terry Nichols were arrested for the murder of 168 men, women, and children. Immediately following the bombing, law enforcement searched furiously for a man whom numerous sources say they saw with McVeigh, and who by some accounts was seen walking away from the Ryder truck—the character whose police composite sketch becomes known around the world as John Doe 2. According to the police description, this man is about five feet nine, muscular, and dark-haired. By some accounts, he drove an older model pickup truck and had a dragon tattooed on his left forearm.

The description of John Doe 2 bears an uncanny resemblance to Kenneth Trentadue, who died mysteriously at the Federal Transfer Center in Oklahoma City after his arrest in San Diego. An autopsy revealed that Kenneth had been beaten unmercifully. It identified forty-one wounds and bruises: His eyes were swollen and black, even the bottom of his feet bruised, and his throat had been cut. Yet officials at the institution told the Trentadue family that Kenneth committed suicide.

When a local reporter brings that to my attention, it is clear to me that Trentadue did not kill himself, because no man can beat himself so savagely before slashing his own throat. I believe Trentadue may have been mistaken for a man he resembles: Aryan Republican Army co-founder Richard Lee Guthrie. Is it possible that federal authorities, suspecting they had John Doe 2 in their hands, tried to force him to talk? Is it possible that investigators or the guards at the Oklahoma holding facility went too far when interrogating him, demanding information that Trentadue did not have? I call Kenneth's brother Jesse, a Salt Lake City attorney, to share my concerns. Jesse knows nothing about the resemblance between his brother and Guthrie, the nation's most wanted man.

While the Justice Department is working to convict what it insists are the only two conspirators, McVeigh and Nichols, its agents are actively investigating a more sinister plot, a plot that is concealed from the public.

23

GLENN'S FUNERAL

July 18, 1997
Eleven months later

Glenn Wilburn was my hero. Glenn used every ounce of his energy the last fifty-eight days of his life, since the bomb ing, searching for the truth. He believed the American public, as well as the victims of the bombing, had been lied to and deceived by the government, but the ultimate victims, of course, were those who lost lives, limbs, and/or loved ones.

The stress of these lies took Glenn to an early grave. If there is one thing I learned from his death, it is that harboring bitterness and anger in your heart is like drinking poison and expecting the enemy to die. Glenn's death certificate says he died of a heart attack, but I believe his anger killed him.

As I think about Glenn's funeral, it seems only fitting that it be conducted downtown, close to the bomb site, since it was there that he began to lose his life. I have been attending City Church, a magnificent old church in downtown Oklahoma City, since the bombing. The structure was built in the early 1900s, rich in architectural design. The cathedral ceiling and windows are intricately etched stained glass. The auditorium is filled with lavishly carved Baroque woodwork delicately detailed with gold inlay. Massive columns support the balcony, which wraps all around the inner walls of the elaborate sanctuary. The floors are paved with exquisite Italian marble.

The church holds a special place in my heart because it has been ravaged by the wrath of the bomb, just as our family has been. The beautiful stained-glass windows were blown out. The structural damage was severe, but the restoration was completed before Glenn's funeral.

When I talk to my pastor and friend, Larry Jones, about Glenn's funeral, he asks, "What do you want me to tell them about Glenn?"

"Just tell the truth," I answer.

And Larry does just that at the funeral service, giving a blistering sermon:

"I don't want us to become a nation, as Alexander Solzhenitsyn said of the Soviet Union, where the lie has become not just a moral category, but a pillar of the state. If I'm not mistaken, we're living in America, and what is taking place frustrates me. I am beginning to see that Americans are living under fear of their government.... I really believe that after the Oklahoma City bombing, if our government had stood up and said, 'This is actually what happened, something went wrong,' and apologized to Oklahoma City and the nation—'We're sorry for what happened, we want you to forgive us'—had that happened, I don't think we would be here, burying Glenn Wilburn today.... You see, as Huxley said, 'You shall know the truth and the truth shall make you mad.' And as Glenn Wilburn began to find out the truth, it did make him mad, and the load he carried literally took him to the grave."

Glenn's coffin is placed unopened at the front of the church. Glenn was a proud man, and I knew he would never want to be put on display for his friends to file by to look at him. We place a picture of Glenn at the front of the church, along with a large, enchanting portrait of Chase and Colton as little angels. The thought that Glenn is now with the babies brings me comfort. His casket is draped in an arrangement of delicate little fresh flowers with a ribbon entwined among the petals that has the word "Papa" printed on it.

When the service is over, my brother Bobby places his arm in mine and supports me down the aisle to the front door. There we are by a steep array of long, foreboding steps. As the bagpipes play "Amazing Grace," I watch the pallbearers struggle with Glenn's coffin on their shoulders to get him down the perilous stairs and into the hearse that is waiting. We get into the family car, and the funeral procession circles the haunting site where the Murrah Building once stood. At first, there is a deafening quiet, and then, glorious bells begin to toll throughout the city in honor of my late husband. There is a holy presence in the air that warm summer morn as Glenn is ushered into the presence of God with two little boys by his side.

24

THE HEAD OF THE SNAKE

April 1998
Three years after the bombing

After Glenn's death, I continue to investigate, no longer caring about my personal safety but driven to find the truth. I had never heard of Robert Millar until Stephen Jones and his investigators brought him to my attention. Since then, I have learned a great deal about him and his critical role in the bombing. He is dead now, possibly the victim of his own evil deeds—a diabolical but fascinating central character in the Oklahoma City bombing, and who knows what else. His persuasive personality and clever brain enabled him to fool the most prestigious law-enforcement agencies in the world.

Robert Millar was born in Kitchener, Ontario, Canada, to a father who, after participating in the carnage that was WWI, had become a pacifist, joining the Mennonite community shortly before Robert was born in 1925. As Robert was growing into manhood, for reasons unknown he rejected his father's beliefs and became involved in the Christian Identity movement. This radical group had its origins in England in the 1880s, and because of its "super-race" beliefs, became a major contributor to the development of Hitler's Nazi party. As it grew in Europe and found its way to North America, it morphed into an antisemitic, racist, and white-supremacist group of cultists who claimed Jesus as their spiritual founder and leader.

Millar, despite his extreme beliefs, possessed natural leadership qualities and was widely recognized as one of the most respected leaders of the Christian Identity movement in the United States. In 1973 he founded Elohim City, a Christian Identity community in a remote location in eastern Oklahoma. Under his leadership, the community drew scores of white-supremacist types from the United States as well as from other countries, all bent on overthrowing the federal government by violent means. To achieve that goal, Elohim became a training facility for domestic terrorists, supporting its inhabitants by raising crops and livestock, but also by robberies and drug dealing when needed.

In the early 1980s, Millar became acquainted with Richard Snell and Jim Ellison, leaders of a similar community in north Arkansas called The Covenant, Sword, and Arm of the Lord (CSA), which had turned violent about that time. They blew up a Jewish community center in Indiana and planned the bombing of a gay church in Springfield, Missouri; but CSA member Kerry Noble actually aborted the bombing of the gay church. He went inside, and when he saw people worshipping the Lord, he thought, “I cannot do this—these people are praising God just like we do”—so they never did bomb or blow up the gay church.

Snell’s path to justice began when he murdered a Black Arkansas trooper in cold blood during a traffic stop, a crime that earned him a life sentence. Later, he and his accomplices robbed a pawn shop in Texarkana, where Snell killed the owner because he thought he was Jewish, which he wasn’t. That murder ultimately sent Snell to the death chamber. Examining

Snell's firearms, federal authorities traced them to the CSA compound, which prompted them to issue warrants for the arrest of Ellison and several of his cohorts. To negotiate a surrender, they brought in FBI special agent Danny Coulson, head of the FBI's Hostage Rescue Team, who later worked on the Oklahoma City bombing investigation. Ellison asked to bring in Robert Millar to talk to his followers. Millar showed up in his tailored suit, starched shirt, and alligator shoes. After four days of discussions, the CSA group surrendered without incident. This took place on April 19, 1985.

Later, at the 1988 Fort Smith Sedition Trial of the CSA, Ellison testified that he and Snell had planned to blow up the Murrah federal building in Oklahoma City in 1983, but failed due to technical difficulties. When the authorities scheduled Snell's execution for April 19, 1995, extremists throughout the country were enraged and swore vengeance. At that point, Elohim became the supreme headquarters for the planning and execution of the bloodiest domestic terrorist act in history, and the architect of that plan was Robert Millar.

But Millar was not alone; there were other key figures at Elohim City.

Perhaps the number-two character was Andreas Strassmeir, a German citizen who joined the compound as the director of paramilitary training and activities. What his cohorts did not know, but what I do know from my investigation, was that prior to joining Millar, he had put in job applications with the Drug Enforcement Agency (DEA).

Pete Ward, also a resident of Elohim City, was driving Strassmeir's maroon 1983 Chevrolet station wagon when he was stopped by Oklahoma Highway Patrol troopers at a roadblock near Elohim City for having no license plate. When Pete couldn't produce a driver's license, the car was impounded. Strassmeir's application for the DEA was found in his briefcase in the back seat of the car.

When Millar discovered Strassmeir's connection to the DEA, he surmised that Strassmeir was working as a paid informant and was keeping the FBI advised regarding the cult's activities. Millar did not expose him. Instead, he fed misinformation to him to mislead the federal agencies. Millar himself also fed false information to the FBI in the guise of an unpaid informant, a role at which he was obviously successful: Strassmeir was not summoned to testify, nor even questioned by investigators, before he left the country after the bombing. It is amazing that he wasn't questioned until a year later, after he had left the United States.

Carol Howe was a documented informant, embedded at Elohim, providing information to the ATF. Her reports to her government handler, as well as what she told me when I met with her, verify that she not only knew about the plan, but also that she was present on a trip to scope out the Murrah Building. She too was not called to testify at McVeigh's trial.

Dennis Mahon, who was not a resident but a frequent visitor to Elohim, was a former Grand Dragon of the Ku Klux Klan. He was a key contributor to the bombing plan and was very close to Strassmeir.

Michael Brescia, Peter Langan, and Richard Guthrie were part of a group called the Midwest Bank Robbers, based at Elohim City. They, and other associates, staged bank robberies throughout the Midwest to support the terrorist activities, including the funding for the bombing project. They were also in place at various strategic locations at the time of the bombing. None of them were charged or even listed as suspects.

While Guthrie was in jail for other charges, he told a reporter that he was going to "blow the lid off the OKC bombing." A day later he was found hanging in his cell, dead from what was reported as a suicide.

I am sure there are others involved, some of whose names are found elsewhere in this book. Still others I have not yet been able to identify.

25

MOTEL 6

October 2005

Shortly after the bombing, whispers of a mysterious law enforcement meeting at the Hilton hotel near Meridian Avenue and Interstate 40 began to circulate. Some claimed that high-ranking officials had gathered there on the eve of the explosion, their presence raising unsettling questions. Among those reportedly in attendance was Danny Coulson, the founding commander of the FBI's Hostage Rescue Team.

It was alleged that Coulson had been in Oklahoma City prior to the bombing, though the official record was murky. His supposed itinerary placed him at the Hilton, perhaps for a classified briefing or a routine security discussion—at least, that's what some believed. Yet, as the dust settled over the ruins of the Alfred P. Murrah Federal Building on April 19, 1995, speculation turned to suspicion.

Why was an elite counterterrorism operative in town before the attack? Was it a coincidence, or did someone know more than they were willing to admit? The official narrative remained firm, dismissing the rumors as conspiracy-fueled conjecture. But in the shadows of tragedy, unanswered questions had a way of lingering, waiting for history to either expose them—or bury them forever.

I was determined to meet with Coulson. At first, the prospect filled me with excitement—a rare chance to uncover the truth. But as I stepped into the courthouse, that excitement dissolved into doubt. The grand marble halls echoed with the steady rhythm of footsteps, the murmurs of attorneys and officials blending into a low, constant hum. Then I saw him—Danny Coulson, standing near the entrance, speaking in hushed tones with a man in a dark suit. He looked serious, unreadable. What was I thinking? Why would he risk answering my questions? Doing so might jeopardize his job or even his retirement. I knew then that as long as he remained on the FBI payroll, conducting or participating in a private investigation would be out of the question.

During a phone conversation with a retired police officer friend in Dallas, he casually mentions to me he just learned Danny Coulson has now retired.

"Are you sure?" I ask, not hiding my excitement.

"Pretty sure," he says. "I have his phone number. I know him, so I am going to call and congratulate him."

My friend gives me Danny's number, so I make it easy for him to meet me. I telephone Coulson and tell him, "I'll drive to Dallas. All you have to do is drive to the Motel 6."

Three days later, I back my car into the spot in front of Room 145. For more than an hour, I traipse between my car and the queen-size bed, carrying twelve years of research, organized into three-ring binders. The binders, two inches thick, fill the trunk of my car and overflow into the rear seat. Each is labeled by topic: ATF, McVeigh phone records, Elohim City, Notes from Terry Nichols conversations, Notes from McVeigh's lawyer, and so on.

After I load the binders in Oklahoma and unload them in Dallas, I realize again how much work I have put into this investigation. While I wait, I arrange the binders by topic, then rearrange them chronologically, then alphabetically. Two hours pass, and I wonder whether Coulson has decided against the meeting. I was surprised when he agreed to meet with me and won't be surprised if he skips out.

My insecurities begin to well up, and I wonder whether I should put everything back in the car and head back home to OKC. By now I trust the FBI about as much as Kennedy trusted Khrushchev. I trust them even less after watching how they concealed and manipulated evidence at the McVeigh and Nichols trials. From the beginning, I believed something was wrong—the facts of this case aren't adding up.

I am torn between visions of Coulson riding in on a white stallion and saving the day, or Coulson folding under the pressure. I am leaning toward the latter when a rap on the steel door startles me.

I slowly make my way across the room to the peephole in the door, look out, and see it is Coulson. He is wearing dark-wash blue jeans, and his black T-shirt stretches tight across his weightlifter's chest, which curves down to a slender waist. He keeps his hair tight on the sides and just enough on top to snatch, but not comb over. He stands silently as I pull the door open.

"Hi, Danny. Thank you for coming," I say.

Coulson takes one step into the room and stops. "What's all this?" he says as he looks at the binders lined across the bed.

"My evidence. It all started shortly after the bombing, when I learned the bomb squad was downtown before the bomb went off. I wanted to know why the John Doe 2 manhunt, the largest in US history, was called off. I decided to investigate, but wasn't sure what to do. I had no experience, so I decided to contact Stephen Jones."

"McVeigh's lawyer?"

"Yes," I answer.

"Why? His client killed your grandsons."

I say, "Jones knew he couldn't get McVeigh off the hook, but he might be able to save him from being executed if he could implicate other guilty parties. So, our motives were different, but our goals were the same."

"So, you actually worked with Jones, to help him defend McVeigh?" Coulson muses. "A bit strange, but I get it; actually, it was brilliant. You know, you would make a great agent—hard to manage, but great instincts."

I continue, "According to FBI witness statements, there were over twenty eyewitnesses who saw McVeigh downtown the morning of the bombing. Not one of them saw McVeigh alone. I contacted each one of them. None of them wanted to help McVeigh by talking to McVeigh's defense team, but they didn't mind talking to the grandmother who was a victim herself."

"What did you learn?" Coulson asks.

"I learned they were afraid. They were not only afraid of the man they could identify with McVeigh the morning of the bombing, but they were also afraid of the FBI. They had been told by agents that they were mistaken. I was shocked to learn they were told that if they talked, they could get McVeigh off. Those interviews were my first real confirmation of the FBI cover-up."

Coulson sits listening intently, then asks, "Why did you call me?"

"I'm hoping that now you're retired you can give me some answers."

"Let's look at what you have."

“Let’s start here,” I say as I pick up the binder I had placed on the off-white Naugahyde seat of a chair. Danny sits down beside me on the worn couch. I open the binder.

“Let’s start with this FBI memo,” I say. “According to this memo, the FBI was investigating members of Elohim City as part of the bombing conspiracy. When did you change your minds, and why?” Coulson looks at me but does not reply. “Why did you quit investigating them? It doesn’t make sense. At the trials we were told McVeigh had no connection to Elohim City, but look at this,” I say as I set the binder on the table.

I pick up another binder with McVeigh’s name typed on a white label stuck to the front cover. I flip it open and turn to McVeigh’s phone records. I snap open the binder and remove a page.

“Look at this—these are McVeigh’s phone records. April fifth, two weeks before the bombing, McVeigh calls Elohim City. Robert Millar’s daughter-in-law answers the phone. She knew McVeigh and told your men he asked to speak to Andreas Strassmeir.”

“I’ve never seen this,” Coulson tells me. *How can that be?* I think, but say nothing.

Coulson sits with his head down, poring over the phone records.

“Do you know about Carol Howe? According to Carol, she was Strassmeir's girlfriend, though he denies it. Take a look at this. She lived at Elohim City, and she was an ATF informant. She warned the ATF that Strassmeir was planning to bomb the Murrah, months before it happened. The documentation is right here.”

Coulson sits quietly, examining the evidence more closely now.

I break the silence. "You guys questioned thousands of people, including McVeigh's third-grade schoolteacher; I've read the interviews. Why in God's name wouldn't you want to talk to Andreas Strassmeir?"

"I don't have an answer, Kathy. But you have my attention," Coulson says.

I flip back into the McVeigh binder, snap open the rings, and hand Coulson another photocopied document. "Speeding ticket—an Adair County deputy stopped him twelve miles from Elohim City." I go deeper into the binder and stop at a red-tabbed page. "He was in Vian in September 1994 and rented a room at El Siesta, seven months before the bombing, twenty miles from Elohim. That's a coincidence? McVeigh's a kid from New York, so what's he doing there? People don't go to Vian, Oklahoma, for fun."

"How do you know no one talked to him?" Coulson asks.

"Right here in his file, the report says Strassmeir has no known connection to McVeigh. He was allowed to go back to Europe without ever being interviewed. His father was the *Chief of Staff* to *Helmut Kohl*."

"I think you're onto something, he says as he picks up the binder marked, Midwest Bank Robbers."

"Ever heard of them? They robbed more than twenty banks in the Midwest. That's how they got their name. They hid out at Elohim City and robbed banks to fund their white-supremacy activities. Michael Brescia was a member of the gang and was Strassmeir's roommate at Elohim."

"Kathy, I have never seen any of this information."

How can that be true? I think to myself.

Coulson opens the binder and I begin to explain. "So, you have a bank robber who roomed with Andreas Strassmeir, Andy the German, as they call him at Elohim City. All you have to do is connect the dots," I say, as I reach across the bed and pick up Jennifer McVeigh's binder. I open the file to Jennifer McVeigh's handwritten confession to the FBI. "Look at this," I quote from a letter Tim wrote to her: "'Something big is going to happen in the month of the bull,'" I read, then explain, "That's April in the zodiac chart."

Coulson continues reading Jennifer's confession: "'My brother gave me three one-hundred dollar bills and asked me to exchange them at a bank, he needed clean money. He told me he didn't rob a bank, but he helped plan robberies. That was his share of the take from one of them.'"

I watch as Danny's face tightens.

Danny speaks. "It's all beginning to make sense now."

"What makes sense?" I ask.

"I was taken off the case a few weeks after the bombing and put on paid leave for the last 10 years, until I retired.

If they had put me on leave without pay, they'd have to tell me why."

"I was a senior agent, one of the most experienced in the country. That's why they put me in charge. When they took me off the case, I was replaced by a newbie. It didn't make sense. I'm not sure what happened, but after what I've seen, I'm not sure what to think. Looks like ATF had prior warning and did nothing. The bank robbers clearly seemed to be involved and the FBI had evidence that tied McVeigh to the bank robberies! Look at this, as I hand him a document the FBI is directing all field offices to search all files of bank robberies that match the M.O. of...McVeigh and his associates! *His associates*. It says that right here on the teletype!"

I continue, "The FBI had to know what was going on, or they wouldn't have named the case BOMBROB. I think they did that because the robbers always had a phony explosive device with them when they robbed a bank."

I watch his demeanor change to anger.

I'm just not sure what I can do. What you need is a Federal Grand Jury"

"How do I do that?"

Coulson says, "It will take an act of Congress."

"Nothings ever easy. I'm not sure how to get that done."

"Nichols needs to tell a Federal Grand Jury what happened. That's the only way to get the answers you're looking for.

"I don't think he will. He doesn't trust the FBI, but I can try." One more question Mr. Coulson, did you know the judge over McVeigh's trial put the twenty-two security videos that surrounded the Murrah Building under seal? If McVeigh acted alone, wouldn't the security tapes prove it?"

"They sure would.... Aren't you afraid?" Coulson asks.

"Who should I be afraid of?"

"The people you could get put behind bars and possibly executed," he replied.

"You might want to think about that." He says as he

opens the door to leave He looks back over his shoulder and says, "Watch your back, kid."

The Federal Grand Jury never happened, but six months later I did connect with Senator Dana Rohrabacher, who chaired an Oversight and Investigations Subcommittee examining the Oklahoma City bombing. He shared with me that federal law enforcement treated the congressional oversight committee as little more than a nuisance, actively obstructing any meaningful investigation into the bombing.

This inquiry should have affirmed the federal government's commitment to transparency and its willingness to uncover and share vital information. Instead, officials from the Justice Department—and possibly the CIA—displayed a troubling lack of responsiveness at critical points in the investigation. Their needless defensiveness undermined the process and cast a shadow over the pursuit of truth.

While much of the official narrative surrounding the OKBOMB investigation holds up to scrutiny, this inquiry could have been far more thorough had federal law enforcement cooperated fully. Congressional investigators have a mandate to uncover the facts and seek the truth, yet they encountered unwarranted resistance in fulfilling this duty. Such obstruction should never stand in the way of justice or accountability.

PART FOUR

The Seeds of Conspiracy

26

RUBY RIDGE INFLAMES MCVEIGH

August 21, 1992
Two years before the bombing

By the late 1980s, the number and size of right-wing extremist groups grew rapidly. An event that fueled that growth was Ruby Ridge.

Randy Weaver and his family built a home in the rugged Idaho panhandle, on the side of a mountain at a place called Ruby Ridge. Weaver and his wife Vicki cleared the land themselves, using the trees they cut down to build a crude structure which Randy constructed with his own two hands. There was no indoor plumbing, so they built an outhouse. The Weavers home-schooled their three children. They were self-contained and lived isolated from the rest of the world. Their social lives consisted of attending activities at the Aryan Nations compound a few miles down the road, an extremist cult whose members called themselves separatists. They believed themselves to be God's chosen people and avoided contact with the outside world. The Weavers shared many Aryan Nation views. The Weavers also attended the services of the pro-Nazi, anti-American Church of Jesus Christ–Christian.

The event that would become known as "Ruby Ridge" became a nightmare for federal law enforcement. It involved hundreds of federal agents, millions of dollars' worth of equipment, and four deaths. One of those killed was a US marshal, another was Randy's wife, Vicki, who was shot in the head by an FBI sniper as she stood in the doorway of her own home, holding her ten-month-old daughter in her arms. The last two were the Weavers' fourteen-year-old son, Sammy, and his yellow Lab dog, Striker.

The case against Randy Weaver began with a gun deal. In October 1989, Weaver sawed off two shotguns and sold them to an ATF informant at the informant's request. Apparently, the ATF didn't think it was a big deal because they waited around until June of 1990 to approach Weaver with a deal. They knew he had been attending meetings at the Aryan Nations compound in Hayden Lake, and they thought he might become an informant if they would let him off the hook on the illegal gun charges. He refused to take the deal, so in December of 1990, a grand jury indicted him for making and possessing an unregistered firearm.

On January 17, 1991, an ATF team, posing as a couple with a stalled car, flagged down Weaver and his wife Vicki on a road near their cabin. When Randy got out to help, they arrested him. "Nice trick," Weaver told the agents. "You'll never do that again." After being released on bond, Weaver didn't show up for a pretrial hearing on February 20. He was lying low on the mountain with Vicki and their children: Sara, sixteen; Sammy, fourteen; Rachel, ten; Elisheba, ten months; and Kevin Harris, a twenty-four-year-old radical whom the Weavers took in. A federal judge issued a warrant for Weaver's arrest, and the US attorney had Weaver indicted for failure to appear. The US Mar*shals* Service was to *serve the arrest warrant.*

There was no way to sneak up on the cabin: The Weavers had purposely built it to be a stronghold against the looters and pillagers of the biblical tribulation they believed was coming. It was high on top of the mountain with a 360-degree view of the forest that surrounded it. The Marshals set up observation posts hoping to find a way to serve the warrants peacefully as the Weavers went about their daily routine.

The Marshals discussed going up to the cabin under a white flag and trying to reason with the Weavers, but after talking with a neighbor they decided it was too dangerous. Weaver had told his neighbor that if federal agents showed up on his property, "I'll take some with me."

The neighbor agreed to be a go-between and deliver the US Marshals' letter to Weaver, asking him to surrender and come out peacefully. Weaver's response was, "You are the servants of lawlessness, and you enforce lawlessness. You are on the side of the One World Beastly Government. Whether we live or whether we die, we will not obey your lawless government."

The letter caused officials to wonder if Randy and Vicki were contemplating a suicide fight to the death. Marshals tried negotiating with Weaver through friends and family, but to no avail.

After several weeks, the chief deputy of the US Marshals ordered that the negotiations cease. The deputy chief had hoped a hard winter on the mountain would drive the family down into town, but it did not. As spring approached, Randy Weaver was becoming famous and an embarrassment to US Marshals. The headline in the Spokane Spokesman-Review read: "Feds have fugitive 'under our nose.'" The New York Times wrote: "Marshals Know He's There But Leave Fugitive Alone." Geraldo Rivera sent a television crew to cover the story.

To the right-wing extremists, Randy Weaver was becoming a folk hero.

Meanwhile, in February of 1992, a new director of the US Marshals Service was sworn in. He said he wanted to solve this problem before the Weavers died of old age. The standoff continued through the spring and summer.

Then, on August 21, things spun out of control when marshals drove out to Ruby Ridge early in the morning to conduct a reconnaissance around the boundary of the Weaver property. As the lawmen moved into position, Weaver's dog began barking and chased the marshals down the mountain. While the marshals ran from the dog, Randy's son Sammy and Kevin Harris joined the chase, trying to stop the dog. One of the marshals shot and killed the dog, which started an exchange of gunfire. Fourteen-year-old Sammy Weaver was shot in the back and a marshal was killed.

With a federal officer killed, the FBI was immediately brought into what now was clearly a major crisis. Who shot Sammy, and why was he shot in the back?

Again, the FBI sent its finest, just as they had done with the CSA. FBI agent Danny Coulson, commander of the Hostage Rescue Team, was brought in to lead the mission. Coulson, along with Larry Potts, the assistant director of the FBI's Criminal Division, drafted the rules of engagement. According to Danny Coulson's book No Heros, FBI personnel heading for the scene were informed that Weaver and Harris would not hesitate to attack any intruder, including agents. Wanting to ensure that their people remained safe, orders were given to consider any adult seen outside the Weaver cabin, or on Ruby Ridge, armed and dangerous and capable of deadly force.

Coulson didn't doubt what the marshals were saying about the danger posed by the family, but something didn't make sense to him. It was the dog that marshals say attacked them. He was a big yellow Labrador retriever, a young dog, not much older than a puppy. Coulson had raised and trained a lot of Labs and other dogs. He knew that Labradors could be protective, but he also knew they were not generally aggressive, especially out in the open. Coulson could *imagine the dog barking and chasing a marshal, but not attacking, as the marshal said in his report. Was there a cover up because a fourteen-year-old was shot in the back?*

*Just before 7:00 p.m., Coulson received a fax. It was a plan of action from the Strategic Information and Operations Cen*ter that needed a sign-off from him. As he read it, his jaw dropped. My God, he thought, we've got a problem. This is not the answer.

Coulson knew what he was reading was absolutely the wrong plan. It was a military assault plan. They wanted to place snipers around the perimeter of the compound, then send in two armored vehicles that would roll forward, equipped with loudspeakers giving orders for the occupants to surrender. If that didn't work, tear gas would be deployed. Then the Hostage Rescue Team was to charge the house, arrest the adults, and take control of the children.

Coulson thought this idea violated everything he had learned from his training and experience. Most operation plans are worked out among the agents on the scene, but this had simply been given to HRT for implementation. I think if Coulson could have made the decision, he would have gone to Ruby Ridge by himself. He was convinced that, despite the threats from Weaver and the tragedies that had already taken place, he could end this thing without further bloodshed. But that was not to be. Orders were orders.

Toward dusk, sniper teams were moving in to set the perimeter. This was the most dangerous part of the operation. If the Weavers were going to shoot at agents, it would be now.

Danny received a report from the HRT helicopter conducting reconnaissance over the Weaver's cabin that they had come under fire. An HRT sniper had returned fire.

He later learned the details of what had actually happened.

At 5:58 p.m., the FBI helicopter took off for a reconnaissance run near the cabin. As the helicopter clattered overhead, and fearing for their lives, Randy, Sara Weaver, and Kevin Harris, all armed with rifles, came out of the cabin and ran to a rocky ledge for cover. Next, the three ran behind the outbuilding known as the birthing shed. When they came back into view, an FBI sniper focused on one of the men. He did not know which one it was, but the guy was carrying a rifle across his chest. The agent later said that he thought the man was preparing to shoot at the helicopter. The agent fired and wounded Randy Weaver.

Now all three people came out from the shed. The first were Randy and Sara, who made a dash for the cabin. Randy entered the cabin first with Kevin Harris a few steps behind. The agent fired just as the man ran into the doorway. He saw him flinch and heard screaming inside the house. After the shots, two armored tanks lumbered up the hill.

A bullhorn boomed, "Mr. Weaver, we have warrants for you and Mr. Harris. Please come out of the house without any further violence."

There was no response, and the tanks were ordered to hold their position. The night passed quietly.

The next morning, Sunday, August 23, the armored vehicles moved up the hill and again called on Weaver to surrender. Again, no response. The HRT, heavily clad in body armor, moved into the outbuildings. An agent entered the birthing shed and radioed, "There's a body in here."

It was fourteen-year-old Sammy Weaver. The boy had been mortally wounded during the gunfight with the marshals when the dog was killed. He had been shot in the back. The marshals told Coulson they had no idea the boy had been hit.

Later it was revealed that when the Lab started barking and chasing the agent, the three marshals took cover in the bush. As Sammy Weaver and Harris came close, an agent rose up, pointed his gun at them, and called out, "Stop, US Marshals!" Then Harris raised his gun and shot one of the marshals in the chest.

The dog turned toward the gunfire and the other marshal shot the dog. As the dog fell to the ground, Sammy Weaver yelled, "You son of a bitch! You shot my dog." Another shot, and Sammy screamed in pain as he made his way to the cabin. From the cabin, a woman's voice cried out, "Yahweh, help us!" A child was screaming, "You tried to kill my daddy!" The marshals thought the commotion was over Kevin Harris. They had no idea it was over the death of Vicki's son.

Coulson thought: What started this insanity? A lousy ATF case involving two guns that had little to do with serious crime. They had enormous federal resources chasing after a mountain man whose only crime was sawing off a couple of shotguns, which were requested by a government informant, and it led to this?

Coulson states in his book that the next day he received yet another directive to assault the cabin. This time he responded:

"Something to consider:

1. Charge against Weaver is BS...
2. No one saw Weaver do any shooting.
3. Vicki has no charges against her.
4. Weaver's defense: He ran down the hill to see what the dog was barking at.
5. Some guys in camouflage shot his dog and started shooting at him and killed his son."

For the next two days there was no activity outside the cabin. Agents with bullhorns were calling out to speak to Vicki Weaver, hoping she could persuade the men to surrender. There was no reply. She was dead.

On August 26, the HRT sent a robot up to the cabin with a field phone, in hope they could get Weaver to negotiate with them. Unfortunately, no one had removed the twelve-gauge shotgun that was attached to the robot. It was not meant to be used against people. The function of the shotgun was to disrupt an explosive device by blowing apart its electronic system, or it could be used to blow the lock off a door. It should have been removed before sending it to the cabin.

Weaver refused to approach the robot or to touch the phone. "Get it the f*** out of here," he yelled.

A break came when Weaver shouted that he wanted to talk to Bo Gritz, a former Green Beret who had become a leading spokesman for militia groups and survivalist movements. He was also running for president on an anti-government ticket in 1992. If Randy Weaver admired Bo Gritz the way Jim Ellison looked up to Robert Millar, Coulson thought they might have found a way in.

When Gritz approached the cabin window, it was dusk. He asked Weaver if everyone inside was okay. Weaver said, "No, my wife was shot and killed last Saturday."

As it turned out, the FBI agent who shot at Kevin Harris missed Harris, but his bullet grazed the wooden door and entered the face of Vicki Weaver, who had been leaning out of the cabin with her child propped on her hip. She had been holding the door open from the inside and calling for her family to get inside. Vicki died almost instantly as the round passed through her carotid artery, exited the other side of her head, then struck Harris in the arm. Vicki bled to death on the cabin floor with her baby still in her arms. Gritz talked Weaver into letting them take Vicki's body down the mountain. Weaver still refused to come out, insisting that he and the girls would be killed.

Coulson went back to the command office; he could not believe that once again they were talking about injecting tear gas into the cabin. How could they do that? They had started with blood on the ground and tempers flaring. Now the violence had ceased; they had a guy that had established a dialogue and could come and go from the cabin at will. They had made great strides...and now they wanted to gas the cabin? Coulson reminded the agents that all survivalists have gas masks, and that the only one that they would be gassing was the ten-month-old baby. "You're not going to do this," he insisted.

The cabin was not gassed, and on Monday morning, August 31, Randy Weaver surrendered.

The shootout at Ruby Ridge not only enraged the anti-government zealots, like Timothy McVeigh, but it also fueled a growing mistrust of national law enforcement by everyday

Americans. After a thorough investigation, the United States Department of Justice awarded Randy Weaver and his surviving children $3,100,000 as compensation for the loss of Vicki and Sammy.

Yet as we shall see at Waco and Oklahoma City, the Feds didn't learn much from Ruby Ridge.

27

WACO: THE LAST STRAW

April 19, 1993
Two years before the Oklahoma City bombing

I also learned from reading FBI agent Danny Coulson's book that on February 28th, 1993, while at home he flicked on the television in the family room to catch an afternoon of golf, only to see a special news bulletin displaying the bloodbath taking place in Waco, Texas.

An ATF agent, dressed in raid gear, crouched by a window on the roof as bullets exploded off of the roof beneath his feet. Another agent scurried down a ladder in a barrage of automatic-weapons fire. Agents could be seen dragging the wounded out of the kill zone. Coulson knew the FBI would be called into this. Then the phone rang, and he was right. He grabbed his keys and kissed his wife goodbye. "I'll call you," he said as he rushed out the door.

On his drive to Waco, Coulson listened to the radio. He learned that around 9:30 a.m., seventy-six ATF agents pulled up to the Branch Davidian compound in a cattle trailer, seeking to serve a search warrant for automatic weapons, explosives, and other illegal arms. As they ran toward the compound, they were peppered with thousands of rounds that came right through the doors, wall, and roof. The Davidians even tossed grenades at medics as they tried to help the wounded. The agents were reluctant to return fire because of the women and children. They did so only when they saw a Davidian with a weapon. Four ATF agents were killed, twenty others were seriously injured. No one knew how many Davidian casualties there could be.

Coulson thought, *Here we go again, getting sent in to clean up the ATF's mess. The ground is soaked in blood, and they expect my guys to bring peace.*

He pulled into headquarters and learned that a crisis management and negotiation team had been lined up. The HRT had not yet been deployed because they had not received formal jurisdiction. Coulson poured over every bit of news footage he could find on the incident. He watched the amazing gun battle over and over.

He recognized one of the wounded as his friend Bill Buford. He had been leading his team up ladders and onto the second-floor roof when rounds from an M16 and AK-47 shattered his leg and hip, and he fell from the roof, breaking several ribs. He was badly hurt, but the reports from the hospital said he was going to make it. Coulson felt bad for Buford, not only because he was injured, but because three of his twelve-man team were wounded.

The more Coulson learned about the ATF raid, the more livid he was that anyone in authority would have signed off on it. The ATF knew that the cult had spent nearly $200,000 on weapons and ammunition in the past eighteen months. They had nearly three hundred assault rifles, many that had been converted into machine guns, and they also had hundreds of thousands of rounds of ammunition.

The boner award went to the ATF spokesperson in Texas who, after the failed raid, told reporters, "The problem we had was that we were outgunned. They had bigger firearms than we had."

ATF officials also knew that David Koresh was waiting for them. Their own undercover agent, Robert Rodriguez, had been posing as a neighbor and prospective convert, when a cult member rushed in and told him he got a tip from a local TV reporter out on the road that ATF was planning a raid on the compound. The cult member was hoping to film the impending raid. The element of surprise means nothing when they know you're coming.

ATF had assigned eight agents to live in an undercover house near Mount Carmel, but they never bothered to keep a log or do a twenty-four-hour surveillance to determine Koresh's habits. They didn't even have a good photograph of Koresh. After the FBI took control, they got a picture of him from his Texas driver's license.

If Coulson had been in charge before the killings occurred, he would have waited and used an HRT assault team to plan a mobile ambush to arrest Koresh. With Koresh out of the way, he felt the chances of getting the other Davidians to walk out would have been much greater. If that had happened, the negotiators would have had something to work with. As things stood now, the negotiators had nothing to leverage. After the deaths of the ATF agents, there was nothing left on the table. Koresh had two choices: He could lead his people out, go to prison for capital murder, and perhaps be executed. Or he could stay in the compound and be "God." He chose to stay.

The HRT was told to avoid getting into a situation where a shoot/don't shoot decision had to be made. Throughout the fifty-one-day siege, not a single FBI weapon was discharged on Coulson's watch.

The Davidians stood watch in a tower that had a 360-degree view of the plains. They also had night-vision scopes, and their fifty-caliber guns could penetrate almost any vehicle. Coulson asked the army for nine Bradley fighting vehicles configured without guns.

Late in the afternoon, on March 1, HRT operators started driving them around. The sight enraged Koresh, who told negotiators he was going to blow them off the map. Knowing that Soviet-designed rocket-propelled launchers were on the black market, the operators were unsure if Koresh could make good on his threat. Coulson went back to the army for two Abrams tanks and five combat-engineer vehicles that could withstand a direct hit by most hand-held rockets.

By the end of the day, the negotiators had spent seven hours on the phone with Koresh, and ten more children had been released, for a total of fourteen. Koresh was promising that everyone would come out and surrender on March 2, if his message concerning the end of the world would be played to a nationwide radio audience. The Christian Broadcasting Network and KRLD agreed to carry it that day, between one and three o'clock.

Coulson was elated, as was everyone working on the case. They were preparing for an elaborate surrender and made arrangements for medical care for any who might need it. They also prepared a safe facility for the children.

Two children appeared shortly after 1:00 a.m. on March 2. At 8:10 a.m., two more children and two elderly women came out, bringing Koresh's message. Several hours later, Koresh's wife, Rachel Howell, gave them the first head count of those that remained inside: forty-three men, forty-seven women, and twenty children.

Koresh's sermon went out over the air at 1:30 p.m., as agreed. At 3:00 p.m., the time he was supposed to surrender, nothing happened. A negotiator got on the phone and called the compound.

A little child answered. "Are you coming to kill me?" she asked.

The negotiator swallowed hard and replied, "We are not going to hurt anyone. We want to help your mommy and daddy to come out."

The FBI ordered a personality assessment on Koresh. After listening in on his conversation with the negotiators and reading up on the history of the cult, the consultant concluded that Koresh would never leave the compound, nor would he allow those he cared for to leave. They were told that Koresh valued his power over others more than life itself, and was extremely proud of it. He envisioned himself a great prophet who would be persecuted and killed like those in the Bible.

Koresh often had sex with girls as young as ten. He preached that God wanted him to be a "sinful Jesus," so that when he stood in judgment of sinners on Judgment Day, he would have experience of all sin and depravity He ordered that the men of the compound were to remain celibate. After giving that command, a few of their wives and daughters bore his children. The conclusion was that Koresh might have a mass suicide-homicide in mind, like the Jonestown Massacre.

Three more children came out on March 3, 4, and 5, but they were the last. Koresh told negotiators that those who remained were his biological children. Over the next weeks, twelve more adults came out, the last one on March 23. The FBI learned that those released were expelled for drinking and noncompliance, and some were just old and weak. It appeared Koresh was giving up those who didn't matter to him.

The children were taught to worship, fear him, and call him "father." Koresh spanked children, including young infants, until they bled. The children who had been released early on told of being beaten with a paddle called the Helper.

The HRT team developed an emergency assault plan in case a murder-suicide pact began. If the adults decided to poison everyone, including the children, Coulson and his men had acquired enough anti-cyanide kits to provide a lifesaving dose for every child and a few adults. They figured the adults were volunteers and the children were victims.

Friction developed between the ranks. The negotiators were at odds with the tactical people. No one could seem to agree on anything. Most of the problems between the HRT and negotiators was lack of communication. The special agent in charge would meet with the tactical team or the negotiation team, but seldom at once.

Negotiators turned off electricity and water. Every night, the compound was lit up with floodlights. Davidians woke up every morning with loudspeakers blaring and Nancy Sinatra singing "These Boots Were Made for Walking"—all designed to unhinge the Davidians and prompt them to surrender. Instead, it had the opposite effect. Their treatment was evidence to them that it was the Tribulation.

Indications from electronic listening devices the HRT had slipped into the compound in milk deliveries was that Koresh was getting stronger. The whole Waco crisis team feared that the Davidians were plotting to burst out of the compound, firing at agents while using children as shields. Koresh could hold out practically forever. He had at least a year's store of

MREs (military "meals ready to eat") on hand, plus a huge tank of water.

The snipers had been out on the line for thirty-eight days, peering through their scopes. No doubt, this was a stressful duty. No SWAT unit or rescue team could use their weapons with the surgical precision necessary to shoot a Davidian charging their lines with an AK-47 in one hand and a baby in the other. No one was enthusiastic about tear gas, but there just didn't seem to be a better solution. It seemed a better option than letting the crisis drag on for more months. Coulson was on board with the tear gas but didn't want it delivered by armored vehicles. He thought it should be fired in with M-79 grenade launchers, but he was overruled by Janet Reno.

Janet Reno asked medical experts for their opinions regarding the side effects of CS gas on children, pregnant women, and old people. Military experts persuaded her that tear gas wouldn't do permanent damage. Reno considered the gas plan for a few days. On April 17, Reno approved the tear gas plan to be executed on Monday morning, April 19. That afternoon, the HRT operators drove their armored vehicles close to compound walls. Koresh was on the phone, raising hell with negotiators. "If you don't know what you're doing, this could be the worst day in law enforcement history."

The negotiators sent a text to the Davidians, asking that it be read to the people inside the compound. "We are preparing to introduce a nonlethal tear gas. We are not going to enter your compound. This is not an assault so do not shoot."

At 6:02 a.m., two armored tanks pulled up to the living quarters. The CEVs (combat engineered vehicles) on the left side punched holes in the first-floor window and sprayed CS gas inside in two fifteen-minute burns. These rooms were chosen because they were farthest away from the area where the children were sleeping. They were also chosen because they were next to a crude, underground bunker the Davidians had formed out of an old school bus. They hoped to prevent people from streaming into the bunker, where they might suffocate from overcrowding.

At 6:04 a.m., reports of gunfire were coming from the building, then heavy fire erupted. The CEVs were being pelted by automatic weapon fire. In an effort to stop the gunfire, an order was given to gas the whole compound.

At 7:09 a.m., the operators reported they had delivered all their CS rounds through the windows, but the walls on the left side of the compound had not been penetrated. To intensify the gassing, orders were given to punch holes in the walls and fire more CS rounds. With the supply of rounds exhausted at close to 9:30 a.m., field officers were asked to deploy more rounds to the scene. They arrived around 11:30 a.m. CEVs were then deployed to knock holes in the rear walls to create an escape route. The last tear-gas rounds were projected into the building about 11:40 a.m.

At 12:07 p.m., images of fires were seen around the compound. There were reports of a man wearing a dark mask, carrying a rifle, and moving back and forth, as if pouring something. Then he was seen kneeling as if to light a fire. Flames shot up.

Coulson was watching on a bank of televisions inside the temporary FBI headquarters among the tent city of law-enforcement officials and reporters. *I told them not to do this. I knew it was too dangerous. We should have waited.*

On the screen was an agent holding a microphone, pleading with Koresh. “Don’t do this to these people. Don’t end it this way. David, don't be a destroyer. Be a savior, lead your people out of there."

The message was repeated over and over. Everyone was waiting for the children to come out. They never did.

Plumes of smoke rose from all around the compound. Gasps filled the room as they all watched the entire compound light up. No one was coming out. As the fire engulfed the building, you could hear gunshots. It was believed that the people who wanted to escape were being killed.

The fire trucks had been kept away up until now, to prevent the firefighters from being shot. Now it was too late. The building was collapsing. As the fire was raging, ammunition was exploding and continued to do so for about four hours. There were 400,000 rounds stored at the compound, plus well over a hundred weapons.

Coulson learned from the medical examiner that seventy-five people died that day: fifty adults and twenty-five children under the age of fifteen, not including the five more that were killed during the February 28 raid.

The autopsy reports were heartbreaking. Joseph Martinez, age eight, died of smoke inhalation. Audrey Martinez, age thirteen, had been buried alive and died of suffocation. Abigail Martinez, eleven, died of a gunshot to the head. "Doe 33," an unidentified three-year-old boy, had been stabbed in the chest. "Doe 51A," a two-year-old girl, died of smoke inhalation. "Doe 53," a five-to-six-year-old girl, had been shot in the heart. "Doe 57," a six-year-old girl, suffocated. "Doe 62" died of blunt force trauma to the head; she had been beaten to death. "Doe 67-2," a seven- or eight-year-old boy, was buried alive. "Doe 67-8," an infant, died of a gunshot wound to the head....

The reports went on and on. Coulson could not finish reading them.

One of the awful consequences of the siege was that it proved to the Branch Davidians that the apocalypse was real. David Koresh had been right when he prophesied from the Book of Revelations. The Tribulation was upon them. Their treatment by law enforcement confirmed it. After waiting for forty-one days to get the Davidians to surrender, why was the decision made to raid the compound on April 19, Patriots Day—a day revered by right-wing extremists?

Still enraged over the April 19 assault by federal authorities on Randy Weaver's family, which ended with the deaths of Randy's wife and son, Timothy McVeigh drove from Lockport, New York to Waco, Texas. He parked on a hill outside the compound where people had gathered to watch the standoff. He was sitting on the hood of his car and watched as tanks moved in. He heard the screams of the children as they were engulfed in flames. Rage filled his heart when he saw armored tanks used by the military being used on American citizens. He swore vengeance.

Waco was the final catalyst for McVeigh's deadly future plans.

28

MCVEIGH'S FORMATIVE YEARS

Timothy McVeigh was forgettable as a boy. There were no entries on his report cards from school, or comments from his teachers, that would indicate that he was special in any way. Tim was a long, tall, gangly kid in school that the students bullied, calling him "Noodle." He had that boy-next-door ordinariness. No one special by anyone's account, not even his mother's.

Mildred McVeigh packed up and left both her husband and son when Timmy was ten years old, taking his sisters with her. Timmy was always closest to his younger sister Jennifer. After his mother left, it was Jennifer that he missed the most. After school was the hardest for him. He would come home to an empty house and sit alone until his father got home from work. Tim's dad, Bill, tried to comfort his son, but he was hurting, too. Their lives collapsed the day Mildred left. Nothing would be the same again.

The McVeighs weren't rich people, but they lived decently enough in the small town of Rust Belt, just east of Buffalo, New York. By the time Tim got to high school he was a good student, but could hardly be called brilliant.

Tim McVeigh attended a local business college after high school. Six months later, he became disillusioned with the books and enlisted in the United States Army. Tim wanted to see the world, and the army was his ticket. He took to military life and needed the discipline and regimentation it brought. His platoon mates gave him a sense of family.

He loved guns long before enlisting in the army. After his mother left, his grandfather, Ed McVeigh, had spent a lot of time with Tim hunting and fishing.

According to his military records, McVeigh became an expert marksman and was a model soldier. He rose rapidly to become a sergeant before heading off to the Gulf War as a gunner on a Bradley fighting vehicle. He became a decorated war hero. He earned a Bronze Star and an Army Commendation Medal while in Iraq. His proudest memento of that time was a photograph of him shaking hands with General Norman Schwarzkopf. McVeigh met him while the general was negotiating the ceasefire with the Iraqi military command at a desert rendezvous.

When McVeigh returned from the Persian Gulf, he planned to be a career man in the military, but he wanted to up his game by joining the Special Forces. Unfortunately, he couldn't hack the physical stress and demands. Tim had lost weight in combat and was out of shape. He knew he wasn't going to make it when he developed blisters on his feet the second day.

When the Special Forces denied him, he was devastated. The disappointment soon turned to bitterness, and, at the next opportunity, he left the service and began to drift. By 1993 he was spending his time crisscrossing the country, visiting his old army buddies in places like Decker, Michigan, where Terry Nichols was living on his brother James's farm, and with Michael and Lori Fortier in Kingman, Arizona.

Very soon, this gung-ho, kill-the-enemy soldier began looking for ways to punish the government for mistreating him. He recruited his friends to help.

29

DECKER, MICHIGAN AND BABY JASON

November 21, 1993
One year, four months, and twenty-nine days before the bombing
Events as I believe they probably happened

At 5:15 p.m. on November 21, 1993, Terry Nichols stood in the doorway of the family farm.

He had grown up in this house. His older brother James ran his mother's farm now. It didn't produce enough revenue for two families, so Terry was going to strike out on his own.

Nichols stripped off his T-shirt and mopped his face. His arms hung from his shoulders. "I'm ready to call it a day," he said.

"What? You done already?" said Tim McVeigh, who had spent the day stuffing the Nichols silverware and bedding into boxes and garbage bags for their move to Las Vegas. "This is not even my crap and I'm still working." McVeigh turned a kitchen chair backwards and straddled it as he stopped working to sip a Miller Lite.

Jason toddled in from the living room and went for Nichols, who bent at the waist and grabbed the boy under each arm. "Upsy-daisy!" Nichols said, picking up Jason and tossing him toward the ceiling.

"It's hard to take you serious with that chink kid running around," McVeigh said. "You got a chink wife and a kid that's one-hundred-percent chink."

"Filipino."

"It's all chink. Dumb idea to let her bring the kid. It's not even yours."

"She wouldn't have come."

"Then you should have dumped her when you had the chance. She cheated on you before you'd been married six months. She'll do it again."

"She was seventeen."

"She's probably cheating on you right now while you think she's looking for more boxes."

"Marife wasn't sure she would ever get to the United States. She didn't know whether she'd ever see me again."

"That's probably what she thinks every weekend when you go to the gun shows."

Nichols ignored McVeigh. Every other woman had cheated on him or dumped him or both. He was twice Marife's age, and he looked older than that.

"They'll never let the kid into Elohim City," McVeigh continued.

Terry tossed Jason again. The boy laughed. "You want something to eat, buddy?" Terry asked him.

McVeigh stood and walked toward the door that opened onto the side of the house where his car was parked. "The sight of chink children chowing down nauseates me," McVeigh said.

"I'm going to put him to bed after he eats," Nichols said.

McVeigh had opened the door, but stopped with his hand on the knob. "That kid's going to cause you trouble. It won't be long before he figures out you're not his real father." McVeigh slammed the door behind him.

At 5:33 p.m., McVeigh stepped out of the kitchen and into the side yard silt. He walked to his car twenty feet away. He opened the door, bent down, and curled in. He banged his knee under the steering column, which happened every time. Before he cranked the engine, headlights flashed in his eyes. It was Nichols's truck. He rolled down his window and waited.

"Marife!" he hollered. He flashed his headlights, then stuck his left arm out the window and waved her over to his car. "Come here." Marife walked to him. "Terry told me what you wrote to your mama," he went on. "You feel like you have three husbands. Which one of us is your favorite?"

Marife slapped his arm. "It's not you." She broke eye contact..

"Aw, come on. Be nice to me. I'm one of your husbands."

Marife swallowed hard and ignored the comment. The light from the dusk-to-dawn pole lamp glinted off McVeigh's dark eyes. Her eyes never left his.

"You didn't do Terry no favor bringing that chink baby over here. If I was him, I woulda told you to leave him where he came from."

"Why don't you leave?"

"That's no way to talk to your husband. You couldn't even wait six months to get over here. You told him that he was the only one. He believes you."

An hour and four minutes later, at 6:47 p.m., Nichols scrambled an egg for Jason, poured him a glass of milk from their Holstein, bathed him, and laid him in his bed. The bed was surrounded by boxes—stacked three and four high—waiting to be loaded onto the truck.

"I want Mama."

"You go to sleep. Mama will kiss you when she gets home."

Nichols pulled Jason's quilt up to his neck and said good night. He was kind to the boy, even if he looked nothing like him, but to whom he was willing to give his last name. When the boy shut his eyes, he walked to the door and pulled it closed.

He didn't have much to offer the children in his life, but he was good to them. His father was an angry, hard-drinking man. He couldn't remember his dad ever tucking him in bed. There weren't too many good memories left for Nichols here.

He went to the kitchen and poured a glass of milk, then sat down at the kitchen table. As he looked out the window and onto the fields, he wondered whether Josh, his son with Lana, remembered the bedtime stories he told him when he and Lana were married. He stayed home with Josh while she sold houses. Every night when he put Josh to bed, he cuddled the boy until he fell asleep.

Josh's memories of his dad have faded. Now, when he tells people about his father, he brags that his dad, and his Uncle James, and their friend Timothy McVeigh, know how to blow up stumps in the field.

Nichols, too, remembers explosions from his childhood—nights when his father would return home late, and drunk. His childhood was filled with his parents fighting.

He looked at his watch. Six forty-seven, and Marife wasn't home. He took the store-brand peanut butter from its place by the sink, shook open the plastic bag that held the Holsum bread, and grabbed two pieces, which he smeared with the peanut butter. He ate, then washed it all down with another cup of milk.

Marife walked into the kitchen as he was finishing his last bite. Her eyes betrayed recent tears.

"You've been gone three hours."

"There are no boxes in Decker. I had to go to Flint." she said.

"What's up with the tears?"

"I'm getting sick of your boyfriend's rude comments."

"My boyfriend? What's that supposed to mean?"

"You spend more time with Tim than with me."

"You're jealous of McVeigh?"

She didn't answer. Instead, she asked, "Where's Jason?"

"In bed."

"Can you get the boxes out of the truck? I'm going to shower."

Nichols walked to the truck. McVeigh's car was there, but moved from where McVeigh had parked it earlier—far enough away that he couldn't see inside it. If McVeigh was in the car, he was lying down.

At 9:03 p.m., Marife and Terry's brother, James, were sitting on the floor in the living room when Tim McVeigh walked into the kitchen from outside. He then walked into the living room and sat on the couch.

"And here's Marife's third husband," McVeigh said. James Nichols didn't understand the joke and frowned. "Marife has told her mama that she feels like she's serving three husbands, me, you, and Terry."

Marife stood. "I'm going to check on Jason," she said.

McVeigh got up and went outside.

James heard the scream and ran to the bedroom. Marife was holding the body of her lifeless son.

⌘

The investigative report the Sanilac County sheriff's detective filed about Jason's death didn't answer the obvious question. How did a two-year-old, alone in a dark room, pull a plastic dry-cleaner's bag over his head and shoulders?

"Upon mother discovering child unresponsive behind door of child's bedroom, child's uncle telephoned 911 while another male subject in the home performed CPR on the child.... Child dead at home but pronounced upon arrival a hospital.... Child's mother very distraught. Requested investigators take fingerprints. She thought this could not have happened by accident, she believes someone has intentionally done this to her boy."

The following day McVeigh packed his things and headed to Elohim City.

30

MCVEIGH AT ELOHIM CITY

The Fall of 1993
Less than two years before the bombing
Events as I believe they probably happened

You won't find Elohim City on any map. The FBI has dedicated an incredible amount of time, money, and manpower to investigating and monitoring the town's activities. Yet, this idyllic hamlet (known to its residents as "God's City," the Hebrew translation of Elohim) remains well hidden, impossible to find without the assistance of one of the few people in the world who've actually been there. Some reports reference Fort Smith as the nearest town, others Sallisaw, Muldrow, or Stilwell. They're all more or less right, but also dead wrong. Elohim City is not "near" any town: Its four hundred acres are situated as far as possible from nearby civilization.

Bad men are drawn to the City of God. The Southern Poverty Law Center calls it the meeting ground for America's most sinister extremists. Many Oklahomans regard it as the most dangerous and mysterious place in the state. There, Tim McVeigh at last found a place to call home. A place where his radical ideas seemed normal.

McVeigh made the sixteen-hour drive from Decker, Michigan to Elohim City in fourteen hours. As his luck would have it, he got stopped for speeding on the last leg of his journey, a few miles outside the compound.

As McVeigh approached the entrance of the community, he was met by Elohim City founder, Robert Millar, and several armed guards. McVeigh politely told Millar that the weapons made him a little nervous. Millar, not missing a beat, sent the armed guards away.

"You lost?" he asked, smiling, in a country drawl. His tone was relaxed and friendly.

"No, I'm here to see Andy."

"Andy the German?" Millar asked.

"That's right."

"Any friend of Andy's is a friend of mine. Come on in."

Millar's home was modest—simple, clean, and with hardwood floors. On the wall hung a large digital clock. Framed photographs of family decorated the coffee and end tables.

Millar settled into his chair. "So, what's your name?"

"Tim Tuttle," McVeigh answered.

"We've been expecting you, Mr. Tuttle. Andy has told me a lot about you." He dialed up his son, John. "John, would you go down to the shop and tell Andy that his friend Tuttle is here?"

In a few minutes Andy knocked at the door and Tuttle/McVeigh stood. The two men greeted each other with a warm handshake.

Andy looked at Millar and said in his German accent, "My friend here is good people. You're going to like him. He was at Waco when the Feds burned it."

"Is that right?"

"Yes sir," McVeigh responded to Millar. "I was in Iraq. *I know about* Bradley tanks. I know what kind of damage those tanks can do. The images of that tank punching holes in that building still haunt me today. Things have got to change. It's not right, the military attacking its citizens."

Millar listened carefully as McVeigh talked.

A knock came at the door. It was Richard Guthrie, a court-martialed Navy Seal who came under federal law enforcement scrutiny after making a threat toward President George Bush in 1991. His childhood friend, Pete Langan, came with him.

"Gentlemen," Millar announced, "I would like you to meet Tim Tuttle."

⌘

McVeigh returned to Elohim City on October 12, 1993, with Terry Nichols and Michael Fortier to discuss "direct action" against the federal government with members of the compound. Millar started off the meeting.

"Our final goal is to overthrow the government and bring the country back to the white Christian country the Founding Fathers established. We must take action. We have to disrupt government and do whatever we can to make the government look suspicious."

Fortier leaned over to Nichols and whispered, "The government is doing a good job of looking bad. Even without our help." Millar added, "A few of these events would cause the white Christians to rally and then the second revolution to begin. Remember our patriot, Richard Snell. The Covenant, the Sword and the Arm of the Lord must be avenged."

"That's right," McVeigh chimed in. "We also must not forget Ruby Ridge and Waco. The ATF and the FBI need to pay for those massacres."

Millar left the room as Guthrie and McVeigh began to talk about how to finance their plans. They needed money, so the rest of the meeting was about bank robberies.

By January 1994, Guthrie, Langan, and Brescia started robbing banks in Iowa, with McVeigh driving the getaway car. The FBI dubbed the gang the Midwest Bank Robbers. As their stash grew, they began to put their plan into action. They began targeting federal buildings for a big event. The federal building in Oklahoma City made sense because the ATF and FBI had offices there, there were plenty of innocents, and they were not well protected.

By autumn, McVeigh and the gang were formulating their plans. Guthrie and Langan, were chosen to accompany McVeigh on his bombing run. Terry Nichols and Michael Fortier, being family men, would remain on the periphery.

31

CAROL HOWE'S FALL FROM EDEN

Early 1994

Carol Howe was eyewitness to what the feds didn't want the rest of the world to know—which is that the Murrah explosion was not a two-man job.

Carol, like Adam and Eve, was born into an Edenic world. If she had remained in the Eden into which she had been adopted on the first day of her life, if she had not been eventually beguiled by a serpent named Dennis Mahon; and if she had never called the phone number "1-800-Dial-A-Racist," she wouldn't have ever known the people she knew; she wouldn't have ever learned the facts she learned; and none of us would ever have heard her name—except perhaps on the Tulsa World's society-page coverage of the Tulsa Junior League coronation.

But Carol Howe fell from the paradisical world she was born into—and, in fact, she left Eden of her own choice. To understand Carol's life and her fall, you must know about her background.

The first and last time Carol ever saw or touched her fallen birth mother was on her way out of the birth canal. The people who gave Carol their name, and her own branch on their family tree, took her straight out of the warming lamp in the hospital into their palatial home.

Carol's father was president of an Oklahoma fossil-fuel extraction company, Sooner City Oil. Her mother enjoyed the luxury of her blessed life and doted on her daughter. Growing up, Carol had a personal nanny and everything a little girl could want. She wore the finest of clothes, took ballet lessons, and even learned to play the violin. She attended private schools, where she maintained a 4.0 grade average. She was a quiet girl by nature, a young lady who never, ever lit up the room. By the time she was twelve, she had read every book that Lucy Maud Montgomery and Aleksandr Isayevich Solzhenitsyn had written, plus Charles Darwin's books; and she had hiked the trails of Prince Edward Island and Rocky Mountain National Park. By the time she was sixteen, she had skied in Switzerland, cycled in France, England, Wales, Ireland, and Spain, then fished and hunted in Chile.

"A good girl," everyone who knew her whispered somberly to one another…after the fall.

Some compared Carol's life to Patty Hearst's, but a significant difference separates them. Carol wasn't kidnapped. Though she grew up in the cushion of bank accounts the size of which Forbes publishes stories about, the money never was important to her. On the evening of her nineteenth birthday, she informed her parents that she was moving to Telluride, a mountain town in a Colorado box canyon with only one road in.

"I'll see you when I see you," she told them. "And by the way, you can keep your BMW. I bought a Volkswagen."

That was the last they ever saw of "their" Carol, the good girl they adopted.

When Carol visited Tulsa again eighteen months later, she wasn't their Carol. This Carol was a troubled girl with a dark side.

Carol *couldn't* say what had changed her, and she didn't blame anyone. The abundance, perhaps, bred disdain for privilege and led her to reject it. And there was the anger. She couldn't identify the cause simply as anger at the man who fathered her and the woman who birthed her and gave her away. Carol couldn't exactly identify the root of her anger; but the black boys were her explanation, and their race was her target, and it began one night when the black boys came to the city park in Tulsa, where Carol had just celebrated her twenty-first birthday with her parents.

Carol enjoyed spending time alone. This evening she had stopped by the park, which once belonged to the federal government—a hundred acres with thirty Quonset huts the US Army had covered with topsoil and Bermuda grass, which gave them the appearance of huge, tipped-over, half-buried garbage cans. During World War II, the Army stored ammunition and nerve gas there. Now, the city of Tulsa stored lawnmowers, water hoses, hoes, shovels, and fertilizer spreaders. Children rode bicycles over the thirty humps, and park-goers sat on them.

It was getting late, but not yet dark. She sat atop the hut with the best view of the duck pond. She sat on its north end, her feet dangling, twenty-five feet above the concrete sidewalk. She was smoking a cigarette, wearing blue jeans and a turquoise T-shirt.

The black boys, who were her explanation, arrived at the park under cover of dusk and a drizzle. They approached her from behind. The significant details of the attack are that it was violent, bloody, and prolonged. Instead of leaving her to lie atop the Quonset, mostly disrobed and in agony, one of the young men shoved her off, and she landed on her feet on the sidewalk below, then fell to her knees. At their trial eight months later, Carol was still recuperating in a wheelchair, her heels left with stainless-steel pins, her left kneecap plastic.

The nineteen-year-old defendant, now a convict, bared his teeth and sneered at her after the jury sentenced him to only five years, with credit for the eight months served. On the drive back to her apartment, she saw the billboard with the "1-800-Dial-a-Racist" phone number.

"I realized I hated them when I saw the billboard," she said to the man who answered the toll-free number. "Does it cost anything?" she asked as she lay on the futon and propped her feet on the arm.

"Not a dime. We just want to keep our race pure."

"I don't even know your name," she said. "What's your last name?"

"Sure, my name is Dennis, Dennis Mahon. I'll meet you for coffee—where? In the morning."

"Call me Freya," she told him.

That is how Carol—who is now Freya, which means goddess of love in mythology—came to know the facts that attorney Stephen Jones needed her to tell in order to help his notorious client, Timothy McVeigh.

32

DENNIS THE MENACE

Months before the bombing

Carol Howe's newfound friend, Dennis Mahon, had been banned from Canada and the United Kingdom due to his connections with terrorist groups. However, he was allowed by federal authorities to be in the United States. It was his connections in Canada that opened doors for him at Elohim City. He was also a former Imperial Dragon of the White Knights of the Ku Klux Klan.

Dennis introduced Carol to Elohim City. It was her relationship with him that gained her access to a terrorist training ground, which most people would like to avoid. Elohim City is located on the Oklahoma and Arkansas border. The residents there call themselves "ultra-militant white separatists." Its members are required to read *Mein Kampf, The Silent Brotherhood,* and *The Turner Diaries.*

Dennis stayed in an old travel trailer with a flat tire, parked on a vacant lot grown over with weeds—quite different from the privileged life Carol came from. Oddly enough, Carol, now Freya, enjoyed life there. She participated in paramilitary training and didn't seem to mind the crude conditions and rough existence out of doors. Pretty little Carol seemed to fit right in, almost like this was the life she was born for.

Carol was letting her carefully coiffured hair go all natural. Her brunette roots had grown out several inches, replacing the fine, bleached-blonde hair. Her straight bangs hung just below her eyebrows. Her face was full and round; she was a pretty girl with the face of a child. "Miss Freya" thrived as she participated in military maneuvers and combat training. She became a crack shot, even getting a homemade swastika tattooed on her left shoulder. She loved the excitement of playing military games and shooting guns. Never again did she want to be vulnerable to attack.

A photograph from Stephen Jones showed Carol wearing a *Schirmmütze*, a Nazi officer's dress cap, which was twice as tall as her face. A Nazi field tunic, cut for Goliath, draped her shoulders.

Dennis and Carol hit it off at first, but later things began to change. While Carol loved her life with her comrades at Elohim City, Dennis became possessive and controlling. His jealousy was making her miserable—so much so that she decided to cool the relationship.

After she returned home to Tulsa, Carols parents bought her a modest home, not far from their own. The months at Elohim City had given her a new appreciation for her parents, and they were elated to have her come home. Meanwhile, Dennis was desperate to rekindle his relationship, but she would have nothing to do with him. He called constantly and, when he got no response, he began to leave threatening messages, so she had her phone number changed.

Three weeks after moving back to Tulsa, Carol enjoyed a late-night dinner with her parents. Her mother had made her signature lasagna, and the dinner was lovely, served on the usual fine china, with long-stemmed water glasses and cloth napkins. All seemed well with the Howe family.

When Carol got home that night, she backed into her driveway and parked combat-style, under the security light. With a cigarette in hand, she walked down the sidewalk to her front door. She put the cigarette between her lips, so to free her hands as she rummaged through her purse looking for her keys. From the corner of her vision, she noticed rustling in the bushes by her front door, and it frightened her. She hurriedly found her keys and began struggling to get the key in the knob.

Suddenly a large figure wearing a ski mask jumped from the bushes and grabbed her from behind.

"You thought you could just ignore me, you little bitch " She recognized the voice. It was Dennis. "You ain't no better than me, living here in your fancy digs."

"Get your hands off of me, you pig!" she screamed.

His breath reeked of cheap wine. He was clearly inebriated. He shoved her inside the door. There, he ripped his mask off and spun her around to face him.

"How dare you ignore my calls," he said, as he slapped her across the face. He leaned in to kiss her and she spit in his face. He was livid.

"You nasty bitch " he said, as he wiped the spit away. "We could have done this the nice way, but you ain't being nice."

Walking behind her with his arms around her neck, he forced her into the bedroom. She struggled to break free and dragged her feet, but she was no match for Dennis, who outweighed her by eighty pounds. In their scuffle, Carol fell onto the bed, with Dennis stumbling and landing on top of her. She began to scream, and Dennis held her by the hair and stuffed a scarf that was laying on the bed into her mouth. He waited for her to tire, then he finished what he had come to do—then he passed out cold.

Carol tried to roll him off but couldn't. She managed to wiggle out from underneath him. Now that she was free, she wasn't sure what to do. If she called the police, would they believe her? After all, she and Dennis had been dating. And worse yet, she knew if she were to get him in trouble with the law, the boys from Elohim City would come after her. They would not take kindly to her causing their boy to go to jail.

33

UNLIKELY INFORMANT

August 23, 1994
Seven months and twenty-seven days before the bombing

Angela Finely stopped shuffling papers when she saw Dennis Mahon's name on a document out of Adair County, Oklahoma.

"J. Edgar has smiled down on us today," she said to Emily Franco, who occupied a desk across from hers at the Tulsa Bureau of Alcohol, Tobacco, and Firearms. "Look what I just found stuck in the middle of our daily briefing stack. It's a protection order against Dennis Mahon." Angela passed it to Emily, who glanced at it.

"Sounds like he really did a number on this girl," Emily said, nodding. "He's an animal."

"So, we need to track down Miss Howe. After what Mahon did to her, I'm sure we can convince her to help us."

Carol accepted their invitation to lunch at El Chico. From their table, the quartet—Miss Freya, Angela, Emily, and a third ATF agent whose name was Irene—watched the tortilla-maker flatten the balls of masa and flip them on the griddle.

"That's what we have in mind for your boyfriend," Angela said. "We need you to help us flip your boyfriend. After what he did to you, we thought you might be interested in getting some revenge."

Carol Howe had placed her elbows on the table, her forearms flat in front of her, her fingers laced. "What do you have in mind?"

"We need you to supply us with information. The second you don't feel safe, leave."

"How can I do that?" Carol asked.

"Every two or three days, make an excuse to leave, and go to a pay phone. Someone will answer the phone round the clock. As a confidential informant your number will be CI 183. Call collect. Say the call is from 183. We will record all your reports. We'll pay you twenty-five dollars a day."

"I don't want money. If I did, twenty-five dollars wouldn't be enough."

"We have to pay," Angela replied as she nibbled at the chips and salsa.

"How will you know when you have enough to take him down?"

"It won't take much. Selling illegal firearms. Bank robbery. Conspiracy to take down the United States government, he's involved in all of it. I just need the evidence to prove it."

Carol agreed, reluctantly, to return to Elohim City. She arrived there on a Monday, knowing that Dennis would be in Tulsa. She saw Millar walking across the compound when she pulled through the gate. He waved.

"Can we talk?" she hollered out the car window.

"Sure, come on in," he said as he walked toward the one-room schoolhouse, where all the children at the compound were taught, grades one through twelve. It was early and the building was empty.

"We've missed your pretty little face around here, Freya," Millar said.

"I've missed you, too. This place is special. It's the only place I ever fit in."

"You left so suddenly. Why did you leave?"

"That's what I want to talk to you about. It was Dennis, he was making me crazy with his jealous ways. It was just so intense I couldn't stand it, so I quit coming. But you guys are like family to me, and I've missed being here. Dennis is a problem for me. Could you talk to him and call him off? I'm willing to be his friend; but just a friend, with no benefits, if you know what I mean."

Millar chuckled. "You don't worry about ol' Dennis. I'll talk to him."

The first person she encountered leaving the schoolhouse was Andy the German. She had seen him around, but never really talked to him. Andy was a tall man with a medium build, dark hair, and bucked teeth that should have seen braces long ago. He had a thick German accent and oversaw paramilitary operations at the compound. She was excited when he invited her to train with the men.

At one point, Andy the German decided to test Howe's loyalty. He made her crawl under barbed wire while he fired a .45-caliber pistol at her feet. Most women would have fled the challenge, but not Carol. She was an impressive soldier and enjoyed the training.

Carol reported to her FBI handler that Mahon was gathering fully automatic weapons and was preparing the group for a race war, as well as a war with the government, in the near future. He was rapidly stockpiling ammunition, silencers, and guns in the bunkers on the compound, while Millar was preaching about the holy war that was soon to come.

As CI 183 submitted her reports on Dennis, she included some things about Andy. She reported that he told her they could not out-breed the enemy, so they must exterminate them. That got the handlers' attention. She asked her informant to start focusing on Andy the German.

It took three months for Carol to learn Andy's real identity: Andreas Carl Strassmeir. She found it on some documents hidden in a duffle bag while he and his roommate were in town for supplies. She also found books on bomb making.

Carol was a natural as a CI. She didn't mind betraying the friends she was making. She felt like Mata Hari in an old movie. She became a seductress. She thought she was luring Andy into her web. Little did she know who Andy really was.

No one suspected Carol. They believed her to be their comrade. She felt like she belonged there, and maybe she did. After all, no one knew who her birth mother was. Carol liked to fantasize about her, and hoped she was more like her than her adopted mother, whom Carol deemed to be weak after her diagnosis with multiple sclerosis.

As men would come and go from the compound, CI 183 learned as much as she could about them. Andy the German's roommate was Michael Brescia. He was engaged to Grandpa Millar's granddaughter. He also was good friends with Richard Guthrie and Pete Langan, who were frequent visitors. There was another man Carol saw less frequently. His name was Tim Tuttle, aka Timothy McVeigh.

On the last night ATF informant Carol Howe spent at Elohim City, she saw all the men of the compound gathered outside around a campfire, drinking beer and smoking pot. Carol knew there was a big secret at Elohim City, but she hadn't been able to find out what it was. She stood behind a tree in the distance and listened intently. She couldn't make out everything that was being said, but she heard enough to realize they were planning something diabolical. Strassmeir and Guthrie did most of the talking.

Strassmeir told the men, "Our goal is to overthrow the government of the United States!" The men cheered. "And you know how do we do that? By spreading the money around to fund 'the movement.' We're doing God's work, as Millar proclaims."

Guthrie shared an article he read in the paper where authorities had dubbed them the Midwest Bank Robbers, and even likened them to the Jesse James gang.

She realized that some of these men were hiding out from the law. Mahon got up to relieve himself behind a tree and saw her. He was unable to make out who it was.

She ran into the woods and hid there until daylight, when she walked calmly to her car parked next to the church and drove back to Tulsa, to the safety of her parents' home.

PART FIVE

Justice on Trial

34

MCVEIGH'S ARREST

Wednesday, April 19, 1995
Ninety minutes after the bomb goes off
Events as I believe they probably happened

There was no "after the bombing plan" for the perpetrators. From what I can discern, the only instructions from Millar and Pastor Richard Butler, (who was founder and leader of the Aryan Nations, which was a white supremacist group whose organization promotes racist ideologies and sought to create a white homeland) were: "Don't come to Elohim City or Aryan Nations Headquarters in Idaho; and don't call or contact either of us." So, when McVeigh headed north from the bomb site, no one knew if he had a plan and, if he did, what it was.

When McVeigh reaches Twenty-third and Broadway, he turns right. Just as he reaches the ramp to the Broadway extension, which will take him to its intersection with I-35 north, the Mercury feels airborne as the shock wave from the blast rocks the northern half of Oklahoma City. Clerks at Penn Square, a large shopping center at Fiftieth and Penn, four miles from ground zero, dive under counters, thinking that an airplane has crashed.

McVeigh, satisfied that the job is done, reaches I-35 and heads north to God knows where. The Mercury he bought in Junction City looks like hell but runs well, and Tim keeps it just under the speed limit. This is no time to attract a speeding ticket. What he does not know is that the license plate that he hastily put on the Mercury has fallen off. The little task of making sure that the tag was secure will have fatal consequences for Timothy McVeigh.

Trooper Charlie Hanger is heading south at ninety miles per hour on I-35, lights and siren on. Twenty minutes earlier he had been summoned to Oklahoma City as a backup for a code-red emergency. At mile marker sixty, he is ordered to cancel that order and return to his normal routing. He shuts off his lights and siren, finds the next trooper-only U-turn spot, and now heads north at normal speed. He is disappointed that all the experience and skills he developed in his twenty-year career are not going to be a part of what now looks like the crime of the century.

Trooper Hanger continues north at seventy miles per hour. He overtakes an old Mercury traveling maybe five miles per hour slower. When he pulls into the middle lane to pass, he notices that the Mercury has no license plate. He thinks, *Surely, I can find something more interesting than ticketing for a missing tag while I'm missing what I should be doing in Oklahoma City. Oh well, I'll drop a ticket on this poor slob and be on my way.*

He slows and allows the Mercury to pass on the right, then pulls in behind and flips on his lights.

"Oh shit!" McVeigh says aloud. "I knew this would happen, but not now…not today!"

As McVeigh slows the Mercury and pulls toward the shoulder, he touches his shoulder holster that contains his Glock pistol. He can easily kill a stupid Oklahoma trooper, but then what? No. He recalls his POW training before he went to Iraq. "Don't volunteer anything. Don't tell them anything about your fellow soldier. If you have to, give up your life. Spit in the eyes before they kill you."

Tim steps out of the car as Trooper Hanger approaches.

"Hands where I can see them," says Hanger.

When McVeigh raises his hands, Hanger's trained eyes spot the bulge on McVeigh's left side under his jacket. The trooper draws his own gun and instructs McVeigh to place his hands on the roof of the Mercury and to keep them there until he is searched. With his left hand he reaches for McVeigh's pistol.

"My gun is loaded," says McVeigh.

The trooper removes McVeigh's gun from the holster. "So's mine," Hanger says, putting his weapon to McVeigh's head. "Put your hands behind your back."

McVeigh complies without hesitation, and Hanger slaps the cuffs in place. He continues the search and finds a large knife in McVeigh's belt.

"We will check your driver's license and see if you're wanted when we get to the jail," Hanger says. "No need to do it now because I'm arresting you for carrying a concealed weapon. Let's go."

When he places McVeigh in the back seat of the patrol car, Charlie Hanger has no idea that he has arrested the man who ignited the fuse that killed and maimed hundreds of innocents.

At the Noble County Courthouse in Perry, Hanger checks the wanted network. Finding nothing on McVeigh, he completes the paperwork. He pours himself a cup of coffee and sits down to watch the news about the bombing, where he would like to be. At this point, the speculation is that the bombers are of Middle Eastern descent.

McVeigh is scheduled to go before the judge the next morning, on Thursday. He is advised that the judge is running behind, so his hearing will be on Friday.

The next morning, Trooper Hanger receives a call at home.

"I understand you are the trooper that arrested McVeigh on Wednesday. Right? Where is he now?" the voice asks after identifying himself as FBI.

Charlie replies, "His hearing was this morning. He had several hundred dollars on him, so he's made bail by now. But I'll double-check that. When I checked his record yesterday, he wasn't wanted for anything. What's up?"

"Find him," the voice says. "He may have some info about the bombing. Get back to us pronto."

Hanger immediately contacts the jail and finds that the hearing was postponed again, this time because the judge's son missed the school bus and the judge had to take him to school. On his way to Perry, Hanger finds out the axle from the Ryder truck has been found, and the serial number traced to the rental agency, which then somehow led them to the Dreamland Motel in Junction City where a Timothy McVeigh had registered in his real name. Lea McGown, the owner of the motel, had identified McVeigh from artists' renderings of the two people who rented the Ryder truck from Elliott's Body Shop.

"Oh my God," says Hanger aloud. "Thought I was missing all the action in OKC, and I had the bomber right here all the time."

Trooper Charlie Hanger is now a national hero.

FBI Agent Danny Coulson is called in to transport McVeigh into Federal custody. Coulson commanded the Hostage Rescue Team at the CSA, Ruby Ridge, and Waco. He flew from Oklahoma City by helicopter to pick up McVeigh from the Perry, Oklahoma courthouse. People are gathered on the lawn outside the courthouse, yelling "Baby killer!"

As Coulson and his men walk into the courthouse that house the sheriff's office and jail, he pauses to scan the crowd. "They don't look very happy," he whispers. "We need to get him out of here ASAP."

Deputies bring McVeigh out from the holding tank. McVeigh looks at the TV on the wall, views the coverage of the bombing, and asks Coulson, "Were there any children killed?"

Coulson answers, "Yes."

McVeigh wants to know how many.

"Nineteen," Coulson says.

McVeigh grins and says, "Good, that's three less than Waco."

Timothy McVeigh is about to achieve the fame he so desires, and the title, "Most hated man in America."

The last picture of Chase and Colton taken before the bombing on Easter Sunday.

Kathy Sanders and her son, Danny, who was an off-duty police officer the day of the bombing. He saw his mother and sister while watching the news coverage on TV. He rushed and found both of Kathy's grandchildren. Both were dead.

Kathy and her daughter, Edye.

Chase and Colton's first and last trip to the zoo with their grandmother.

Chase and Colton, the ultimate little he-men.

The America's Kids Daycare. Nineteen children died in the bombing, including their teacher Ms. Brenda, shown in this picture with them.

The bombed-out Alfred P. Murrah Federal Building. The daycare was on the second floor. (Photo by David Allen.)

Edye hanging a memorial picture on the fence in honor of her boys. (Photo by David Allen.)

Kathy and her family at the Memorial that is held every year to remember those who perished. This picture is the 12th anniversary. Kathy's new granddaughter, Emjay, is sitting on her lap.

After the bombing, a fence was erected to keep people back from the rubble. Visitors to the site hung mementos on the fence in honor of those who perished. (Photo by David Allen.)

Chase and Colton's funeral. The saddest day of my life. (Photo by David Allen.)

Carol Howe, also known as Confidential Informant 183, who was planted inside at Elohim City for the ATF. She told her handler that the people at Elohim City were planning a bombing and that one of their targets was the Federal Building.

The largest manhunt in history was being conducted and within weeks, it was called off. The FBI said they were mistaken. Twenty-two eyewitnesses saw Timothy McVeigh the morning of the bombing, and not one eyewitness saw him alone.

The Dreamland Motel in Junction City, Kansas, where McVeigh stayed the week before the bombing. There were men seen coming and going from his room all week. The FBI was never able to identify these men.

Kathy Sanders visited with Carol Howe on many occasions. She was living under an assumed name and feared retribution from those she informed on at Elohim City and the FBI, who was doing nothing to protect her.

Andreas Strassmeir lived at Elohim City and went with Carol Howe on three different occasions to target buildings to blow up. According to Howe's reports, they were targeting the Federal Building. Timothy McVeigh also called Elohim City the week before the bombing, two minutes after calling the Ryder company, and asked to speak to Strassmeir, who was allowed to leave the country without ever being interviewed by the FBI. However, the FBI did interview McVeigh's third grade schoolteacher.

This is the aerial view of Elohim City. The white building at the bottom is the church where Kathy and her daughter, Edye, attended a worship service at the compound.

Kathy Sanders preparing to fly over the compound; she wanted to know everything she could about the compound.

The Israeli Flag placed in the doorway of the Church of Jesus Christ–Christian at the Aryan Nations. The members wipe their feet on it before going into worship.

You walk down the isle of the church, and you see a life size bust of Adolf Hitler to the right of the pulpit.

One of the buildings on the compound has
a large Nazi Swastika on the roof.

There is no stained glass, only Nazi flags.

Pastor Richard Butler, founder of the Aryan Nations.

35

CAROL RECALLED BY ATF

April 21, 1995
Three days after the bombing
Events as I believe probably happened.

On April 19, Carol Howe had been sitting Indian-style on the couch in her Tulsa apartment, her gray cotton T-shirt gown stretched tight from her shoulders to her knees, watching the *Today* show. Suddenly, Matt Lauer interrupted Katie Couric to say they were cutting to a breaking news story. As she watched the unfolding images, she said aloud to herself: "They did it. They really did it!"

Two days later, Carol answered a knock on her door and was greeted by a man and a woman in black suits who flashed their FBI identification.

"You buffoons!" she growled. "I told you they were going to blow it up."

The agents didn't flinch at Carol's invective. "Ms. Howe," the female agent said, "we need your help. We have a warrant for your arrest. We've been instructed to invoke it only if you refuse to come voluntarily."

CI 183 elected to go voluntarily. She pulled on navy linen slacks and a gray sweatshirt for what normally was a two-hour trip. With the FBI on the gas pedal, they covered the distance in seventy minutes and total silence.

They drove to the command center at ground zero. The agents had lowered the car's windows so Carol could smell the smoke and scorching paint on the burned-out pickups and cars. The acrid air seemed short on oxygen, and Carol was aware of every lung-scorching breath she took.

The agents exited the car. Carol, seated in the back seat, stared. The scene, framed through the rear window, appeared as if it were on a television screen, the same way the scene had appeared two mornings before when NBC cut to live coverage.

Carol had been here six months earlier, a week before Thanksgiving, in the back seat of another car, with Dennis Mahon in the passenger seat and Andreas Strassmeir driving. They had stopped in exactly the spot where Tim McVeigh would park the Ryder truck on April 19.

"This is the one," Dennis had said.

"What about the daycare?" Carol asked.

"Forget about the daycare! The Feds didn't take no pity on the Branch Davidian children. Good book calls for an eye for an eye, and I reckon this is it."

Carol had looked up from the street level toward America's Kids Daycare on the second floor. She watched as a little girl pressed her face against the glass, peering down at them.

On the tense return to Elohim City, she lay back in the seat, eyes closed, with thoughts of the little girl who peered down on her from the daycare running through her head. By the time Strassmeir drove through the gates at Elohim, Carol was certain the boys in the front seat intended to do what they'd been planning for all these months. She didn't know exactly how they planned to pull it off, but CI 183 knew it was past time to call her handler at the ATF.

⌘

The female agent who brought her from Tulsa opened Carol's door and motioned for her to follow. They escorted her inside the command center, where half a dozen agents lay about on the floor on air mattresses. Carol saw that one of the desks was covered with photographs of dead children.

The agent put Carol at a desk next to a window, through which she watched a man in a khaki jump suit tie an identification tag onto a black watch band strapped to a forearm and hand. The man dropped the arm into a clear plastic bag. Carol turned her head in time to grab a trash basket and get it under her mouth before she wretched.

An agent offered her a blue washcloth, moistened, cool, and told her, "I'm Agent Rex McMurray."

McMurray started laying out headshots and artist sketches on the desktop. Carol recognized and named Michael Brescia and Richard Guthrie.

"We know you've been working with the ATF. That's why you're here. We need your help."

"You're two days too late. When I tried to tell them, nobody would listen."

"So, what can you tell me about those two?"

"Brescia shared a room with Andreas Strassmeir. Guthrie hung out at Elohim City. They robbed banks together."

"Hey! Hey!" A man's voice rose above the hubbub. He pointed toward the television that sat atop two steel file cabinets in a corner of the room. "They made the arrest."

The color bar across the bottom of the TV screen said: "Suspect in Oklahoma City bombing arrested by FBI." The typist misspelled Oklahoma.

On the screen, a dozen or more men appeared at the courthouse door and moved quickly through it. Most of the men were police from various agencies, some wearing blue uniforms, some tan. The man in the middle of the group wore the orange uniform of a county jail. His hair was clipped in a military-style buzz cut. A brief flash of silver from his midsection showed the agents had cuffed him. An FBI agent followed behind, on the prisoner's right shoulder, and an FBI agent walked ahead of him, on his left shoulder. Noble County deputies, Perry city police, and Oklahoma state troopers walked by his side. The TV broadcasters said nothing. As they moved the man in orange jumpsuit toward a full-size van, the only sound was the growing murmur of onlookers and the barking of an unseen dog. The van left the courthouse and then left Perry in the escort of five police cruisers.

The network replayed the exit from the Noble County courthouse. They slowed the footage and drew a circle around the face of the man in orange. Connie Chung narrated over the scene.

"Authorities are telling us the suspect's name is Timothy McVeigh, and that he was arrested shortly after the bombing on Wednesday. The state trooper who arrested him had stopped him because there was no license tag on his Mercury Marquis. McVeigh spent two nights in the Noble County jail and was about to bond out when the FBI called the jail."

Carol stared at the face in the red circle on the screen, only vaguely hearing Connie Chung's words. "Who is it? Who is it? Who is it?" she whispered. The screen cut to a photograph of the suspect's license, and the memory clanked into place. "Tim Tuttle. That's Tim Tuttle."

Carol tapped McMurray's arm. "I've seen that man at Elohim City," she said and pointed at the television. "His name's Tim Tuttle."

McMurray stood from the table and walked three desks over, where he spoke to another man in a black suit. The two of them returned to Carol.

"Let's find a quiet place and talk about Tim Tuttle," McMurray said.

Carol followed, and the trio picked up two more agents by the time they walked into a small office and shut the door.

"Tell these agents what you told me about Tuttle," McMurray said.

Carol recalled three times when she saw Tuttle at Elohim City, and she told them about the evening he showed up in Oklahoma City, when they decided the Murrah Building was the right target. Carol started to cry. "Why hadn't they listened?"

McMurray told her, "Ms. Howe, we need you to go back to Elohim."

Seeing the pictures of the dead children gave her the courage she needed.

Fewer than twenty-four hours later, on the first Sunday after the bombing, CI 183 drove her Volkswagen through the gates into Elohim City, which was uncharacteristically quiet. No rubber basketballs pounding on courts of red clay. No children chasing chickens or dogs. No gathering of the superior race at the garage while mechanics ground serial numbers off engine blocks and firearms. No pseudo-soldiers parading the grounds with their thirty-eights hanging off their hips.

Carol saw women pulling weeds in the communal vegetable garden. She parked and walked over.

"Where is everyone?" Carol asked Millar's granddaughter, Rachel.

"The men are away."

"Every one of them?"

"See for yourself."

"Where'd they go?"

"If I knew, I wouldn't say." Rachel brushed her hands together, picked up her basket, and scurried off.

Carol spent the rest of the day in her room, leaving only for a sandwich in the dining tent. Sometime after eleven that night, she was awakened by a pounding on her door. She opened it a crack, and Dennis Mahon shoved in his foot, then pushed the door open.

"Blast it, Freya! This is important."

At that, Carol's knees went to rubber, and she couldn't resist the door when Mahon shoved on it.

"I'm not going to hurt you," he told her. "I need your help."

"What do you want?" she asked.

"If anyone asks you where I was on Wednesday, you tell 'em I was at your house in Tulsa."

Fearing for her life, Carol agreed.

When Mahon left, Carol ran out the back door to her Volkswagen. She turned the key. The engine cranked but failed to engage. "Start. Start. Start!" she shouted.

At the sound of the engine firing, one of the men looked out the window of the chapel. She didn't recognize him. She shifted first gear to second in a hurry, hung a U-turn, and sped toward the gate, gravel spraying behind her like the wake behind a speedboat.

36

ARYAN REPUBLICAN ARMY

Early 1996

Jennifer McVeigh admitted her brother asked her to exchange three one-hundred-dollar bills for clean money. He told her he had not participated in a robbery but was somehow involved in the planning of it. The money represented his share of the bank robbery proceeds.

In early 1996, a group of white militants known as the Aryan Republican Army (ARA) had been arrested for bank robbery. Newspaper reports referred to them as the Midwest Bank Robbers, since they'd been holding up small Midwestern banks since 1992, sharing the proceeds with a variety of neo-Nazi groups. Their crime spree was so prolific that authorities likened them to the Jesse James gang.

The FBI broke the case with the arrest of Richard Guthrie after a two-mile chase through Cincinnati, Ohio. His accomplice, Peter Langan, was lucky to have survived capture. His white van was shot to pieces by the FBI, US marshals, and local police, though Langan never fired a shot himself. Grazed in the head by a bullet, Langan managed to crawl out of the wreckage alive. Guthrie entered a plea bargain and named names. His information led to the arrest of alleged fellow gang members Kevin McCarthy, Scott Stedeford, and Michael Brescia. All were former skinheads from Philadelphia who played together in a heavy metal band called Cyanide. They had been at Elohim City and had gone through terrorist boot camp under Andreas Strassmeir.

McCarthy and Stedeford used to stay with Strassmeir when they were in the area for rest and relaxation between robberies. In fact, they were with him at Elohim City immediately before the Oklahoma City bombing in April of 1995, according to McCarthy's statement to the FBI.

Brescia's role seemed to be different from the others. Although he participated in the robbery on August 30, 1995, where $9,845 was stolen from Bank One in Madison, Wisconsin, robbery was not his main function in the ARA. He served as second in command of paramilitary operations at Elohim City, under Strassmeir. Many investigators around the country believe that Brescia is John Doe 2.

Richard Guthrie told reporters his deal with the government included a promise to provide them with information about organizations "whose goal is the overthrow of the United States government or to engage in domestic terrorism." He also confirmed to the media that some of the unrecovered money from the bank heists was "spread around" the white separatist movement. How much information the government actually received from Guthrie is not public knowledge and may never be.

Prison guards found Guthrie dangling from an air vent in his cell with a sheet wrapped around his neck. The cause of death was listed as suicide. He was found a few hours after telling a reporter for *The Los Angeles Times* that he intended to write a tell-all book "that would go a lot further into what they were really doing." This happened just nine days after Guthrie signed the plea bargain.

The ARA was modeled after the Irish Republican Army and the Aryan Resistance Movement, the military arm of a Nazi organization called The Order. In the early 1980s, The Order was the most dangerous terrorist group in the United States. They robbed $3.8 million dollars from a Brinks armored car; they also planted bombs and killed people in a campaign against the Zionist-occupied government. The Order was broken up by the FBI in 1984 when the leader, Robert Mathews, entered into martyrdom by burning to death in his cabin rather than surrender to the FBI.

Mathews left behind some very specific instructions for terrorist tactics, according to "Commander Pedro" in the ARA film, *The Aryan Republican Army Presents: The Armed Struggle Underground*. "The first rule was that terrorist cells must be kept separate from other units, and they must be broken down into even smaller units called teams. It was recommended that no unit be comprised of more than six members. This unit is then broken down into two- or three-man teams.

Every member of The Order is expected to obtain at least one, preferably two, false identities. No member is to divulge his new identity to anyone, not even to his team leader. All sensitive communications must be made from pay phones; calls must be placed from pay phone to pay phone. Every member of the Order and the ARA is to have at least one ten-dollar roll of quarters with him at all times.

The ARA was clearly attempting to rebuild The Order. "Our goal was to open the door to overthrow the United States government," admitted Kevin McCarthy, one of the bank robbers.

When the FBI busted two ARA safe houses in Ohio and in Kansas in February 1996, they found a recruitment video called *Armed Struggle Underground.* The tape starts with an IRA song, "The Patriot Game." The tape proceeds with a grimacing "Commander Pedro" sitting in a command bunker with a ski mask covering his face. Commander Pedro explains:

"The goal of the ARA is the overthrow of the US government, the extermination of America's Jews, the deportation of all blacks, and the establishment of an 'Aryan Republic' on the North American continent. Linger at your own peril. We have endeavored to keep collateral damage and civilian damage to a minimum. But, as in all wars, some innocents shall suffer, so be it. We call ourselves the Aryan Republican Army because in some of our tactics, and some of our goals, we have modeled the organization after the successful and yet undefeated Irish Republican Army. We understand the meaning of ethnic cleansing. We will deal with informers ruthlessly and permanently. For actively working with our enemies, you will be terminated. If you just like to run your mouth, you'll be kneecapped." At this point Pedro holds up an automatic pistol, and an electric drill. "Either one, I can assure you, are extremely painful."

The ARA was equipped for terrorism. In the busts, the FBI seized a shoulder-fired rocket launcher, Semtex explosives, hand grenade canisters, eleven pipe bombs, and an arsenal of M-14 rifles. It also found high-quality false ID badges and driver's licenses in the names of US marshals and FBI agents.

From watching this video, you would never guess the menacing Commander Pedro is also a transvestite. He is known as "Donna" at the chapter of Crossdressers and Friends in Kansas City.

His real name is Pete Langan.

This cell appeared to also be raising funds for the Aryan revolution. Over a period of two years, between January 1994 and December 1995, they netted more than $250,000 in well-planned robberies across the Midwest. Wearing Ronald Reagan and Count Dracula masks, they robbed small-town banks and seized the cash at hand. They would amass anywhere from $3,000 to $30,000 within ninety seconds. They never tried pushing their luck by trying to get the big haul from the vault. To deter police, they would leave disarmed pipe bombs in Easter baskets and Christmas stockings. By the time the FBI cracked this cell, the group had carried out a total of twenty-two bank robberies.

After learning about this organization, I began to suspect that the Midwest Bank Robbers could have been connected to the Oklahoma City bombing. I was troubled by Richard Guthrie's mysterious suicide after announcing he was going to write a book that would tell what they were really doing. I contacted Guthrie's partner, the very colorful Pete Langan. Pete was a high school dropout from suburban Washington, DC, and the son of a CIA officer. I found the menacing Commander Pedro seen in the recruitment video serving a 240-year-sentence in a federal prison in Florence, Colorado—the same place Tim McVeigh was serving his time. We began to correspond. The following excerpts are from one of the letters Pete wrote to me:

> Dear Kathy,
>
> I was a little uncertain how to respond to your request to tell you more about facts, times, and places. A person in my position must be very careful about what they say and write. But I think I can give you a general

> idea of what I know. Court transcripts and FBI documents show this: Kevin McCarthy claims to have been with me in Kansas on April 19, 1995; he also told FBI investigators he had been with me for the three days prior to that. But the FBI also knows he was in Oklahoma (Elohim City) and Fort Smith Arkansas on the 16, 17, and 18, and 19 of April. I can state for the record without any reservation Kevin McCarthy was not with me in Kansas at any time on 19 of April 1995. Records will show that these obvious contradictions were known to the FBI and others.
>
> They gave a witness against me in this case a lie detector test (Sean Kenny) and he was shown to be untruthful and deceptive. But they never gave a lie detector test to Kevin McCarthy (to my knowledge). If they had, the results would have been required to be turned over to me. If they did not, it would be grounds for a new trial. A person must wonder why the FBI ignored leads in Oklahoma, the ATF informant Carol Howe, and all the other mysterious goings on at Elohim City. Anyone seeking the truth would ask questions and publish the answers. To date, no one in the government has stepped forward. In fact, it's the feds, not the defense attorneys, who have gone to court to suppress evidence.

After reading Pete Langan's letter, I had to wonder how many people could be involved in this crime. Why would Kevin McCarthy be lying about his whereabouts on April 19, 1995? It seems to me that the government was willing to overlook the complicity of the Midwest Bank Robbers in the Oklahoma City bombing in order to protect their informants. Peter Langan had become a problem, and the government wanted him out of the way. At his trial, expert testimony established the device left at one of the banks was a destructive device. The FBI manipulated testimony and got Langan convicted of planting a bomb, which in reality couldn't blow up a birdhouse. The other members of the gang plea-bargained, providing information in exchange for lighter sentences, while Langan is locked up for life in a supermax prison. The others are free men today. That's just wrong on every level.

37

KILLER EYES

November 3, 1997
Two years, six months, and fifteen days since the bombing

Our eye contact in the courtroom is accidental.

The first few hours, Terry Nichols sits with his eyes focused on his mother, careful not to let them wander from her face. In one careless moment, however, his eyes drift from her face and onto mine, and our eyes lock. I sit silently looking into the eyes of the man who helped kill my grandsons.

This isn't the first time I have locked eyes with a killer. The first encounter was the first day Timothy McVeigh appeared in a courtroom. When McVeigh entered the courtroom, he resembled a young college student. The defense team welcomed him as if he were a celebrity by shaking his hand and patting him on the back. They were all laughing and joking. It was offensive to me, and I could tell the other survivor family members felt the same. It was evident McVeigh was enjoying his newfound notoriety.

The longer I watched his smiling face, the angrier I became. McVeigh was no celebrity. He was a cold-blooded killer who had the audacity to appear in front of those whose family members he had murdered—with a *smile* on his face!

His haughty presence sickened me. I began to stare at him intently. After a while, I could tell he was becoming uncomfortable with my glares. He locked eyes with me in an effort to make me stop. We had a stare-down. I was not about to back down. After several minutes he mouthed to me, "What do you want?" I said nothing. I simply continued to stare. I eventually won the stare-down between the two of us, so credibly that McVeigh scooted his chair back, so his lawyers blocked his view of my face.

This time is different. I am the same grandmother, it is the same crime, but it is a different killer. The difference: McVeigh was never remorseful and had been safely locked away on death row for months, awaiting happy hour and the special midazolam cocktail the feds were shaking up for him.

⌘

By the time my eyes met Terry Nichols's eyes in the Colorado courtroom, I see this man differently. What I recognize is that this man, whose gaze holds me tight, is a mother's son.

At the beginning of the trial, at the start of jury selection, even before I locked eyes with him, I had met his mother. It was an innocent encounter. I noticed her the moment she walked into the courtroom. The woman entered alone, sat alone, spoke to no one, never turned her head left or right. During the two morning breaks, she stood alone in the hallway. She had pinned her gray hair into a bun, which gave her a passing resemblance to TV Sheriff Andy Taylor's Aunt Bea. The hem of her black wool coat, which hung below her knees, was wet and dirty where it had dragged against the mounds of September snow, scraped into four-foot piles by the plows.

The trial broke for lunch, and in the federal courthouse cafeteria, where I paid two bucks and a quarter for a turkey-and-cheese sandwich, I saw the woman was alone at a table.

"Are you expecting anyone?" I asked.

"Only trouble," Aunt Bea said, and smiled. "I'd be happy for the company. You don't even have to say a word."

"I'm—"

"I know who you are," she said. She laid her fork, laden with a chunk of cantaloupe, on the edge of her plate. Her hands disappeared beneath the table, and she hung her head. "Your grandsons were Chase and Colton. *Are* Chase and Colton."

"Did you lose someone in the bombing?" I asked.

The woman didn't raise her face. "You might say," she replied, "that I lost a son. But he's still alive." I remained quiet. She went on. "They say my son killed your grandsons. My son is Terry Nichols."

Now I understood why she was alone. How awkward she must have felt to be in a strange city, where she knew no one, with her son on trial for mass murder. We sat silently sharing a meal, and our pain.

⌘

After lunch, back in the courtroom, two FBI agents escort Terry Nichols, along with the federal bailiffs, to the defendant's tables. We are an hour into the afternoon session when Terry Nichols's eyes drift from his mother's to mine. His gaze holds tight, and perhaps the reason I allow it is because I feel so sorry for his mother, whom I had met in the cafeteria. I feel the instinctive discomfort of accidental eye contact. Discomfort turns into confusion. I should be angry at this man for his crime against my family. But I have no anger. All I have is sadness for Joyce Nichols Wilt. Her boy is on trial for murder. This is her boy, whom she had cradled in her arms as an infant.

Our eyes are locked. I do not know what to do. His mother is sitting beside me, and the families of the victims of the crime are in the courtroom. Rather than glare, I simply nod my head slightly. At my gesture, Nichols' eyebrows lift, and his eyes seem to open wider. Then he returns my greeting with a nod as slight as mine.

Thus begins our daily ritual, which I do not fully understand.

As the trial drags on without the identity of the other people involved in the bombing, I tell his mother, "Terry has got to testify. The victims deserve the truth."

"He's scared," Joyce says.

"Read this note I've written to him."

And Joyce does. "I am sure, Terry," the note begins, "that you were as surprised as I was the first time our eyes met in the courtroom. Since that day, I have watched you carefully. You cried when your lawyer mentioned your children. I think you are a man with a big heart. I'm not sure how you got involved in this crime, but I pray you will find the courage to take the stand and tell the jurors who helped you and Tim build the bomb at Geary Lake. Why should you take the fall alone? The truth could set you free."

"Will you take it to him?" I ask, and Joyce does.

That night, after her visit with him, she calls me.

"It's like I told you. Terry's scared. If he talks, they'll kill his family."

"Who is 'they,' Joyce—the FBI, or his friends at Elohim City?"

38

THE NICHOLS TRIAL

December 1997
Two years and seven months since the bombing

Prior to the trial Timothy McVeigh submitted to a poly graph test. The interrogation room was small and sterile, the pale, fluorescent light casting sharp shadows on the walls. McVeigh sat stiffly in the chair, his face staring blankly, looking straight ahead. The polygraph machine hummed faintly beside him, its wires snaking across the table, their sensors affixed to his fingertips, chest, and arm. The examiner, a man with graying hair and an expression of indifference, glanced at the machine, then back at McVeigh.

"You understand how this works, right?" the examiner asked, his voice steady but probing.

McVeigh gave a slight nod, his lips pressed into a thin line. His military training had taught him to remain calm under pressure, but the faint twitch at the corner of his mouth betrayed an undercurrent of tension.

"Good," the examiner continued. "Let's get started."

The questions began. McVeigh answered them calmly, his voice even and controlled. The machine scribbled its jagged lines across the rolling paper, each stroke a snapshot of his responses. The examiner watched, his trained eyes parsing the peaks and valleys of the readout.

"Did you plant the bomb in Oklahoma City?" the examiner asked finally, the question hanging in the air like a drawn blade.

"Yes," McVeigh replied, his tone matter-of-fact. The machine's pen moved in rhythmic waves, as though it too, accepted his answer without hesitation.

"Were there others involved in planning or carrying out the bombing?"

McVeigh's gaze didn't falter. "No."

For a moment, silence filled the room, thick and oppressive. The machine, however, told a different story. Its lines spiked erratically, the chaos on the page imaging the turmoil McVeigh's face refused to show.

The examiner's eyes narrowed as he studied the data. He didn't say anything, but the sudden change in the readout was as loud as a gunshot. He cleared his throat and continued with the script, but the air between him and McVeigh was filled with unspoken tension.

The session ended shortly thereafter, the wires detached, the machine powered down. McVeigh leaned back in his chair, his posture relaxed but his jaw tight. If he noticed the examiner's lingering stare, he didn't let it show.

Later, as the examiner delivered his findings to the investigators, his voice was grave. "There's clear deception on the question about others being involved."

The room was silent. The agents exchanged uneasy glances. The evidence against McVeigh was damning, but the polygraph results hinted at a larger conspiracy. Yet the decision came swiftly and decisively: the polygraph results would not be introduced at trial. Too unreliable. Too contentious. And too dangerous to the prosecution's airtight narrative.

For McVeigh, it was a small victory in a trial he knew he would ultimately lose. But as he sat alone in his cell that night, staring at the gray walls and listening to the distant hum of fluorescent lights, he couldn't shake the image of those jagged lines scrawled across the polygraph paper—proof, perhaps, that even in silence, the truth had a way of clawing its way to the surface.

Of the scores upon scores of people who perished in the bombing, Timothy McVeigh and Terry Nichols could only be charged in federal court with the deaths of the eight federal agents who perished.

I had come to this trial hoping to find answers, but Judge Matsch seemed to be pulling for McVeigh and Nichols. I wanted to know why the FBI didn't investigate Elohim City. ATF informant Carol Howe had warned her handler of the potential bombing Strassmeir and Mahon were planning.

Stephen Jones, McVeigh's attorney, found none of the witness statements pertaining to Mahon and Strassmeir because the names had been purposely misspelled. The prosecution was hoping they would slide right past McVeigh's defense team. The worst misspelling was "B-o-b L-a-mar. Ask any computer to search for Robert Millar, and not even the most sophisticated of programs would come up with Bob Lamar. Elohim City was simply EC. Strassmeir was spelled as Strasmeyer and Mahon as Mehaun. Carol Howe was referred to only as Carol: Without a last name for 'CAROL,'" and with all the misspellings, they simply fell through the cracks.

Judge Matsch refused to allow ATF Informant Carol Howe to testify, the woman who sat in front of the Murrah Building with Andreas Strassmeir and Dennis Mahon when they chose the Murrah as the target. Judge Matsch declares that Carol's testimony is irrelevant. Jurors hear about that extra leg, but no one explains that the leg may have belonged to a bomber who didn't make it out alive. The back-breaking straw, though, is the judge's seal on the twenty-two security videos, which agents retrieved from cameras all around the Murrah. Twenty-two tapes that would have recorded all manner of significant evidence, and the judge keeps them under wraps. No one, not even the judge, offers a good explanation for this, because there is none.

The FBI hadn't done anything as simple as run the fingerprints, according to FBI Agent Louis Hupp, a short pudgy fingerprint specialist, who combed his thinning white hair over his bald spot, left to right. "Yes, sir," he told the defense attorney, "I recovered several excellent sets of latent fingerprints and palm prints from the Dreamland Motel. We also recovered several good sets from the automobile Mr. McVeigh was driving when the state police arrested him shortly after the bombing."

"And did the results of your analysis produce the identity of any suspects?" the defense attorney asked.

"The fingerprints were never analyzed, sir," Hupp said.

"You never ran the prints?"

Hupp's face went red, which looked especially bright under his white hair. "No, sir."

"Why not, Agent?"

"I was told that the money and time required to analyze them was not an efficient use of agency resources."

The defense attorney was incredulous and so was I.

During a break, I spoke with John Hersley, who had become the chief case agent in Oklahoma City. "We'll run the prints," he told me, "after the trial. We don't want Nichols's attorney to have anyone else to accuse and take the heat off Nichols."

Michael Fortier told the FBI that his mother-in-law, Ila Hart, would provide his alibi for the day of the bombing, but she refused to do so when the FBI asked her if she would be willing to take a polygraph test. Instead of prosecuting him, they offered him a plea deal for testifying against McVeigh. His wife Lori went free and never spent a night in jail, yet she made the phony driver's license which enabled McVeigh to rent the Ryder truck. She watched as McVeigh used Campbell's Soup cans to show her how he planned to build the bomb. She testified that she wrapped the blasting caps used in the bombing for McVeigh. She said she disguised them to look like Christmas presents.

Michael Fortier was caught lying under oath three times, yet the government still honored the plea deal. He was sentenced to only ten years. Why did the FBI give him such a sweet deal? Did he finally get his story right? The one they wanted him to tell?

39

STRANGE TURN OF EVENTS

December 22, 1997
Two years, eight months, and four days since the bombing

Terry Nichols's federal trial ran nine weeks, and then the jurors duked it out for forty-one hours over six days. Just days before Christmas, the *Rocky Mountain News* editorial wrote, "Should the jurors grow faint of heart or merry of spirit and fail to convict Nichols of murder in the first degree, they can still convict him of negligent homicide and stamp his ticket for a one-way ticket to the execution chamber, compliments of the federal government."

I was not optimistic. If the jurors didn't have the courage to send him up on first-degree murder, what was the chance they'd sentence him to death on negligent manslaughter? The vote to give him the needle would require unanimity. At last count, that was something not found in the jury box.

On the sixth day of deliberations, the jurors' collective nerve failed. They went for guilty on the lesser charge. "Merry Christmas," someone in the back yelled sarcastically.

In its editorial, the *Rocky Mountain News* opined: "Involuntary manslaughter is what you give a drunk driver when he crosses the center line into the path of an oncoming vehicle, kills himself and an entire family of a man, wife, and three kids."

When Judge Matsch finally gaveled the courtroom quiet, he asked each member of the jury whether that was the verdict he or she had reached. When the twelfth juror answered yes, the judge had to grab his gavel again, but this time, the courtroom was beyond his control.

Wrote the *Rocky Mountain News*: "You do not convict a man of involuntary manslaughter when he built a bomb that killed 168 people. The jurors might as well have turned Terry Nichols loose for all the justice they served to the survivors." This is the fact the survivors all knew: Terry Nichols voluntarily engaged in mass slaughter. Add the three babies who died in the womb, and you have 171 victims. But what about the leg? It's clear someone who is missing the leg died in the explosion. If that is correct, the death toll rises to 172.

The jurors could have found him guilty of murder in the first degree. Instead, they voluntarily found him guilty of involuntary manslaughter. They didn't punish him for building, and successfully launching, a weapon of mass destruction. They let him off the hook and convicted him of merely conspiring to use it. His lawyer, Michael Tigar, convinced the jurors that when the bomb Terry Nichols helped to build exploded, he was back home in Kansas lovingly frying bacon for his wife and children. That was all the jurors needed to hear. He merely built the bomb, but wasn't there to actually light the fuse because he was at home with his family.

Everyone in the courtroom was surprised and disappointed. When you lust for a man's blood, and all he suffers is a flesh wound, it's hard to accept. At least the jury *didn't* turn him loose, but to some they might as well have unshackled him, bought him a new suit, and boarded him on the front seat of a Greyhound bus.

A cousin of Jannie Coverdale, who also lost two grandsons, stood from her seat in the fourth row and wailed. Two of the women jurors hid their face in their hands, and one wept. Judge Matsch pounded the gavel three times and stood and pounded again. "I will personally clear this courtroom if you don't control yourselves," he said in a voice halfway between a yell and a bellow.

I stood stunned and remained silent. This was the best news Joyce had heard since the day the agents arrested her son. I wasn't going to add to her anguish.

Terry Nichols, who should have been grateful, frowned when the foreman read the verdict. Surely, he didn't think the jurors would acquit him? Judge Matsch told the jurors to return at 9:00 a.m. sharp on Christmas Day to decide Nichols's sentence.

"Tomorrow," I said to Joyce, "or the day after, this part will be over."

On the other side of the courtroom, it was Jannie Coverdale herself, not her cousin, who stood. "They had receipts for fertilizer and phone records. What else did they need?"

The judge looked directly at Jannie. He wrapped his right palm around the business end of the gavel, and the handle jutted through his index and third fingers. He aimed it at her. "Ma'am, sit down. These jurors don't have to answer to anybody for their decision."

Jannie ignored the judge. The finger she pointed at Michael Tigar, Terry's lawyer, trembled. "I hope you choke on your steak tonight," she said. "You're buying your supper with money soaked in my babies' blood. You said Terry Nichols was a family man. You said he was building a life, not a bomb."

The bailiff suddenly was standing between Jannie and Michael Tigar, and with a hand on each of her shoulders, he turned her toward the exit.

"Yeah, you're good," she shouted, as the bailiff pushed gently against the top of her back and guided her toward the exit. "The jurors swallowed that whole, without even chewing."

Joyce stood in tears. I put my arm around her and asked, "Could I buy your dinner?"

"Thank you, Kathy. I know you've lost some friends over our friendship. I'll go to dinner, but I'm buying."

We hugged, then walked out the doors into the hallway.

"Call me when you're ready," I said as Joyce walked outside. I turned back to locate a water fountain.

A mother whose twenty-three-year-old daughter had been a teller at the third-floor credit union, was talking to a newspaper reporter. "Sometimes I feel like my heart's—" She stopped until the sobs stopped. "Forty-something hours, those jurors. This the best—"

At that moment, I crossed her field of vision. Her stare was unrelenting and angry.

"I guess you're happy for your friend," she said. "I'm sure your grandsons are proud you have taken up with that woman."

I walked to the water fountain. I bent forward, brushed back my hair, and prepared to sip the cool water. The fountain sprayed me in the face. As I straightened and wiped my face, a hand touched my right elbow. A man in a black suit was standing at my side.

"Michael Tigar would like a word with you."

"You're mistaking me for someone else."

"No, ma'am, Mrs. Wilburn."

"What does he want?"

"He'd prefer to tell you himself. Do you mind?"

"I'll listen to him."

The man turned, and I followed. "Who are you?"

"His son."

My newly honed instinct told me to ask to see his driver's license, but I didn't. I followed him down the hall, around the corner, to an exit that wasn't visible from the lobby. He shoved open the door and held out his hand to motion me to climb the stairs ahead of him.

"My dad suggested the back stairs would be better."

The door at the top of the third flight of stairs opened into a hallway on the fourth floor. I waited for my escort to take the lead. We passed two closed doors; at the third door, the younger Tigar rapped lightly with the back of his knuckles, then he led me into a conference room.

The first thing I saw was white U-Haul packing crates stacked eight boxes long and four boxes high. A huge rubber tree with mammoth leaves that touched the ceiling stood in the corner. An aloe vera plant sat in the middle of the table, its long fleshy green spindles sprawling over the side of a terra-cotta pot.

Michael Tigar's voice brought my attention to the right side of the room, where a dozen people sat around the far end of a rectangular table. Five on one side, six on the other, and Michael Tigar at the head.

"Thank you for coming, Mrs. Wilburn."

"Please, call me Kathy."

I walked to the closest end of the table and rested my hands on the top of a high-back leather chair. My chest heaved slightly from the exertion of the climb up the stairs. Tigar, who had been seated, stood, and unfolded his six-foot-four frame until he loomed over the table and the rest of his team. He had loosened his tie and removed his jacket, and looked out at me from beneath Leonid Brezhnev eyebrows that grew over his eyelids like gnarled fingers. His salt-and-pepper mop of unruly hair hung below his ears.

"Get comfortable," he said and looked to his right at his wife, Jane Tigar. She, too, was a lawyer, with neatly groomed side-parted black hair and a tiny frame. Ron Woods, a former FBI agent who now practiced law, sat next to her. I recognized the other faces, but didn't know their names.

Tigar cleared his throat again and rested his hands on top of his chair.

"Mrs. Wilburn…Kathy, we have one last challenge. We avoided the worst outcome, but the jury still can impose the death penalty." He crossed his arms. "I presented everything I had in the trial. There is nothing more I can say to persuade the jurors for the penalty phase. We've discussed a lot of options, most of them nonstarters. But my wife suggested an idea that we'd like to run past you. Mrs. Wilburn, short of intervention from heaven, the jury's probably going to recommend the death penalty. I would like to ask you if you if would you be willing to take the stand and ask the jury to spare Terry's life?"

"Why would you ask me do that?"

"To save a man's life. You are actually our only hope."

An involuntary "ha-huh" escaped my throat, a half-laugh, half-whimper. I looked from him to Jane who looked at Ron. I stared into every face around that table. A sob erupted from the same depth as the involuntary laugh. Eleven sets of eyes were locked on me. The twelfth set, the one that wasn't locked on me, belonged to Jane Tigar, who had spun around in her chair and appeared to be looking out a window.

"Do you know what you're asking me to do?"

"Intellectually? Yes."

Mrs. Tigar turned back in her chair to face me. "I don't think I could do it," she said. "I've got children, but we've got to be sure we did everything possible to save his life."

"The other families already think I've betrayed them. They hate me for my friendship with his mother."

"Yes ma'am, I know," Michael Tigar said, "but they lack your compassion."

"I've lost my boys. I've lost my husband."

"I wouldn't ask if I had any other good option."

"Can you stand there and tell me that Terry is innocent?"

"Yes." He looked at his wife again and said: "Of murder."

"Of murder?" I asked.

"He's innocent of murder," she replied.

"What's he guilty of, then?" I asked.

"Of being a shy, timid man who falls easily under the sway of stronger personalities. He didn't intend to kill anybody. He thought the building would be blown up in the wee hours of the morning when no one was inside. Did you see his face when he heard the verdict? He didn't think anybody would die. He honestly thought they were going to let him walk. For Terry, blowing up the Murrah was going to be no different than blowing up the stumps on the farm. Just a bigger stump."

"With people in it," I said.

"There were not supposed to be people in it. He is not a criminal. If he hadn't met Timothy McVeigh, he would be farming blueberries in Kansas."

"Did he help build the bombs?"

"Yes."

"Then your definition of innocence is quite a bit different from mine. If he's innocent, put him on the stand and let him explain what happened."

"The prosecutor would shred him. Terry would stumble over his words. He would make a terrible witness."

"Do you know what you're asking? Total betrayal of every person, living or dead, that was in that building. You're asking me to betray Glenn, Colton, and Chase."

I wept and leaned my neck backwards and looked at the ceiling. No one spoke. I put both palms to my eyes to dry them. A chair squeaked. I put my hands in my lap. I looked at Tigar. I moved my head slowly and looked at the face of every person at the table.

"You get me a meeting with Terry Nichols. I want to know the names of every person who helped to kill my grandsons. I want to know whose fingerprints are on this crime. Get me that, and I'll take the stand."

"I'm on it," Tigar said.

40

THE VERDICT

December 23, 1997
Two years, eight months, and four days since the bombing

I did not get an opportunity to talk with Terry Nichols. When the Nichols trial was over, I was not the only one who left the courtroom with unanswered questions. Even the jurors questioned the facts that had been presented. They did not like being lied to. They had heard enough evidence to know from the eyewitnesses at Geary Lake that there had to be at least one John Doe 2 and probably more. But the government continued to hold to its contention that Timothy McVeigh and Terry Nichols had masterminded and conducted this crime on their own.

Beth Wilkinson, US Attorney for the prosecution, referred to John Doe 2 in her closing arguments as "a mysterious Elvis sighting" and "Timothy McVeigh's phantom friend." How Ms. Wilkinson could make fun of so many credible eyewitnesses—people who had seen Timothy McVeigh with other people in the downtown Oklahoma City area the morning of the bombing—was a mystery.

The prosecution failed to call the eyewitnesses who could place Timothy McVeigh at the scene of the crime. If they had, they would also have to admit there were "unknown others" involved in the bombing. What was really going on?

When the jury deliberated the first time, they voted ten to two to acquit Terry Nichols. Two jurors managed to persuade the other ten to change their minds.

Following the trial, the jury forewoman, Niki Deutchman, told CNN:

"It would have been much easier for the jury to make a decision about Timothy McVeigh's role in the bombing than Nichols because the evidence was much clearer. It was hard to tell how involved Nichols was. The evidence was circumstantial and did not prove beyond a reasonable doubt that he knew the building would be blown up with people in it."

There was a wide range of opinion among the jurors. The government dropped the ball. There was a lot of evidence that indicated others were involved in this crime. The decision was made early on to limit the investigation to Timothy McVeigh and Terry Nichols. A decision was made not to pursue the others involved. The government did not prove to all the jury members that Nichols was greatly involved in this whole process, only that he was somewhat involved. Nichols wasn't directly present or implicated with anything.

"The jury could not agree on the sentencing process, so Judge Richard Matsch declared the jury hung. There would be no death penalty and Judge Matsch would decide Nichols' prison sentence. A majority of jurors thought Nichols was innocent. The FBI conducted over 30,000 interviews but made no tape recordings of any of them. It would have been very helpful in the nine and one-half hours the FBI interviewed Nichols if they had taped the interview. The notes provided by the FBI, from the interview, in no way reflected nine and one-half hours of conversation. The FBI evidence was handled sloppily, evidence was misplaced, some was rained on, and some rust-stained. Witnesses indicated they had been badgered by the FBI and stopped talking to them."

I was proud of Niki Deutchman that day for speaking the truth, and I thought she presented a good case. The jury had weighed the facts, but could not agree on Terry Nichols's guilt. However, Niki's statements made some families of the bombing victims very angry. They were irate with the jurors for questioning the FBI's conduct and for wanting to know more about others involved in the bombing. They wanted revenge. They wanted to put the tragedy behind them. They wanted the case solved, so they could go on with their lives, knowing the perpetrators had been caught and punished.

I thought there was a problem with the government's theory and wanted *everyone* involved in the crime to be caught and punished.

41

TERRY NICHOLS'S CORRESPONDENCE

December 30, 1997
Two years, eight months, and eleven days since the bombing

When Terry Nichols didn't get the death penalty at his federal trial in Denver for the eight federal agents he was convicted of killing, he was moved back to Oklahoma to stand trial for the 160 civilians. It was Oklahoma's backup plan. Oklahomans wanted him to die.

Terry Nichols's first correspondence with me arrived a week after the jurors in Denver spared him an appointment with his Maker. The envelope was on top of other mail in the box, as if the letter carrier knew who had written to me, and placed the envelope so I wouldn't miss it.

Each letter of my name and address was perfectly formed and spaced, as if he had written with a typewriter. At first, I didn't want to open it. I wasn't looking for a pen pal, and if I were, it wouldn't be the Oklahoma City Bomber. My curiosity about the letter won out, and I slit it open to find a thank-you card he had made. On the front of the card, he had written Kathy in the same small letters that were on the front of the envelope. Below my name, he had written, in larger letters that leaned left, *Thank You.* A pair of butterflies circled the words, and across the bottom, he had colored tiny red flowers blooming on bright green stems.

"Dear Kathy." I moved to the living room and sat on the sofa, so I could steady my left arm on the arm of the sofa. "Thank you for befriending my family. I know they really appreciated you, as did I. Seeing a kind face in the crowd meant a lot to me...."

That was the first of many letters, which grew increasingly more personal but always stopped short of anything I really wanted him to tell me. His entire world, he wrote, was a gray concrete cell. He was allowed to leave only one hour a day to go outside, weather permitting, and was segregated from all other prisoners. I am sure it is a miserable existence.

I was willing to dance with the devil to get to the truth I had so persistently been chasing; and who would know more about the bombing than the bomber himself? I told him about my new grandson, resisting the temptation to say, "The one you didn't kill." I added, "If you'll send me your phone number, I'll call."

Three days after I sent it, he called from the Oklahoma County Detention Center. My mouth and tongue went dry, as if someone had swabbed out my mouth with a fist-size ball of cotton, and I could hardly move my tongue.

"Hello, hello, hello," I said, before I picked up the handset. A recorded voice informed me that I was receiving a call from inmate. There as a pause, and then Terry Nichols said, "Terry Nichols."

"Will you accept the call?"

"Yes."

"Hello. Hello. Hello."

"Kathy?" he said in a voice that was as unexpectedly delicate as his handwriting. This conversation was the first of many, all of which were short on substance. But I could endure the small talk, on the chance it eventually would lead to "The Big Talk."

"I'm hungry for a hamburger. Can you come pick me up?" Terry asked.

"I'd love to, Terry, but I have this aversion to being shot at," I said, and we both laughed. I asked, "So what's really for supper?"

"White bread, baloney, mayonnaise, brown beans, and canned pears. Supper and lunch," he replied.

"Yummy," I said, and asked, "Do you have a window in your cell?"

"Tiny one. On my tiptoes, I can see out. I can see a Dog Chow billboard."

"I know the sign. I'm going downtown tomorrow morning. I'll stop by and wave. Be at your window at ten o'clock, I'll be standing on the sidewalk outside the jail. See if you can spot me."

I arrived ten minutes before ten, parked parallel, and put a quarter in the meter. I stood in the grass, between the sidewalk and the curb, and looked at the top floor of the jail. I counted time by the number of times the traffic light at the intersection went from red to green. On the fifth yellow light, I saw an arm at one of the windows. I raised my arms straight in the air and swayed them, left to right.

My telephone rang at seven that evening. "I saw you!" he said. "I forgot how pretty you are. If I can arrange it, would you be willing to come see me?"

I agreed to the visit.

"I'll put you on my visitor's list. I'll call Hermanson in the morning. He'll work it out."

Brian Hermanson, his lawyer for the state trial, didn't like the idea. "Why do you want to meet Terry?" he asked me.

I told him I wasn't sure, but that we had been corresponding by letter and conversing by phone for months. The line went quiet.

"I didn't know that. I would have never agreed to it." Hermanson told me. "But if it's gone on this long, and makes my client happy, I'll make the arrangements on one condition. You are absolutely forbidden to discuss Nichols's pending trial or his alleged crimes. Do I have your word of honor on this?"

"Deal," I said, although I wasn't sure I would keep my end, once I was in there. But that was my only way in, and I wasn't above crossing my fingers behind my back. "Deal," I repeated.

"If you go out of bounds, he'll tell the guards to take him back to his cell. End of conversation."

We also agreed that neither of us would disclose the visit to anyone.

To be honest, I was not sure why the unprecedented visit was so important to me. This *was* Terry Nichols, one of the men who'd slaughtered my grandchildren. Adding insult to injury, Nichols's bomb had stripped away the spirits of my late husband and deeply wounded my daughter. In any case, I knew I wanted to talk face to face with this infamous man. Who else would know more about the bombing than one of the bombers?

42

TERRY NICHOLS'S VISIT

January 1998
Two years and nine months after the bombing

Arrangements were made, and I got my visit with Terry Nichols. As I entered the county jail, I prayed no one recognized me. After all, Oklahomans would not take kindly to someone visiting the man who did $652 million of damage to their city and killed so many of its citizens.

I had been in the room, alone, for five minutes. I could hear the noise of the jail behind me. The space before me, on the other side of the bulletproof, soundproof glass, was a vacuum. I set my eyes on the round silver ball that was the doorknob. I didn't see the knob turn, didn't hear anything, so I jumped when Terry Nichols appeared through the door without any warning. Two guards filed in behind him. While one removed his handcuffs, the other walked to the glass, pulled out a chair, and picked up the handset Terry would use to talk to me.

"You'll have thirty minutes, ma'am," the guard said. "I'll tap my wrist when your time is about gone so you can wrap it up."

Before I was ready for the moment, I was face-to-face with one of the men who took the life of my grandsons.

Terry Nichols was only five foot nine. After three years in prison, his skin was the color of biscuit dough, which made his standard-issue, bright red uniform look all the brighter.

The 1980s-style eyeglasses, which he had been wearing the day he was arrested, had been replaced with wire frames and thick, round lenses. You could have mistaken him for a librarian or a post-office clerk. For a moment, he and I simply stared at one another. I looked into his face, and he seemed to look through mine, then he picked up the telephone handset.

Something gripped my brain, as if a bony hand were palming and squeezing it. I couldn't recall a single thing I had planned to say. The silence was so dense I could more easily have broken the glass between us with a head butt than I could have formed words on my tongue. *Say something!*

"You look like one of Santa's elves in that red suit."

The observation surprised Nichols, and his shoulders relaxed. The crimson started on either side of his nose and flowed to his ears and hairline, like a tide sliding in on the beach. "Tell my mother," Nichols said. "She'll think that's funny."

"What else do you want me to tell your mother?" I stared straight into his eyeballs, willing his to be still. But he looked up, down, a flitting glance into my eyes, as if he were about to let me in, and then his soul retreated into the sockets. He closed his eyes and turned his head to the left and kept it there.

"Tell her I don't sleep much." Complete silence followed. After a moment: "All night, the screams and crying sound like a zoo. Like chimpanzees screeching. I hear a peacock all night." I allowed the silence to hang. *Is Terry Nichols one of the animals who screams all night? Does he cry? Does he beg for someone to help? Does he actually believe someone will?*

At that moment, the glass between us fogs over. My arms felt heavy, so I rested one elbow on the countertop, and I dropped the telephone handset onto the counter....

"Mrs. Wilburn. Mrs. Wilburn. It's time," says a man, who helps me to stand, then walks me through a door to the other side of the glass, a door that wasn't there when I came into the room and disappeared as soon as we were through it. Once I was on the other side, I see Terry Nichols, strapped to a gurney, his arms strapped beside him, soft side up, an IV tube stuck in the flesh below his elbow. A rubber tube snakes from his arm and through a portal in the wall behind him. Somehow, I know the executioner is behind the wall, and the tube runs to a syringe the executioner holds in his hand. He is awaiting the governor's call to the warden, who will then rap on the wall and say, "Sir, it's time." A chaplain stands to Terry's left, and the warden stands behind him. The warden flips a light switch to the "on" position. I hear the whir of electric motors, and I know the motors are parting the curtains that open onto the witness room. I keep my back to the windows, my eyes on Terry Nichols, and the office clock on the wall above his head. The hour hand is on the twelve; the minute hand is almost there; and the second hand is slogging its way to the midnight hour. The phone rings and the warden answers. "Yes sir, Governor," he says. Terry's eyes plead for his life. As the plunger is pushed and the syringe empties, muffled shouts erupt behind me. The witnesses are cheering. I look around the room. The tiny witness room is packed with people whose faces I can't make out because my vision is blurred. But as my eyes adjust, and my vision sharpens, I realize the witnesses are all children. And as the faces come fully into focus, I recognize everyone. I see Peach Lyn, Baylee, Danielle, Zachar, Anthony, Elijah, Aaron, Jaci, Ashley, Tevin, Dominique, Kayla, Blake, Gabriel, Antonio,

Tylor, Lee, and a baby with no name. All the children, everyone who died by Terry Nichols' hand. In the front of the room, Chase and Colton are cheering, jumping and high-fiving, banging on the glass, banging, banging, banging…

My eyes snapped open. I had slipped into a daydream that was so vivid that I was surprised to hear Terry's voice. But there he was, upright in a chair and not dead of a fentanyl overdose. The banging that had awakened me was not Colton and Chase rapping on the window, but one of the guards on the other side of the glass, tapping it with a steel key.

"Ten more minutes," he announced.

I picked up the telephone handpiece, which had fallen onto the countertop. Terry, still talking about the night screams of animals, never knew I had slipped away. "All night, the screams and crying sound like a zoo. Like chimpanzees screeching. I hear a peacock all night."

"Terry…" I paused. "Tell me about the bombing."

"You promised not to ask."

Yeah, but to whom did I make the promise? To the lawyer for hire who is defending the man who killed my boys and 166 others? I promised a convicted killer? Promises are for civilization.

"I need to know."

"Who d'ya want to tell?"

"This is for me."

He took the plastic beige handset from the side of his face and balanced it on his right shoulder and looked at the ceiling. Whether this was willful rudeness, defective social skills, or guilt, I didn't know. But whatever he intended, he set every red root of my hair afire. I stood so quickly that I scraped my lap against the counter. I put my face next to the glass, the handset in my right hand and pressed against my chest.

"Stop wasting time!" I screamed.

He waited a moment, then smirked. He returned the receiver to his ear, and the talking end of the handset to the side of his mouth. He wagged the handset up and down, as if the receiver was riveted to his ear.

"I will tell you something that you have to keep to yourself," he said, his voice growing loud when the phone neared his mouth and softer on the trips up and down.

I sat back down. "I'm listening."

"You can't tell anyone."

"You have my word."

"You gave your word you wouldn't ask about the bombing."

"You killed my grandsons." The strain of holding my tongue hurt like a bad tooth.

"I will know if you tell anyone."

"You have my word."

"When my trial is over, if you haven't told anyone, I'll answer every question about the bomb."

"You have my word."

"You tell anyone—"

"You have my word."

"The FBI searched my house in Kansas. But they didn't go in the crawl space. At the bottom of the stairs in the basement, there is a crawl space. There're two doors on the floor that go into it. I buried two boxes of blasting caps there. Under two piles of rock that are a foot deep. They are wrapped in plastic. I'll know if you tell anyone, because if this gets out, they'll be in here to beat it out of me."

"What was it for?"

"Backup."

"When did you bury it?"

"That's all. Thank you for taking care of Mother."

One of the guards behind Terry tapped the watch on his left wrist. I returned the handset to the phone cradle and stood. With nothing else to say, I pressed my right palm against the glass. That was another baby step in the process of forgiving, although I didn't know it, and that certainly wasn't my intention. I wanted to squeeze every bit of information out of him I could.

Terry's eyebrows arched in surprise when I palmed the glass. The guard over his left shoulder had slipped his right hand under Terry's armpit and was helping him stand. Terry stared at my open palm for a second. As the guard to his right attempted to replace the cuffs on Terry's wrist, he shook his arm free, leaned toward the glass and placed his hand against it, a little higher than mine. We held the position for a few seconds. I looked into Terry's eyes, but he was looking down.

I turned and took a couple of steps toward the door. I stopped and looked back.

Terry Nichols and the guards were already gone. Our handprints on that cold soundproof glass were the only evidence we had been there.

PART SIX

Face-to-Face with Evil

43

THE DREAMLAND

Spring of 1999
Four years after the bombing

I go to the trials of McVeigh and Nichols hoping to find answers and find none, so I continue to search.

I have come to the Dreamland Motel hoping to find answers. Dreamland is the place Timothy McVeigh spent the last four nights before the bombing. Men were seen coming and going from his room, but the FBI was never able to identify them. I am here hoping to learn more.

An American flag is tied to a bent aluminum pole that angles out from the top of the office and over my Jeep in the parking lot. The flag pops in the Kansas wind. I get out of the car and the door slams behind me. A burst of wind blows my long red hair up over my face, covering my nose and eyes. I struggle with the loose hair to pull it back and into a ponytail.

The nicest car in the Dreamland Motel's parking lot is a thirty-two-year-old 1967 red Ford Galaxy. I drop the bottle of water I am holding. It rolls three-and-a-half parking spots to the north and stops against the front driver-side tire on the Galaxy, which the driver has backed into the space. When you back your car into a spot, I have learned since beginning my investigation, it's called combat parking. It's a tactic maneuver terrorists and robbers dreamed up, which allows for a quick getaway. I hurry across the parking lot, the wind pushing at my back, to retrieve my water bottle from the tire of the Galaxy, which is missing its hood, exposing all its engine. Sunlight glints off the chrome pieces, which stand out among the rubber belts and rusty pipes. All four windows are down, which allows a clear view of the interior. The shifter knob is a chrome skull. The white leather upholstery in the back seat is rotten, ravaged by sun and rain. Cigarette butts lay ankle deep in the floorboard on both sides of the car.

With my bottle of water in hand, I walk to the Dreamland office and open the door. The wind nearly rips the aluminum knob from my hand, and the effort to close the door against the wind hurts my right shoulder. Two steps inside, I stop and try to smooth my hair as my pupils adjust. The still air in the little lobby feels humid-hot after the blowing wind outside.

"Room?" asks a woman behind the counter.

"Are you the manager?"

"Owner," she says, "and maid and hostess. I even make the coffee," she adds, in what I took to be a German accent.

"I read in a newspaper that Timothy McVeigh stayed here."

The owner-hostess parts her lips to speak, but she does not. She stands silent, her mouth opens slightly. Then she closes her mouth. Her brown eyes never leave mine.

"Are you a reporter?"

"No ma'am. I'm looking for the other men who were seen with McVeigh here."

"Hmmm. Is that right? Do you really want a room?"

"Yes, and I don't want just any room. I would like Timothy McVeigh's room."

She stands looking at me quizzically. "Why would you want to do that?"

"Because Timothy McVeigh murdered my two grandsons."

I let the silence hover over the moment as Lea McGown, the owner, contemplates my odd request.

"I thought you looked familiar. I remember your two little boys. I'm quite sure I've seen you on TV. The boys were Chase and Colton. Right?"

"Yes ma'am. I'm Kathy Wilburn, their grandmother."

Her brown eyes begin to fill with tears.

"I was the first to identify him," Lea McGown says. "FBI agents showed me the artist's sketch. Took a second. But I knew, and I showed them where he signed the register. I'd show you, but they took all my records, and still have not brought them back."

I stand quietly.

"Room 25," she says then. "Are you sure?"

"Yes ma'am, if any of those men are still around, I'd like them to know I'm getting close. I'll spend the rest of my days hunting them down."

She takes a key from a hook and hands it over the counter.

"The room's just like he left it."

44

ROOM 25

Spring of 1999
Four years after the bombing

Mrs. McGown thumbs me to the right. I look at my reflection in the mirror behind the counter and my hair is a mess. I step out of the office, turn right to follow the sidewalk. Then I take in an intentionally deep draw of oxygen, straighten, and cover the short distance to the red door of Room 25, five feet north of the Galaxy.

The door's paint is peeling in half-inch strips to reveal faded green. The proprietor has stuck a rectangular, gold-on-red *No Smoking* sign beneath the room number. Room 25—the shabby room where a man had laid his head two nights before he killed my grandbabies. As if he's going to observe a no-smoking rule. I take the key, insert it into the knob, turn it, turn it harder, and push it open.

The door-frame-shaped rectangle of sunlight paints a Salvador Dali slab of light on the shabby green shag carpet that looks as if you could walk into it. The shag is worn smooth and flat three feet into the room. The back of my knees quiver and I hesitate. The room reeks of a million cigarettes smoked long ago. The nicotine has glazed the walls a sticky brown. Someone has burned a hole, the size of your standard motel-room glass ashtray, into the green shag. To my left, a single-wide window opens onto the parking lot.

Without turning around, I wrench my left arm behind me and pat the wall between the door frame and the window to find the light switch and flip it. The switch turns on a forty-watt bulb in a goose-neck chrome lamp, mounted above the bed's headboard, which is screwed to the wall. The bedside tables are aluminum TV trays with gold-color legs. The chenille bedspread, a dingy floral print, is nappy and worn thin, bald in spots. The spread hangs irregularly below the mattress line.

I draw open the curtains, but the light only slightly improves the room. I step into the rectangle of doorway sunlight. The sun warms my jeans, but not enough to stop the quiver in the soft spot behind my knees. I walk to the bed, sit on the edge of the nappy spread, beneath the forty watts of electric light. I turn to my right and each pillow, right in the middle, where a head will lie.

"Right here," I say as I pat the pillows, unsure if I am speaking aloud or only in my brain. I push up from the bed, walk around the end, and into the bathroom. The linoleum floor is ripped at the threshold, where mold creeps out. I pinch the edge of the shower curtain, which hangs stiff and rigid, pull it back, and silverfish scatter across the bottom of the tub. The ceramic in the toilet bowl hasn't been white for many years. I push the seat up with my right foot. The underside is speckled brown, as if someone has choked on his chaw and spattered tobacco juice.

45

MISTER MCVEIGH'S VISITORS

Spring of 1999
Four years since the bombing

I park my Jeep, non-combat-style, into the slot in front of Room 25. I pull my suitcase from the seat behind me, lock the Jeep, and return to our room—mine and Mister McVeigh's.

I set my suitcase on the dresser. Mrs. McGown knocks, and I jump. "Towels, and new sheets," she says. She edges past me and places the linens and towels on the dresser. She walks to the head of the bed and yanks back the chenille spread to reveal a knotty blanket. Mrs. McGown throws the pair of pillows onto the wooden table by the window. She walks to the window and pulls the curtains shut. Then she yanks back the blanket to reveal a dingy white sheet, which she yanks off to strip the mattress bare. "Back in a minute," she says, and walks out. She leaves the spread, the blanket, and the sheets in a pile at the foot of the bed.

My resolve to sleep at the Dreamland is diminishing with each layer Mrs. McGown strips from the bed. My stomach begins to churn at the thought of sleeping in this place. I am no longer sure this is a good idea. I am beginning to fear that my night at the Dreamland could turn into *Nightmare on Elm Street.*

I stand by the pile of bedding. I kneel and finger the scratchy wool blanket as I eyeball the discolored old mattress Timothy McVeigh has lain on. Timothy McVeigh had lain here premeditating, hours and days before the bombing.

I am willing to crawl into Mister McVeigh's skin to learn the truth, but I am not certain I can crawl into Mister McVeigh's bed. What exactly was I thinking I might accomplish by sleeping on the mattress where Mister McVeigh slept before he drove the Ryder truck to Oklahoma City?

"If mattresses could talk…" I say aloud.

"What's that?" Mrs. McGown asks as she returns to the room through the door she didn't close completely when she left.

"If these mattresses could talk…."

"I imagine they can," she replies. "They speak DNA, but the FBI was never interested, as far I could tell, in anyone's DNA but McVeigh's. I wasted so much time answering their dumb questions, but they always told me I was not right. They never believed what I told them."

"Why would they do that?"

"I don't know, maybe because it didn't fit their picture. I'm very disappointed with the system, and I'm not helping them anymore; I can tell you that. If they did something wrong, they need to admit it. But I promise you I saw with my own eyes that McVeigh wasn't alone in this room. When he came here to rent a room, he drove up in a beat-up yellow Mercury. Later was when he showed up with the Ryder, and I wasn't the only one who saw them. Hilda, my maid, cleaned this room every day and said that on Monday morning, April 17, around 9:00 a.m., she started to unlock the door of Room 25. She thought McVeigh had already left, but as she started to open the door, a man appeared and handed her some towels.

This man, she said, was not McVeigh. He was dark and not so tall, and she thought he looked like one of her people—referring to her native country of Puerto Rico. She also said he had big strong arms. The FBI didn't believe any of us. It made us all mad."

"Did anyone else see McVeigh with other men?"

"There was David King, and his wife. They were guests here most of April. He and I both noticed McVeigh back an old, faded Ryder truck—jerky, jerky, jerky, like he doesn't know how to drive a truck with a clutch. He was going to run into the building, so I hollered at him and ran over. I saw David laughing because McVeigh looked like a little boy in trouble. He apologized and quit trying to back into that spot and parked on the grass. Then the rear tires start sinking into the septic tank. I sent my boy over to ask him to park in front of the office.

"That was on Sunday. The next day, McVeigh was here with a new truck. I noticed the switch but didn't see the men. David said he remembered this clearly because they blocked access to *his* parking spot. He says McVeigh was accompanied by two men, who helped him attach a trailer to the truck. I saw the trailer. Even David's mother saw the Ryder truck parked at the Dreamland on Sunday, April 16, as she was bringing an Easter basket to her son. But nope, FBI says we're all wrong."

Mrs. McGown unzips a plastic package and pulls out a new plastic mattress cover. She unfurls the cover like a sail. Together, we slide the plastic cover over the mattress and snug the elastic corners. We stretch the fitted sheet over the mattress, spread the new top sheet, the new blanket, and the spread.

"McVeigh stayed here four nights?" I ask.

"That's right. Four," Mrs. McGown says. "April 14, 15, 16, 17, and left the morning of 18. Parked the truck there," she says, pointing out the window to the parking lot near the Dreamland sign. "We get lots of U-Haulers," she continues while she folds the bedspread back. "He wasn't different, really, than the others. People are moving all over the country. Rental place just up the highway."

As she fluffs the pillows, lays them aright, and turns to leave, she asks, "How old were your grandsons?"

"Colton was two," I say. "Chase, almost four. They were as much our sons as they were our grandsons. Our daughter was only twenty-two and already divorced. They had been living with us for a year. We got off our routine that morning, and I didn't kiss my babies. Timothy McVeigh killed them before I ever kissed them goodbye."

"I'm so sorry about your babies. I wish there were something I could do. After I identified McVeigh, the FBI never believed another word I said. They came every day for three weeks with the same dumb questions. They wanted me to say Timothy McVeigh was alone when he came here, but he was not, and they didn't want to hear about the other men who were in and out of his room. Every night, I walk the property, all the way around the building. That Friday night, Good Friday, I heard voices in McVeigh's room. Men's voices. No, McVeigh wasn't alone."

She turns and looks over her shoulder.

"That window there," she says, pointing to the back wall. "The curtains were closed, but the window was open. I heard two men talking, at least two. It wasn't the television I was listening to, which is what the FBI tried to convince me. Even the Chinese delivery man told them, when he brought food to McVeigh's room, the man who paid him was not McVeigh."

"There a good hardware store nearby?" I ask.

"Sure, Good Value is two blocks down the road."

46

THE LONG NIGHT

Spring of 1999
Four years after the bombing

Timothy McVeigh slept here, and so did Kathy Wilburn. To be precise, I stayed the night here. But I slept in the manner to which I have become accustomed, which is hardly at all.

The night wind at the Dreamland whistles through the window screens, and the floor-length curtains pop and flap. The temperature has dropped twenty-two degrees since sunset, and as I lie (not sleeping) in Timothy McVeigh's bed, the thermometer falls to 64 degrees. I know because I rouse out of bed to check the thermometer, hanging by a nail on the wall.

This evening, before I lie down to not sleep, I drive to the hardware store and buy a bottle of Pine-Sol, a roll of paper towels, a box of plastic gloves, a three-pack of Ivory bath soap, and distilled water in a plastic gallon jug. At the diner next door to the hardware store, I brush a previous customer's left-behind salt off a gold-flecked table, sit on the worn-out navy-blue cushion, and order a cheeseburger with no onions. I return to our room—mine and Mister McVeigh's—with my supplies and my travel-size toolbox. I slip the disposable gloves onto my hands and fill the sink with hot water, pour in half the bottle of Pine-Sol, remove the plastic wrap from the paper towels, and wipe down the toilet. I rip the wrapper off a bar of Ivory, wash my face and body using three wash cloths that once were white. I am not about to step into the shower—not even in shoes. I brush my teeth and rinse the toothpaste from my mouth with distilled water from the hardware store. Still in my traveling clothes, I sit on the mattress and ease back until my head rests against the pillow.

On April 16, one of the nights Timothy McVeigh slept in this bed, a tornado ripped up Miami County, two counties east of here, and five people died. Why not Junction City? Why not Dreamland, Room 25? Tim McVeigh, and two or three of his compadres (if I'm right, and I am), would have been gone with the wind funnel. All God had to do was just move the tornado two counties west. But God didn't, and here I am, chasing a demon even as mine are chasing me. I'm traveling in McVeigh's footsteps, hoping to find the truth.

I have mapped out my route to truth. The route starts at the Alfred P. Murrah Building, and one of its byways led me here to Junction City, where Timothy McVeigh, and others unknown, built their bomb. A bomb with wheels, packed with ammonium nitrate.

The Dreamland is my first stop. The next is Elliott's Body Shop, to visit with the man who rented the Ryder truck to McVeigh. While I'm this close I want to see Fort Riley, the place where Timothy McVeigh talked up his view of truth and justice to his old pals Terry Nichols and Michael Fortier. My last stop is one I am dreading—Elohim City.

I am traveling light as I steer the Jeep out of the Dreamland parking lot. Inside the cab, I have a canvas tote bag with a rope handle, a new sixteen-ounce jar of Jif peanut butter, a box of crackers, and six twelve-ounce plastic bottles of Diet Coke. I can't shake the feeling that Timothy McVeigh is in the Jeep, too—riding shotgun. The presence of the "man" whose bed I have just shared makes my spine tingle.

The windows are down, and the sixty mile-per-hour wind whips my ponytail. I'm sure it is my imagination, but I can't shake the eerie feeling. I brake and steer onto the grass shoulder, coasting, slowing. I have no idea how far I have traveled since the Dreamland—no idea where I am. As I thought about what Mrs. McGown told the FBI, I can't figure out why they didn't believe her. Surely, they would want to catch everyone involved in the Oklahoma City Bombing, or did they have something to hide?

47

WHATEVER HAPPENED TO JOHN DOE 2?

Spring of 1999
Four years after the bombing

After "the blind sheikh" tried to blow up the World Trade Center with 1,500 pounds of fertilizer packed inside a Ryder van, Ryder, as one reporter wrote, "was the rental truck that nine out of ten terrorists prefer." Timothy McVeigh rented his Ryder from Eldon Elliott, whose auto body repair shop was just up the road from the Dreamland. Mr. Elliott was one of dozens of eyewitnesses who saw John Doe 2 with McVeigh. "Makes me sick I rented that bastard my truck," Mr. Elliott told the FBI.

I obtain and read the witness statements I get through McVeigh's defense team, but I want to hear for myself what the witnesses have to say. Elliott's is my first stop after leaving the Dreamland. Three body men inside Elliott's garage stop their work and stare as I park my Jeep and walk to the front door of the business office, with my red hair blowing wildly across my face.

When I pull open the door for the second time in two days, I am standing at a counter where Tim McVeigh conducted business. I sense the lingering evil, just like I did when I checked into the Dreamland. At the Dreamland, McVeigh counted down the minutes as he planned the bombing with his friends. But here, this is the place where he rented the Ryder that he turned into a rolling bomb.

"Howdy," says the man behind the counter.

"Hello," I reply, without resting my arms on the countertop glass, which is smudged with the greasy prints of hands and fingers that have been who-knows-where.

"What can I do you for?"

"I'd like to speak to Mister Elliott."

"I'm Elliott."

"I'm Kathy Wilburn, sir. I lost my grandchildren in the Oklahoma City bombing."

Eldon Elliott wipes his eyes with the back of his right wrist, the only clean spot between his fingertips and his elbow. His greasy blue jeans hang low in the front, with his paunch exposed between his waistline and his green plaid shirt. His red hair is wiry, a short Caucasian afro.

"I'd like to talk to you about the bombing."

"I've seen you on television. I remember your grandsons. I'm so sorry. I can't imagine losing one of my grandkids."

"No, you can't."

"Could I get you a cold drink?" Elliott asks.

I accept the Royal Crown soda he hands me.

He says, "When I heard the Oklahoma City explosion was another truck bomb, I prayed it wouldn't be a Ryder because I knew it would be bad for business. But it was worse than that. It was one of my Ryders, and I rented it to him."

I say, "I'm finding it hard to believe that on the day McVeigh rented the bomb truck, he stopped down the road from here, at McDonald's, left his car in the parking lot, walked up the hill in the rain, came in here alone, rented the truck alone, and drove off alone. Is that what you told the FBI?"

"No ma'am, it didn't happen that way. I remember McVeigh, I sure do, and he wasn't by himself. Heck, I walked out to the truck with him and his friend. I was this close to both of them. I showed them the gas tank was full and told them about refueling it before they brought it back. The FBI says I was confused and thinking about Todd Bunting, and that I saw that boy the day after. Not so, I wasn't in the shop the day Todd Bunting came, and I never even saw Todd Bunting."

As I lean on the counter, I wonder whether any of McVeigh's fingerprints can still be here. A man comes in from the side door, opening into the garage.

"That's Tommy," Eldon says. "He'll tell you."

"Tell her what?" Tommy asks.

"This lady's grandboys died in the bombing."

I walk two steps toward Tommy Kessinger and extend my right hand. "Hi Tommy, I'm Kathy Wilburn. I'd like to talk to you about what, and who, you saw when McVeigh came in to rent the truck."

"Okay, sure, I was sitting over there, by the wall, eating popcorn and drinking a root beer. McVeigh and the other guy came in the door. McVeigh done all the talking and paperwork. I told the FBI the boy with McVeigh was wearing a blue-and-white hat and that he was wide across the shoulders, medium height. He was muscled up. They acted like I was too dumb to remember what I seen. I told them you don't have to be smart to know if you see two fellas or one."

Mr. Elliott turns toward a woman, visible through a window, who is at a desk in an office behind the counter. "Vickie!" he hollers. The woman looks up. Mr. Elliott motions for her to come. "Vickie filled out the rental papers," he says. "Tell this woman."

"You talking about McVeigh?"

"Yeah, and the other guy."

"Okay, the other guy stood right there next to McVeigh. I talked to both of them. McVeigh's birthday was listed as April 19, 1974. When I saw it, I wished him a happy birthday and told him I'd been married longer than he'd been alive. His name on the license was Robert Kling. Made me sick when I realized that he used that date for a reason. He probably thought it was hilarious."

Elliott chimes in, "I haven't been able to sleep since the bombing. Tell her what else, Tommy."

"What do you mean, 'What else?'"

"About the face artist. Tell her about that."

"FBI sent an agent to talk to me about John Doe 2. He showed me a book with a bunch of faces and told me to point out the one that looked the most like the guy I saw. So that's what I did. Next thing I knew, the FBI sent Miss Boylan in here to talk to me. Jeanne Boylan is a sketch artist in high-profile cases. She drew the Unabomber and told me that the FBI uses her for hard-to-crack cases. She starts asking me questions about the guy I had seen with McVeigh. She didn't know I never seen him face-to-face."

I say, "Do you know how to reach Miss Boylan?"

Eldon finds Ms. Boylan's number on a pad in the drawer under the counter and punches the number. She answers right away, and he explains why he is calling. "I'm going to put you on the speaker," he says. "That okay?"

"That's fine," she answers.

"I have Kathy Wilburn with me, she is the redhead you may have seen on the news. She lost two grandsons in the bombing. She's asking questions about the bombing, and I told her she needs to talk to you."

"I know who you are, Kathy," Jeanne says. "So sorry about your boys, how can I help you?"

"Thanks, Jeanne, if you can just tell me about your visit here, I would appreciate it," I say.

Eldon pushes a tall, cushioned bar stool to the counter for me.

"Okay, I remember it clearly. An FBI special agent contacted me and asked if I would be willing to work on the case. Of course I was, and I work differently than the typical in-house bureau sketch artist. I work strictly from a witness's memory. I don't show them pictures because it taints the witness's memory. After I talked to Tommy, I called the agent. 'What the devil are your boys thinking? I've got the witness right here. They showed him pictures and bullied him into picking one. The witness never saw the suspect from the front, all he saw was a profile. You grew John Doe 2 a bunch of hair, nobody knows whether he had hair because he was wearing a ball cap.'

"The agent was angry, I could hear it in his voice. 'Go back to your hotel. Don't say or do anything until you hear from us.'

"That night an FBI agent I had never met before showed up at my hotel. It was past midnight. He knocks and shows me his badge through the peephole. Then he says, 'The information you provided today is wrong, it does not exist—so be smart and forget it.' After all this time, working with major law-enforcement people, this was the first time I was really afraid...not of the criminals...but of the FBI."

On June 14, 1995, two months after the bombing, the Justice Department announces they are terminating the hunt for John Doe 2. According to them, he doesn't exist. The twenty-two people who saw McVeigh downtown the morning of the bombing were all wrong; and now Tommy, Vickie, and Eldon, every one of these eyewitnesses, apparently were all blind.

48

CITY OF GOD

Spring of 1999
Four years after the bombing

According to the information I had gathered from the Stephen Jones defense team, I believe McVeigh first came to Elohim City in the fall of 1993. The trip coincides with phone records and a speeding ticket issued to McVeigh in September of 1993.

In her reports, ATF informant Carol Howe states that McVeigh had a meeting with Strassmeir, Guthrie, Brescia, and Langan. Millar started off the meeting by telling them all again that the final goal was to overthrow the government and bring the country back to the white Christian country like the Founding Fathers intended. He told the men, "We have to disrupt government and do whatever we could to make the government look bad." Millar thought a few of these "events" would cause the white Christians to rally, then the second revolution would begin. Millar had sworn revenge on the ATF and the FBI for Ruby Ridge and Waco. When Millar left the meeting, the remaining men discussed the robberies and talked about checking out some federal buildings for a big event. They said they needed money, so the rest of the meeting was about bank robberies. By January 1994 they started robbing banks in Iowa, with McVeigh driving the getaway car.

They were soon calling themselves the Aryan Republican Army. McVeigh's recruits included David Lynch, a skinhead from Port St. Lucie, Florida, whom he met at a gun show. In addition to his belief in white supremacy, Lynch was a drug dealer. He was a major distributor to the skinheads and militia guys.

Thoughts from the reports I had read are flooding my mind as I sit shotgun, my daughter Edye gripping the wheel, guiding us through the gates og Elohim City. The name lingers in my head—City of God in Hebrew. The irony is suffocating. "No one's going to believe we've been here" I murmur, reaching for my massive camcorder. I hoist it onto my shoulder, pressing record, determined to capture proof of this moment.

Then I hear it—Edye's voice, sharp and panicked.

"Put the camera down, Mom. Put the camera down!"

The fear in her tone sends ice through my veins. My stomach drops. Something is terribly wrong. Without hesitation, I fling the camera to the floor.

She stops.

I stop.

And suddenly, everything feels deadly still.

Edye stops the Jeep as I struggle to close the window completely, a large German shepherd smashes his nose into the glass, leaving a smear of saliva. We stay in the car. Two men in green camouflage T-shirts step in behind the dog, each of them brandishing a long gun. I recognize one of the guns as a .22 with a scope—don't know what the other one is. They point the weapons in our direction. The shorter of the two men calls off the dog while the one wearing shabby jeans with a canvas belt steps toward my car.

"How can we help you, ladies?"

"We're here to see Pastor Millar."

"You armed?" he asks.

"No, we are not." I reply, my voice unsteady. My gaze locks onto my daughter, fear tightening its grip around my chest. What have I done? What have I led us into?

"He's in the church. Leave your belongings in the car and follow me."

Inside the crude domed structure, which looks more like a Smurf house than a church, the seating for the worshipers present is arranged horseshoe-style. Four men are at the opening of the horseshoe on the left side. They have an electric guitar, an electric keyboard, an acoustic guitar, and a drum set. A hand-lettered cardboard sign, which hangs from the drummer's high-hat, identifies the musicians as the Iron Cross Band. The worshipers circle up and march around the church as the Iron Cross plays "Onward Christian Soldiers." Their voices rise in volume as the men with side arms brandish them in the air.

This isn't your old-time religion.

Millar watches it all from his chair, sitting at the podium to the right, with two wives flanking him. Whiskers encircle his mouth and cover his chin. He twirls the ends of his white moustache. He doesn't stand like the others, just observes it all with a condescending, paternal smile. When the song ends, the men all sit down. The children, dressed in ragged playclothes with dirty faces, file to the front and begin to sing "Jesus Loves the Little Children," with the second line changed to "The white little children of the world." And the rest: "With yellow hair and eyes of blue, he loves white children through and through. Jesus loves the white children of the world." As the children finish singing, the band continues to play. Millar finally stands, raises his right hand, and the music stops.

His sermon is about one of their members, James Ellison, the founder of The Covenant, the Sword, and the Arm of the Lord, whom he calls "King James." He appears to be a hero to the Elohimers, which is hard to understand because he surrendered to a young, unarmed US attorney and future Arkansas governor, Asa Hutchinson.

The surrender came on April 19, 1985, ten years to the day before McVeigh actually accomplished what King James had been bragging about. Mr. Ellison had been telling all the impressionable young white supremacists that he was going to knock down the Murrah Building with a rocket launcher out of revenge for the death of Gordon Kahl, one of their members who died in a fiery shoot-out with the FBI two years earlier. Instead, King James caved like the coward he was. Asa Hutchinson saved King James's life by talking him out instead of taking him down.

Now, here we are, fourteen years after King James surrendered. He is fresh out of prison, sitting three chairs to my left as Millar praises him—ignoring the fact that Ellison had exposed other CSA members so the feds would shorten his sentence.

"I see we have a guest," Millar says, his gaze locking onto Edye and me. His voice is smooth, calculated. "Sister, please, won't you introduce yourself?"

Edye stays seated, her eyes fixed on the floor. I can feel the weight of her silence, the reluctance pressing down on both of us. Regret coils in my stomach. What have I done? I shouldn't have brought her here.

The room is thick with expectation. A dozen pair of eyes—cold, curious, fanatical—watch me. My knees tremble as I rise, forcing myself to stand tall, to remember why we came. We need answers. And to get them, I have to make them believe we belong.

"I'm Kathy Wilburn." I say, then motion for Edye to stand. She hesitates, but slowly rises beside me.

"This is my daughter, Edye. Her two sons died in the Murrah daycare."

I let the weight of my words settle before adding, "We are the ATF's worst nightmare My two grandsons died in the Murrah daycare. I am ATF's worst nightmare."

Millar's face lights up; he stands and begins clapping. Then the entire church, man and woman alike, rises and the room erupts in a thunderous applause. "Amen, ma'am!" the man beside me shouts as he raises his right hand for a high five.

"Boys!" the reverend shouts. "Let us praise the Lord!" We stand, watching the people raising their hands to God, and wonder, *Did all of them know about the bombing, or was it just God's chosen few?*

49

DANNY COULSON'S BOOK SIGNING

March 29, 1999
Three years, eleven months, and ten days after the bombing

I walk to the back of the Barnes & Noble bookstore. The now-famous FBI agent, Danny Coulson, is talking about escorting Tim McVeigh out of the Noble County courthouse on Friday, April 21, 1995.

"Hundreds of people are jammed onto the front lawn. Hundreds of angry people were yelling, 'Baby killer! Baby killer!'

"Timothy McVeigh was the most hated man in America, and I was holding him by the arm," Coulson said. "We knew some of these people were packing heat; after all, this is Oklahoma! When I got there to pick him up, a Noble County deputy pointed to some locals huddled in a lively conversation. Some were armed; we hoped none of them would want to back-shoot a police officer. Six of us formed a circle around the killer. I prayed this wouldn't be another Lee Harvey Oswald moment."

Three dozen people sit in front of Coulson in Barnes & Noble chairs. Several hold a copy of his new book, *No Heroes*. As an FBI legend, he is popular with crime followers.

I am sitting in an overstuffed chair in the back of the crowd. I met Danny Coulson a few years earlier, outside the fence at the Murrah Building, which was decorated with tributes to the victims. He was the FBI's special agent in charge at the time. Not sure if he will recognize me, and even less certain if he will speak with me.

Danny Coulson created the FBI's Hostage Rescue Team. He was present at some of the FBI's most famous standoffs, with some not ending well. He helped negotiate the peaceful surrender of The Covenant, The Sword, and the Arm of the Lord in western Arkansas. He was also at Ruby Ridge and Waco.

I wait until he signs the last book, then approach the author's table. "Remember me?" I ask.

"Um…maybe," he says. "Give me a second, I'm remembering the red hair."

"Kathy Wilburn," I say, extending my right hand. "My grandsons were in the daycare."

"At the fence, we met at the fence, the day the dog found the leg! How're you?"

"I'm making it."

"I saw you on *Prime Time*," he says. "That was a long time ago."

I'm still looking, Danny. "Can we talk?"

"It depends on what you want to talk about," he says.

"Just some questions," I say. "I'll buy a book if you'll give me fifteen minutes."

"No bribes," he laughs. "But I'll give you a book. Let's get a coffee."

We find a table away from the other tables. Coulson faces the entrance, obviously from habit. We make small talk until the coffee comes, then I say, "Tell me, if you can, how you got involved?"

"I was working in Dallas. The first thing I did after I saw the bulletin was call Bob Ricks, the special agent in charge of the FBI's Oklahoma field office—we go way back. He asked me to come quickly. Before I got out of Dallas, a reporter I knew caught me on my car phone. She was talking Middle East terrorists. I told her, wait, wait, forget it—the bombers were American made. 'Look for the Bubbas,' I told her. 'This has Bubba stamped all over it.'"

"How'd you know already?" I ask.

"The date was April 19. I knew it as soon as I looked at my watch and saw the date. I did the math and calculated that it had been two years, to the day, of the Waco standoff with the Branch Davidians. I'll never forget that date. If I'm perfectly honest, I was expecting something. I knew as soon as I heard it. It was payback.

"I worked in the Waco case. It was a nightmare for the FBI. Ten years before that, on April 19, 1985, I was in Arkansas conducting the raid on The Covenant, The Sword, and The Arm of the Lord. No one died there, but the standoff was intense and lasted for days. April 19's been a bad date for me."

I say, "I know, me too. Unfortunately, I didn't learn about the significance of that date until after the bombing. Had I known, I would never have had my grandchildren in that building. Days after my grandchildren's deaths I learned about Richard Snell."

"That's right. He was there at the CSA raid."

"Danny, can you tell me if it's true he planned to blow up the Murrah Building back in 1985?"

"It's true. It came out in his sedition trial. They were going to blow up the building using a rocket launcher, but when it went off in the arms of its maker, they took it as a sign from God that it wasn't time yet."

"Authorities knew that April 19 is revered as 'Patriots' Day' to these extremist groups. Do you think it's possible they intentionally scheduled Snell's execution on this date as a slap in the face to the movement?"

Coulson tapped sugar from a white packet into his coffee. He sipped, smacked his lips, scowled. "It was a bad day, alright. They should not have executed Snell on that day. His execution fanned the flames and made him a hero. Some hero—he murders a man he thought was a Jew, and later killed a black Arkansas state trooper in cold blood."

Coulson pauses and sips his coffee before he continues talking. "Like I told you, the moment I heard about the bombing I knew the Bubbas did it. When I got the call, I raced to Oklahoma City. I parked down the street from the Murrah, as close as I could get, and ran to the command center. It was total chaos. As soon as I got out of my car, I could smell death in the smoke. Our worst nightmare. I was shocked when we called off the search for John Doe 2, when I knew several witnesses had seen a second man with McVeigh just before the bombing, witnesses who described the suspect to the artist who created the wanted poster."

"It's good to hear you say that—it gives me hope. I'm here because I need your help," I tell him.

"McVeigh's dead and Terry Nichols is in the pen. How can I help you?" he asks.

"I don't believe for a second that those two were the only ones involved in the bombing. Can you tell me you do?" Coulson sits silent and stoic. I continue, "Mr. Coulson, if you have children, I hope they are never murdered. And if they are, I hope you don't find yourself sitting in front of someone who could help you, only to find they are unwilling. You know this isn't right. You know there must be more people out there."

A man's voice rises above the bookstore chatter. "Hey Danny! I heard you were signing books. Did you sell them all?"

Coulson walks around the table. "Hey, man!" he says as he shakes his hand. "Good to see you." Coulson gathers up his things. I watch as they leave the building together.

What now? I think. *Does Ricks know that Danny is beginning to rethink the bombing?*

No answers, just more questions. I never planned to be a detective.

50

THE LAND OF HATE

September 1999

This time, I left my daughter at home. After what we endured at Elohim City. I couldn't put her through that again. The Aryan Nations' compound in Hayden Lake, Idaho, is several miles outside city limits in a remote location. It is truly "No Man's Land"—down a long, dark, foreboding driveway surrounded by dense foliage.

When I get closer, the sign nailed on a tree proclaims *Whites Only* in big bold letters. I can see several buildings nestled in the woods. One has a large swastika painted on the roof. As I drive up to the main gate that Saturday afternoon, several skinheads sit in the shade of some large trees in front of a building called Church of Jesus Christ–Christian.

A wave of fear courses through me as I am approached by a guard and a vicious-looking Doberman, who is not glad to see me. I nervously ask to see Pastor Richard Butler, the patriot of the Aryan Nations. I must appear harmless to the evil-looking men because, after a few questions, they take me to Butler's home.

I am surprised to meet a frail, elderly man, sitting in a recliner. His skin is leathery and wrinkled from spending too much time in the sun. On the chair next to him is a bouquet of dried roses. His wife had died several months earlier, and he left the roses in her chair as a reminder of his lost love.

Butler appears to be a harmless old man in the winter of his life. But I soon learn how deceiving appearances can be. I introduce myself and tell him I am there because I do not believe the story the government is telling me about what happened in Oklahoma City. Butler smiles cagily, agreeing with me that you can't trust the feds.

We visit for more than an hour. He shares Scripture with me from a King James Bible, twisting the words to convince me the whites are God's chosen race and would be the only race to enter the gates of Heaven. I listen silently, stunned. This old man, who looks like a role model for anyone's grandfather, is the head of the snake, the messenger of hate and destruction.

Butler invites me to attend services the following morning. I agree because I am sure this place and these people are connected to the bombing. The next morning, I put on my Sunday best and return to the compound. Everyone is gathered under the shade trees. It is like the old-time camp meetings I had gone to as a child—only this time all the men are wearing Nazi uniforms.

When I enter the foyer of the church, I have to avoid stepping on Israel's flag, which has been placed on the floor as a doormat. When I walk into the church, I see a bust of Adolf Hitler by the pulpit. The service starts with a hymn of praise, from the same type of hymnal I had sung from all my life. It is filled with wonderful old hymns, such as "Amazing Grace" and "How Great Thou Art." I am sickened when we are asked to bow our heads in prayer and every right arm in the building, including those of the smallest of the children, flies up in the air to salute Hitler.

When Butler rises to present the morning sermon, he introduces me as his guest. He explains that God has put a new message on his heart that morning, and it is for me. I am appalled as he proceeds to explain why there had to be a bombing in Oklahoma City. Outwardly, I try to remain calm, but I will never forget Butler's bone-chilling words. "One man's terrorist is another man's freedom fighter." He says McVeigh was a great man and a martyr for the cause. I am not sure I will make it through the grotesque sermon. I plead with God to see me through this debauchery Butler calls a worship service. Somehow, I keep my composure.

When the service was over, Butler and I return to the shade of the beautiful old trees. There I can feel a refreshing breeze. I need to escape. The weight of the hate surrounding me in the compound is crushing. As I sit under the trees, talking with Butler, he refers to himself as a racist but defines the word as "one who loves his race." He points to the two Doberman dogs—Eva and Fritz—that serve as sentries for the compound. Butler tells me they are purebreds, the top of the line. Then he points to an old black dog.

"Do you see that old n***** dog?"

I respond with a nod. By this time, I am so upset I can't find words to speak.

"Old n***** dog has no more a soul than a Jew, an Asian, a n*****, or a homosexual." Butler says he and his followers are dedicated to keeping their race pure, just as Hitler had tried to do. I am repulsed by his sick theology but know I don't dare let it show.

Butler invites me to Sunday dinner with him and some of his Nazi friends. I feel icy glares as we enter the restaurant. I want to crawl under the table and hide my face, so embarrassed am I to be seen with neo-Nazis. Some of the men in our group wear large swastika rings on their fingers. When the waitress brings our food, we pause and bow our heads in prayer. How can these hypocrites have the nerve to ask God to bless their food? They don't need to be praying over food. They needed to pray for their souls!

When Sunday dinner is over and we are saying our goodbyes, Butler kisses me on the cheek. He whispers in my ear, "Don't worry, honey, you will see your boys again."

I cringe. I feel nauseated and dirty. When I drive out of their sight, I use a tissue to rub my face, repeatedly, where he had kissed me. It is as if I cannot remove the evil slime from my face or remove the stench of this experience from my mind. It takes several hours for the nausea to subside. It is hard for me to believe such an evil place exists—and in America!

PART SEVEN

Dealing with the Hate

51

JOSH NICHOLS'S VISIT

June 2001
Five years and two months after the bombing

I have been corresponding with Terry Nichols for almost five years. I'm one of his only friends. He has promised me that when his state trial is over, when he is no longer under threat of the death penalty, he will tell me everything, and I believe him.

I first met his ex-wife, Lana Padilla, when I was in Las Vegas visiting with Carol Howe. Lana painted a picture of life after marriage to a notorious public figure. She was guilty by association in the public eye. The same could be said about her son, Josh.

When Terry tells me that Lana and his son are coming to Oklahoma to visit, he is very excited. He has been concerned about his son. Four years have passed, and Josh has refused to talk to him and has never opened one of his father's many letters.

Three weeks after McVeigh's execution, I get a call from Lana. She and Josh are on their way to Oklahoma City.

"Josh was upset by McVeigh's execution," she tells me. "He spent the summer before the bombing hanging out with McVeigh and his dad on the family farm in Michigan. McVeigh was his friend and he loved Tim. Josh had no idea that when he was having fun on the farm with his dad and McVeigh, blowing up things, they were really learning how to build a bomb. It's really messed him up."

I invite Lana and Josh to stay in my home while they are in town, but she is not sure Josh will feel comfortable doing that. I tell her I understand, but at least to come by for dinner.

That evening when the doorbell rings, I answer and there stands Josh. He has slimmed down since the last time I saw him and is a head taller than I am. I have no idea what to say, so I look up at him and say, "I knew you were coming so I baked a cake."

That breaks the ice. Josh and I stay up into the wee hours of the morning talking about his life since the bombing. He tells me he is having trouble at school. His classmates call him "Bomber" and other filthy names laced with obscenities. Josh is bullied by students and adults, who sometimes physically attack him in groups, then leave him crying and bleeding in the streets. The mistreatment began when he was twelve and continues. At thirteen, he gave up and dropped out of school. At fourteen, he began to fight back publicly against his assailants, and privately against his demons. Drugs and alcohol gave him temporary relief. Often, police found him drunk and high while aimlessly wandering the streets of Las Vegas late at night. Feeling sorry for the troubled youth, sometimes the Vegas police officers took him home instead of to jail.

Josh and Lana wind up staying in my home for four days. I cook for my guests because I am uneasy about being seen with them in public. I fear for their safety, as well as mine. Lana had earlier told me how she and Josh had been abused with shouted threats and profane name-calling from Oklahomans during their last visit to the state. I don't want them to experience that again—or worse—during their trip, which had partially been motivated by my invitation. Besides, I want to learn more about Terry Nichols—husband, father, and bomber. Lana is very forthcoming.

After the bombing, Josh and his mother were held by the FBI in a hotel room for several days. They suspected that Josh could be John Doe 2. He was interrogated for days. During the trial, the prosecution subpoenaed Josh to testify against his father. Lana filed an objection and put a stop to it. She did not want Josh to be responsible for saying something that could get his father executed. She told agents that only five months before the tragedy, as Nichols was leaving for the Philippines, he had entrusted her with a package that he ordered her to not open for sixty days. Shortly after dropping Nichols off at the airport, she defied him and opened the mysterious bundle. It contained notes from Nichols to McVeigh. One urged McVeigh to "go for it" and ended with the words, "By the time you read this I will be gone."

"I sobbed," Lana tells me. "I was convinced he was going to commit suicide." She tells the federal investigators she had discovered a bag containing $20,000, which Nichols had taped to the back of her kitchen utensil drawer, along with his last will and testament, addressed to her.

She says when she read the letters, she told her oldest son, Barry, she was afraid Terry was not coming back.

In the letter, Terry had asked her to take care of some things in a storage locker. Lana and Barry went to the locker and were shocked to find it contained more than $60,000 in silver and gold bullion. Also, there were wigs and masks (which I believe were used as disguises by the Midwest Bank

Robbers, Elohim's Richard Guthrie, Michael Brescia, and Peter Langan).

Nichols's letter to McVeigh ended with these words: "This letter would be for the purpose of my death."

"I didn't hear from Terry until he'd showed up at my house three months before the bombing," Lana recalls. "He was furious because I had opened the package. So, what does he do? The next day he clears everything out of the storage and disappears, again!

"I answered all of the FBI's questions, and I let those agents question Josh, too," she continues. "It went on and on and I told them everything I knew." Finally, agents ended the interrogation by asking Lana, directly, who was really behind the bombing. "I told them it seemed to me that Tim was the leader and Terry was the follower."

On the third night of our visit, Josh's words catch me completely off guard. "Would you take me to the memorial for the people that died in the bombing?" he asks. This young man, who was afraid to come to Oklahoma City, now wants to visit the memorial garden where who knows what might happen, and with me—a grieving victim whose grandchildren are represented by two of the "Memorial Chairs!"

Lana, Josh, and I are on our way to the memorial. As always, I am awed as I walk up to the giant gate. More so, accompanied by my unlikely guests. Many Oklahoma City residents are finding it hard to move on with their lives. I am afraid of what people might think or do if we are recognized.

What would Glenn be thinking? What would anybody I know think? Of course, I know the answer. They would think I have lost my mind. I look around to see if anyone recognizes me. I feel confident they won't recognize Josh. He has changed so much. He is inches taller and pounds lighter since his last exposure by the media circus. But Lana is with me as well, and I am hoping nobody recognizes me.

When we get to the memorial, I escort Josh and Lana to Chase and Colton's chairs. As I pause at chairs 60 and 61, which represent the lives of my young grandsons, with my arm around the bomber's son, I am deeply moved. I am also confident that one day his father will tell me everything.

52

TOM SANDERS, MY GODSEND

September 19, 2002
Seven years and five months after the bombing

Glenn had been dead for five years, and I discovered loneliness is cumulative—the sense of it becomes stronger year after year. By 2002, I was lonely to the bone.

Dale Phillips, a member of the Oklahoma City Bombing Commission, was in business with Tom Sanders, a financial planner in Little Rock, Arkansas, whom I had never met. Phillips insisted that I accept a telephone introduction to Tom.

I wasn't looking for anyone to play "matchmaker" for me, and I didn't like blind dates. But a telephone chat couldn't hurt, I reasoned. Besides, Dale and I had worked closely on post-Murrah issues, and I felt I owed him the courtesy of granting his request. Reluctantly, I took a call from Tom.

Even from the sound of his baritone voice, I decided he was a classy guy. He said he was coming to Oklahoma City for a board meeting the following week. He asked if I would have dinner with him. I accepted.

As the date approached, I decided I didn't want to chance a relationship with someone living 345 miles from me. On the day of my first scheduled date with Tom, Edye asked me to babysit my grandson Glenn, and I consented. Over the phone, I told Tom why I couldn't meet him, and he graciously offered to let me take Glenn to dinner with us. I refused and had no reason to think I would ever hear from Tom again. After all, I had canceled only a few minutes after he'd driven from Little Rock all the way to Oklahoma City.

The next day, Tom sent me a sweet email. He complimented me for putting my grandson first and thanked me for taking time to visit with him. Between the lines, the email communicated that he knew I'd brushed him off, and still he complimented me? *How great* is *this guy?* I thought. I felt like a total witch. I apologized and told Tom I would see him if he ever returned to Oklahoma City. I knew he'd be back because he had that business here.

Tom returned to Oklahoma City the next weekend—and it wasn't for a business meeting. I deduced a lot from that. I told Tom upon arriving at my house that he could pull into the driveway. I would admit him through the garage. Why did I do that instead of receiving him through the front door? He probably thought his visit was unimportant to me. To this day, I often admit guests through the garage. It's how I do things.

Understand: At this point I had never seen Tom in person, and he hadn't seen me. He stood in my driveway when I raised the garage door, and it was like the raising of a curtain for a theatrical production. I liked what I saw, he looked the way he sounded—dignified. Is it possible to look brilliant? If so, he had that appearance, too.

We went to dinner, and on our first date I asked him if we could share one meal. He teases me to this day about it. He says that I was a cheap date and that sealed the deal for him. Besides not being hungry, I didn't want to take advantage of him.

In a brief time, our relationship took a romantic turn. But then I broke up with him. “I’m sorry, but you live so far away from Oklahoma City where my daughter and grandson live,” I told Tom. “I don’t want to be in a long-distance relationship.” Then I cried about my stupid decision for a week. Love, after all, doesn’t always respect geography.

Tom, a bachelor of twenty years, didn’t give up. He convinced me that we would make it work. He owned a condominium in Oklahoma City that he’d bought earlier for his mother. She no longer lived there due to her declining health. He said he would keep it for me to stay in, and I could go back to Oklahoma to visit my family anytime I wanted.

I resumed seeing Tom Sanders and married him one year later. He was a blessing I wasn’t expecting. He accepted me for who I was and, just as importantly, for what I was.

Tom and I had been totally candid during our courtship. He knew, for example, about my obsessive mission to discover what *really* happened before and during the Oklahoma City bombing. He was aware I had befriended and forgiven Nichols, the convicted murderer who, I was sure, would one day tell me everything about Oklahoma’s killing field. I even told Tom I had once been seriously suicidal. He knew I intermittently sat up late to watch a home movie of Chase and Colton as they played with Edye. He knew that sometimes, when I least expected it, I cried myself to sleep.

How many women, with baggage like that, are accepted into a storybook marriage? How many men would grant the acceptance?

Tom Sanders is my godsend.

53

NICHOLS WANTS TO TALK

October 6, 2006
Eleven years, five months, and seventeen days since the bombing

On May 26, 2004, Terry Nichols's Oklahoma trial ended, after his conviction on 161 charges of first-degree mur der. He'd been found guilty on each. The jury deadlocked on the death penalty. He was remanded to federal custody, and was sent to Federal ADX Florence, a supermax prison in Colorado.

More than ever, I urged Nichols to disclose what really happened that day of the Oklahoma City bombing, and to tell what he knew about the others who were involved. I reminded him that his story could be a deterrent to young people who might otherwise pursue a criminal life like his.

As a favor to my cause and to me, Tom had asked Jay Bradford, a former Arkansas state senator and close friend of former President Bill Clinton, to cut through the red tape of the prison system so I could arrange an interview with Nichols. I had been trying for months to see him, but I had a problem. In order to interview a prisoner at ADX, a visitor had to have known the inmate before he committed the relevant crimes, and I hadn't known Nichols then. It didn't matter to prison officials that I had visited him many times while he was in state custody.

I also contacted Michael Radutzky, senior producer for *60 Minutes*, and explained my dilemma. *60 Minutes* wanted the story and agreed to help. Ed Bradley was assigned to the story. My struggle to pair Nichols with the broadcast powerhouse became a running battle between the federal prison system and CBS.

Tom was with me every step of the way as we waded through the quagmire of penal system bureaucracy, which eventually suppressed the truth about Nichols and the bombing. Working with CBS provided an adventure for me. According to prison guidelines, working journalists were allowed to interview an ADX Florence prisoner. I approached the prison officials again, this time as a journalist. I met the prison's guidelines as a special correspondent for *60 Minutes*.

So, *60 Minutes* has a rule that prohibits anyone other than regular correspondents from doing interviews. Because Nichols refused to talk with anyone but me, CBS made an exception, and the CBS legal department agreed to take on the prison system. I thought, *Surely this is it!* Then I received this letter:

> Dear Ms. Sanders,
>
> This is in response to your correspondence in which you request permission to meet with inmate Terry Nichols.
>
> The Bureau of Prisons makes every effort to accommodate media personnel if the request does not negatively affect the security and operation of our institutions. It is my determination, based on my sound correctional judgment, that to grant your request at this time could pose a risk to the internal security of

> this institution and to the safety of staff, inmates, and members of the public. Therefore, your request has been denied and you will not be permitted to meet with inmate Nichols at this time.
>
> Robert A. Hood
> Warden

This maximum-security prison housed the worst of the worst, including Ramzi Yousef, mastermind of the first World Trade Center bombing; Ted Kaczynski, the Unabomber; as well as Timothy McVeigh. And yet I, a housewife, now living in Little Rock after my marriage to Tom Sanders, and someone who had visited Nichols before, someone with no criminal record, might pose a security threat to the staff and inmates? Just how might I do that? Beat them with measuring spoons? How would I *endanger* members of the public? The public was locked outside!

I didn't need the wisdom of Socrates to suspect the federal government's fingerprints were all over this rejection letter. Why would the prison care who, other than past criminal associates, spoke with Nichols? *60 Minutes* had already broadcast an interview with McVeigh when he was incarcerated at this very prison.

Somewhere, some agency with power wanted to keep Nichols quiet. Nichols's interview would explain why the Oklahoma City bomb squad was downtown before the bomb exploded. Did they have a warning? ATF agents were brought in from around the country before the bombing. ATF officials admitted to me that they were working on a sting operation the night before the bombing. But they would never admit the Murrah Building was their sting's objective.

Why had the hunt for John Doe 2 been called off when twenty-two eyewitnesses saw McVeigh downtown, accompanied by another man, the morning of the bombing? Not one witness spoke of seeing McVeigh alone.

Earlier, in the courtroom, I had listened as FBI agents admitted they never ran fingerprints recovered from McVeigh's car. They said it wasn't cost-effective. Really? The federal government spent $82.5 million investigating and prosecuting McVeigh and Nichols. The cost of processing fingerprints would have paled by comparison. What were they hiding? Could identifying more John Does and the fingerprints reveal the identity of government agents who were involved in the failed sting operation?

The *60 Minutes* lawyers repeatedly contested the prison's virtual gag order against the news organization, and now me. They sent letters to Warden Hood, and they initiated other procedures. Meanwhile, I continued to pray that God would let the interview happen. Nichols wanted to come clean by finally revealing the truth. Surely God wanted the same thing, I reasoned. So, *60 Minutes* producers, lawyers, and I resumed submitting interview requests to Warden Hood. Each was denied.

A strong grapevine prevails inside prisons. The word was out that Nichols wanted to rip the lid off the Murrah bombing regarding who was involved and why. Inside the walls, Nichols heard that his life was in danger. Pressure to do the *60 Minutes* interview was mounting. More than ever, he wanted to do it soon.

In October 2006, Nichols called me unexpectedly while I was riding in the car with Tom and his friend Jay Bradford.

This time, Nichols insisted he wanted to do the interview *now*, regardless of prison approval.

"Tom, it's Terry," I said to my husband, who was sitting behind the wheel. Of course, Jay knew about my peculiar friendship with Nichols. But suddenly, the former senator was sitting three feet away as I talked to the high-profile prisoner, which made me uneasy. While Tom and Jay could not hear Nichols on the other end of the telephone line, I sensed they were hanging on to every word. Both were respectfully quiet, but I could feel their tension. I'd never talked to Nichols in front of anybody, including Tom. It felt painfully awkward.

When I announced who was calling, Tom had abruptly veered our car to the shoulder of the road and turned off the ignition, to reduce road noise, so I could hear. Nichols was surrounded by thick walls of steel and concrete nestled in the foothills of the Rocky Mountains. Depending on the weather, and reception, cell phone transmission was sometimes spotty. After we had exchanged a few pleasantries, Nichols blurted the words Tom and I had been waiting all year to hear: "Kathy, we can't afford to waste any more time. Who knows what might happen to me. Let's make this interview happen! If they won't let you inside the prison to see me, let's do it by phone. I'll tell you everything."

Nichols had given the green light to his full disclosure about the Murrah bombing's planning and implementation, all to be broadcast from Maine to California. He had just sanctioned everything I had pursued for years—traveling thousands of miles to interview dozens of people, and more. I was sure the work Tom and I had recently done would now enable Americans to learn what really happened on that fateful day and who was involved. People would hear why the bombing planners did what they did, and exactly who helped them. Nichols was going to reveal the motives behind the madness.

My heart was racing. I wanted to rejoice, but knew I had to remain calm.

Nichols seemed excited to a degree I had never seen or heard from him. I was convinced he truly intended to give full disclosure, trusting his newfound faith to see him through whatever was in store for him. His vow to tell the whole truth to the world was already setting me free from the agony of unanswered questions, those lingering mysteries that had plagued me since 1995. I wanted to shout praise to God for what Nichols was promising. Instead, I remained low-key and methodical, mindful of the need to keep him calm.

Nichols knew I had met Ed Bradley. He also knew I had been engaged in dialogue with *60 Minutes* producers. That was the reason he finally decided to come forward; either the Holy Spirit moved him or was working for all of us. I told him I'd tell the *60 Minutes* people about his long-awaited decision, and he was happy with that.

And so—an unexpected and matter-of-fact telephone call by the side of an Arkansas road was going to change the world, I thought to myself. Nichols's story might finally implicate other people. They might finally be arrested and tried.

Before the telephone conversation ended, Nichols and I chatted about insignificant matters. Then, as he was easing into his farewell, I braced myself to say what I wanted to say.

"I love you, Terry," I said.

"I love you too, Kathy," Nichols answered.

Unavoidably, I felt embarrassed. The car became pressurized in a way I could feel. The former Arkansas senator remained completely silent, except for what might have been a gulp. As soon as Nichols was off the telephone, I began to explain our conversation.

I told Tom and Jay that Nichols wanted to get the interview done—now. Since he and I couldn't get clearance to do it live, we would do it by phone, using Nichols's monthly allotment of two fifteen-minute phone calls. We would record the calls back-to-back. Nichols had set the date for November 9, 2006. On that day, the world would hear the rest of the story about the Murrah bombing. Terry Nichols had said so.

54

60 MINUTES'S BIG STORY

October 2006
Eleven years and five months after the bombing

The day after my excited call from Nichols, I resumed my coordination efforts with CBS and the *60 Minutes* pro duction team. Months earlier, Nichols had made it clear he didn't trust his story to anyone but me. He was afraid a direct interrogation by Bradley might make him look bad. For lack of a better word, I was amused.

Nichols was serving life without parole after multiple convictions for murder. His name and face had been plastered across print and broadcast media around the world. But he didn't want to *look bad*? Was it possible for anyone to make him look worse?

60 Minutes wanted the story so badly that the producers agreed for me to do the interview. I would interview Nichols, then Ed Bradley would interview me. That was unprecedented in *60 Minutes*'s history. I thought the plan showed how passionately producers wanted this interview. They thought it would be the story of the decade, and so did I. Think of it; a surviving victim of a horrific crime interviewing one of the perpetrators.

After a point, someone inside the prison began to manipulate my mail to Nichols. My letters were regularly and mysteriously lost. Once Nichols and I were certain someone routinely tampered with our mail, we devised a scheme. We would begin each letter with a reference, by date, to previous letters. We could then determine which letters were missing.

I wrote to Nichols and said I would send my last three letters again. I sent a copy of each by regular and by certified mail. The certified letters would provide a record of the prison's having received them, including those not forwarded to Nichols. Tampering with US Mail is a felony, even among prison officials. After I began following the regular mail-certified mail steps, my letters to Nichols were suddenly delivered to Nichols in a timely manner.

Nichols was very guarded in what he said in his letters because he knew they were read by prison officials. We felt our phone calls were also monitored. He told me he was going to tell me about Mr. Big, a name he said has never surfaced before. He was scared he'd be killed if the others involved knew what he intended to reveal to *60 Minutes* and to me.

While waiting these many months for the Nichols interview, I learned through Stephen Jones that McVeigh had been given a polygraph test after his arrest. The only question he didn't pass was when asked if he acted alone downtown the day of the bombing. McVeigh said yes, which proved to be deceptive. So I was hoping to learn more about Mr. Big.

Brian Hermanson, Nichols's attorney, wanted this incredible interview to happen. He told me the world would be stunned when Terry Nichols shared his story, and he did everything in his power to help. Prison policy allowed Nichols to call Hermanson frequently. Before each call, the attorney notified me. I then told Hermanson what to tell, and what to ask, his client. Nichols responded to Hermanson, who in turn communicated the prisoner's messages to me. The three of us were persistent in non-stop scheming on how to make this blockbuster interview a reality.

Through it all, Nichols and I bonded more deeply. The man who'd always been so secretive about the details of his criminal escapades was now striving to make them public. Nichols and I had a common cause: We both wanted to expose the truth.

In our hearts, we were confident that, with CBS's help, this interview would occur. Nichols even asked me to prepare a list of questions I intended to pose on national television once the permissions and logistics had finally been arranged. Our plan called for me to give the list to Hermanson, who would give it to his client, so I began crafting these questions:

- Are you going to tell the truth?
- You and I would have never met if my grandchildren had not died in the Oklahoma City bombing. How would you like me to remember you?
- Why have you waited so long to come forward with the truth?
- Eldon Elliot, owner of Elliot's Body Shop, and two of his employees testified that Timothy McVeigh was accompanied by a man when he came to rent the Ryder truck. Do you know the identity of that man?
- Why do you think everyone involved in the crime was not prosecuted?
- Do you believe people inside government agencies participated in or knew about the bombing before it occurred?

- Is there a Middle Eastern connection to the Oklahoma City bombing?

These are seven of forty-eight questions I prepared for Nichols. I neglected nothing about Nichols's and McVeigh's role in the bombing. I also cited names of people implicated in various other investigations but who were never charged.

As Nichols's legal counsel, through privilege, Hermanson read my questions. He shared them with only Nichols. He simply told me I was going to be amazed by Nichols's answers.

Nichols finally became impatient with the prison's overt efforts to prohibit the interview. So, he devised a plan to work around the system. Like all inmates, Nichols had to schedule his phone calls in advance. He was approved for two fifteen-minute telephone conversations with me on November 9, 2006. While prison personnel had committed to the day, none would commit to the requested hour.

I called *60 Minutes* and spoke to a producer and relayed all this information. I had tried for eleven years to secure this interview, and *60 Minutes* had tried for a year. Now it all seemed to be coming together.

The news show's producers summoned me to New York regarding the pending interview with Nichols. They knew Ed Bradley was ill, and that we'd been working on this opportunity for a year. They didn't want to postpone it any longer. Who knew if we would ever arrange it again?

The plan was for me to use the *60 Minutes* studio. Nichols would talk to me by telephone under prison officials' noses! Then, later, Ed Bradley would interview me about my interview with Nichols.

I boiled with excitement. Rushes of adrenaline felt like fire in my veins. I had spent untold sleepless nights mourning the losses of Chase and Colton. Now I can't sleep because of my anticipation. The little silver lining on my cloud of human loss was finally going to glisten. Just as I'd always been told, there really is a God, and he really does move, but not until he's ready.

55

THE INTERVIEW

November 8, 2006
Eleven years, six months, and twenty-one days after the bombing

Brimming with excitement, Tom and I arrived in New York City on November 8, 2006. During previous visits to America's largest metropolis, I had felt a bit overwhelmed by confusion at the airport and the logistical nightmares of trying to negotiate my way in the city. This time, I was oblivious to all of it. Instead, I just pushed through the congestion while yearning to reach CBS and to hear Nichols's answers.

After hailing a cab, Tom and I sped from the airport in Newark, New Jersey, en route to the network's studios on West Fifty-seventh Street in Manhattan. The cab driver picked up on our sense of urgency and really put the hammer down, but I wasn't scared. Sheer excitement about reaching my destination numbed my fear.

Upon arriving, Tom and I signed in and took a seat in a waiting room. For the first time since leaving Little Rock that morning, I wasn't in motion. But my head didn't feel that way. My world was spinning fast, I couldn't step off, and I didn't want to.

While awaiting *60 Minutes*'s senior producer, Mike Radutzky, Tom and I saw reporter Leslie Stahl walk past. I admired Ms. Stahl—and anyone else who was remotely a part of the news organization that was going to help me answer the haunting questions behind the Oklahoma City bombing. Employees were gathered at the front desk laughing. It seemed that Mike Wallace, a legend in his own time, had been sitting behind the CBS telephone switchboard taking calls, as if he was the receptionist. Someone said the receptionist couldn't be found, so Wallace walked from his office to her seat and fielded random calls himself. Imagine callers' surprise when they dialed a listed number answered by Wallace's unmistakable voice.

Soon, Tom and I were approached by Radutzky, who led us to his messy office. Radutzky had to push piles of paper off his couch to make room for Tom and me to sit. The room looked like an indoor landfill, and I loved it.

My eagerness to see Ed Bradley again was percolating. I hadn't seen him since an earlier show done with Murrah survivors, including me. How many times had I watched him bust corrupt politicians and underhanded officials on national TV? He was a champion of the First Amendment. Bradley was a handsome man who looked incredibly trustworthy. I was excited to work directly with this celebrated journalist. I longed to thank him for taking an interest in my probe of the bombing and the principal players behind it. Yet he had no idea that I had been host to them in my home, or that I had visited them in theirs. I felt this telecast was a miracle in the making, a God thing. I yearned to thank God aloud, but I didn't want to scare Radutzky. He obviously had a lot on his mind, and I was about to hear why.

Ed Bradley was very ill, the producer told us. I could feel my spirit sinking, and Radutzky must have sensed it. He rushed to restore my morale, and said the Nichols story would be shot tomorrow, as it had been too long in the planning, and no one wanted to start over. If Bradley couldn't do the story, then Katie Couric would, he said. I wondered if she would remember our first interview on a windy rooftop the day after the bombing, or our second interview on the five-year anniversary of the explosion.

Any lull in my mood was lifted when Radutzky and I began evaluating my questions for Nichols. The senior producer initiated a crash course on how I should steer the interview, how I should not allow Nichols to go off-track, or to linger on any one subject. No one in the studios knew when Nichols would call, just that he would call today.

Nichols was unable to specify the time of our interview, as he had to wait for the prison officials to bring the telephone to his cell. The next morning, the stress among the technicians, cast, and crew rose slowly but palpably. They went about their various tasks like the professionals they were, including the adjustment of the lighting around a sit-in—a man sitting in my assigned chair.

A studio makeup artist applied my facial highlights, and someone else dabbled with my hair. I simultaneously felt special and out of place. All of this behind-the-scenes activity seemed a bit dramatic to me. I would have enjoyed it had I not been stressing about a call from Nichols, awaiting a conversation that would be recorded in one take. The arrangement did not allow for mistakes. I hadn't felt this type of pressure since my time at the white supremacy compound in Idaho.

What if Nichols doesn't call? I asked myself. *I've sparked all this activity among all these important people. And I'm depending on a man who has nothing to gain but the clearing of his conscience? He once had no conscience. Was his spiritual conversion enough to prompt him to keep his word, and to call me within the timeframe he promised? Nichols had to be fragile, given his separation from the entire world. Now, I'm trusting him to speak out on the nation's most powerful television news program! Have I asked too much of him?*

I was ashamed of my doubt. But the notions were spontaneous—and resistant to my efforts to suppress them.

Technicians altered my cellular telephone—the phone with the number Nichols had been given to call. I was then shown how to work a device that would enhance the audio quality of my interview. Finally, there was nothing left to do. Everyone in the studio had executed every necessary task. Nothing remained but time and creative ways to pass it.

A quiet settled over the studio, as people uneasily stood at the ready, awaiting a ringing telephone that would again throw them into action. I felt like I was dressed up with no place to go. I had been told not to leave my designated studio spot, not even for a restroom break. And so, I waited, and waited some more, feeling the nervous energy of a teenage girl waiting for the phone to ring.

The sound of a ringing telephone finally burst out. It seemed louder than a fire alarm. The twenty or so CBS crew members bolted to their assigned places. With all in place, I was given the cue to answer my phone. I nervously fumbled a little while trying to press the right button.

The caller was a close friend from Texas. She was calling to thank me for a painting of Mary and Jesus I had done for her. When I told her why I couldn't talk, she was stunned. I told her I would call her back.

For an instant, the room fell silent. Then someone chuckled and soon the whole studio broke into laughter. As it happened, Vickie's call provided a little comic relief for all of us.

Soon enough, though, Radutzky had his fill of waiting. He ordered an associate producer to call the prison to see if Nichols was proceeding with the interview. These CBS people were accustomed to rigid deadlines and were unaccustomed to unduly waiting on anyone. Now, they were stalled by bureaucrats in a faraway prison who might be flexing their control over Nichols simply because they could. That theory was confirmed when the associate producer called the prison and asked if Nichols was going to call, and received an indefinite answer. I could see Radutzky's patience wearing thin. Nonetheless, he continued to wait with the rest of us—until he received notification of what must have been an emergency. He shared the news with no one but darted from the production room.

"What will we do if Nichols calls now?" I said to no one. "Who's going to run this show?" I felt sure that someone was second in command—and surely that person could do the job.

Radutzky returned within minutes, asking Tom and me to follow him back to his office. He didn't seem to be in as big a hurry as he'd been earlier while awaiting Nichols's call.

"Kathy, I have bad news," the senior producer said, behind a closed door. "Ed Bradley has died."

I could see Radutzky's lips moving, but for an instant, I didn't hear his voice.

"We knew Ed was sick, but we didn't realize the severity of his illness," Radutzky went on.

I think he continued talking, as I think his lips continued to move. Perhaps he had lowered his voice. I could no longer hear a thing.

In minutes, I would see the most esteemed people in the dispassionate world of television journalism as they really were. Despite their sometimes-jaded personalities, their tears flowed as they heard the news of Bradley's death. By now, it was late afternoon and the grief-stricken broadcasters shut down the set without a call from Nichols.

I totally understood. I knew what it was like to lose family, and the *60 Minutes* cast and crew clearly were family with different last names.

Tom and I expressed our prayers and condolences and left the sad building. The day, which had begun with so much promise and excitement, now shifted into slow motion, replete with sadness for the loss of a great American, and loss of what might be the only opportunity for Terry Nichols to tell all.

During our tranquil flight home, I thought about Bradley—specifically when he interviewed me and a few other grieving families of bombing victims. I'd seen his empathy for the emotionally wounded. I had looked forward to making another memorable recollection with him, but now it was too late. He had passed from life to legend on the very day that was to happen.

I heard from no one at *60 Minutes* before Bradley's funeral or during the days afterward. I didn't call anyone at CBS, out of respect for their bereavement.

A few days later, I received an unexpected call at my home from Joyce Wilt, Nichols's mother. Nichols had told Joyce to apologize to me that he didn't call on the appointed day. He felt awful about it. He said officials notified him, the day he was to make the call, that my name had been removed from his calling list—permanently. My future conversations with Nichols were eliminated in 2006. He had learned of the permanent ban as he prepared to dial my phone to start the *60 Minutes* interview.

All that work by all those CBS people, and eleven years of my life spent chasing the truth known only by Nichols, had evaporated by the purging of my name from an in-house calling list. I felt stunned, numbed, and defeated. Now, how would I ever procure information that only Nichols possessed? I had proven that prison officials had censored our mail. I knew he could never reveal what he knew in a letter. And now I couldn't talk to him on the telephone! Nichols feared for his life. He wanted to share his story with the world before he was shut down. Now it is too late.

Lost in a swirling fog of competing emotions, I suddenly felt very sentimental about my relationship with Nichols. Then, for seemingly the thousandth time since the Murrah blast, I suppressed my emotions and composed myself, from habit and determination. I pondered what might be my next scheme to transform the very private Nichols into a public oracle of truth regarding what really happened on that fateful April morning eleven years ago.

56

PLAYING THE GAME

November 12, 2006
Eleven years, six months, and twenty-four days after the bombing

Following Joyce's shattering announcement, we devised yet another plan. She expected Nichols to call her, at her Michigan home, on the next Sunday. She said if I were there, I could have my interview.

"I'll be there!" I almost shouted. "I'll be there! If prison personnel want to play games with me, I'll play. I won't let them beat me," I said.

In the wake of Joyce's call, I was instantly rejuvenated. I could have gone bear-hunting armed with only a switch. Mine was an adrenaline high times ten, or so it seemed.

Joyce was willing to let me come to her home in Michigan to use her call for my purposes. The tireless people at *60 Minutes* promised to meet me at her house. I somehow felt they wanted to do this for all the right reasons, as well as a new one. They were determined to commemorate Ed Bradley, and the last story he almost told.

This would be the second chapter from the same playbook. Only this time, Nichols would call his mother and I would answer the phone. Prison big shots would have no idea I would be on the line. At that instant, perhaps while collaborating with Katie Couric, I would begin my questioning of

Nichols as *60 Minutes* recorded the phone call. My queries would be fast and direct. Nichols, no doubt angry about my removal from his calling list, would tell the truth with all the force and fury he could muster. This interview could actually be better than the one planned inside the *60 Minutes* studio, I realized. One more chance. I was ready for the next step.

Joyce had been wonderful to call me. I had lost my grandsons to the grave, and she'd lost her son to lifetime confinement. But there was a difference, I realized once my euphoria began to subside. Granted, our offspring were gone forever from our lives. And one day, I would talk to my grandchildren in Heaven. But Joyce could still talk to her son by telephone now. If I let her participate in my plot to record Nichols, the prison that removed me from Nichols's calling list might remove Joyce's name as well. How would she ever live with that?

How would I live with it, knowing it was my fault?

As Sunday drew closer, I became convinced these bureaucrats, who for reasons not yet known, denied a grieving America the truth, would certainly not hesitate to deprive a mother from talking to her son. I called Joyce, I called *60 Minutes*—and I called off the entire plan.

As a result of my decision, Americans have never heard Nichols speaking for himself, and I have never heard his voice again. From one mother to another, I just couldn't go through with it. I hope Americans understand. At times, to this day, I'm not always sure I do.

I'm satisfied the Colorado warden didn't take me off Nichols's calling list because I was a security risk. The very thought is laughable. He was merely following orders from someone higher in government bureaucracy—of this, I'm entirely confident. Nothing Nichols would have said to me, and *60 Minutes*, would have affected the prison. It would have affected people who are still at large.

But who are they? And why was I taken off Nichols's calling list?

57

THE PRIEST WHO CONFESSES

October 2006
Nine years and five months since the bombing

Father Frank Murphy savors a large sip of the Irish whiskey, then another, and leans back in his chair. "You're my kind of person," he says. "You don't ask questions about the Bible. You haven't asked me whether your Aunt Millie made it out of Purgatory, and you pour Jameson freely." He loosens his shirt and removes his Roman collar. His glass is already two-thirds empty, and Tom freshens it. Things are going the way we hoped—Father Murphy is well down the path to inebriation.

We are here visiting with the priest in a reception room inside Coury House at Subiaco Abbey, the Benedictine enclave in western Arkansas which includes Subiaco Academy, where my husband Tom attended high school.

We had traveled east on Interstate 40 for nearly three hours, after one of Tom's board meetings in Oklahoma City. Tom, at the wheel, draped his left arm, at the wrist, over the steering wheel.

"You loosen up every time we are within smelling distance of Subiaco," I said, rubbing his right shoulder.

Within half an hour, we could see Subiaco, a knockoff castle on a hill that Swiss monks built in 1878.

At the front desk of the Coury House, we pay for one of the remaining three rooms. Tom knew that a chaplain of the Terre Haute prison, where McVeigh was executed was attending a retreat at Subiaco. The hostess invites us to join the reception.

"Bet he knew McVeigh," Tom whispers to me as he points out the priest. "Let's find out."

We introduce ourselves. The red splotches on the father's cheeks, his rosaceous nose, his world-class belly, and his holding a wine glass in one hand and a brandy snifter in the other, suggest Father Murphy's preferences in beverage extend well beyond tap water. I ask to speak privately, so the three of us go into the small reception room, the better to ply the father with alcohol.

We had been visiting fifteen minutes before I took the first sip of my wine, then set my glass on the table.

"Father, we may have more in common than you think," I say, then wait. "Our grandchildren were killed in the Oklahoma City Bombing."

Murphy looks at his glass, then empties it and sets it down. He slides down in his chair, so his back is straight, like a two-by-twelve board. Topside, his prodigious belly looks as if it might split the very fabric of his robe. He laces his fingers together and rests the flats of his hands across his bulk.

"Were you," I begin, then hesitate. "Tom thought he heard you say you work with prisoners at Terre Haute. Were you there when McVeigh was there?"

Tom adds ice and more Jameson to Father Murphy's glass and returns it to him. The ice cubes rattle against the sides of the glass, the only sound in the room. Father Murphy stares into the drink as if he expects to find a response swimming in the liquor. Then he speaks, uttering, it seems, one syllable at a time. I can't discern whether the liquor or the memory is slowing him.

"There?" he repeats without raising his gaze. "There? Oh yes. I was there. Very much there."

"Did you know him?"

Father Murphy picks up his glass and rattles the ice. Tom refills it as the priest holds his arm out straight, the glass shaking by the hand that holds it. My impatience drives me to ask again. "Did you know him?"

Father Murphy empties the glass in three quick gulps, snapping his neck back each time, the lip of the glass never leaving his bottom lip.

"I need to know everything Tim McVeigh knows. I'd crawl into his skin if I could find out. I've been investigating the Oklahoma City bombing for years, and I don't believe McVeigh was the lone bomber in downtown Oklahoma City the day of the bombing. I'm hoping you might know something that could help me solve this crime."

"Probably not," he says. Then he stops. "You must realize I cannot break the seal of confession."

"Seal of confession!" I blurt out loudly. "Then you did know him! You took his confession."

Tom gives me a voiceless message to ease up. I paused for a long moment. "Father, I am sorry if we seem too intense. Enjoy your drink and let's talk about something else."

A little blurry-eyed now, but still articulate, he says, "No, dear, my heart goes out to you. I know how frustrating this must be for you. As I watched the news after the execution, I kept wondering why the FBI and other law enforcement did not pursue the others involved in this crime. You are right.

Something's not right here. I'll tell you what I can without breaking my vows.

"I visited Tim every day for two weeks before the execution. I serve all prisoners, no matter what, if any, faith they profess. But I know Tim was Catholic, so I offered to hear his confession; but every day he refused. I could tell he was becoming more nervous as doomsday approached. Finally, forty-five minutes before the injection, he sent for me. He was awkward and hesitant. I tried to relax him, knowing he had not been to confession for many years, since his youth. He finally eased a bit and started talking…I can't tell you how hard it has been for me to hold this inside."

His head drops a bit, and he looks up to the ceiling. Then he looks at Tom, then at me. He reaches for Jameson support once again. I start to say something but don't—let the screaming silence continue.

"I have to be careful what I say. I took the vow as a young priest."

"I know you did, Father, but please don't let murderers run free because of your oath. You need to help me."

"The church does not exist to do the work of investigators."

"So, you can forgive a murderer, but it would be wrong for you to help me? Pardon my French, Father, but that's nuts. Do you really think God wants you to put your neck on the line to protect the people who killed Chase and Colton? Obviously, it's easy for you to forgive and forget," I say. "You don't have children. Or grandchildren."

My words startle Father Murphy, who looks up from his whiskey glass for the first time in several minutes. There are tears forming in Father Murphy's eyes as he holds out his glass.

Tom takes it, adds ice and a generous pouring of Jameson. His words are beginning to slur.

"I took my vows before I knew men killed innocent people to make a political point. But you must swear not to divulge to anyone from whom you derived this information. I believe there is a reason that only God knows that we happened to meet here, in this place, at this time. So, reason number one is that I believe our meeting is God's work. Second, I believe your motives are real and that you and the other victim families have a right to know. Finally, Tim did not confess what I am going to tell you. He did confess some things that I am not going to tell you, but that I can swear to you are not relevant to your search."

No more Jameson. Father Murphy pushes his glass away and looks directly into my eyes, tempting me to turn away—but I don't.

"Tim reiterated to me that he served in the army in the Middle East, even killed several of the enemy, and was decorated. Then he applied to the Special Forces and was denied—supposedly because he didn't have the physical stamina, but in his mind because he was becoming obsessed with the downfall of the United States, brought on by the politicians. When he left the army, he was full of what he believed was patriotism. Tom and Kathy, I know you know all of this, so I'll cut to the chase. He told me he was proud to die for the cause. This is the part you are interested in. He was proud because he was leaving behind a number of his comrades who participated in the organization and execution of the bombing. He said these people were now in Oklahoma, Kansas, Arkansas, Florida, even foreign countries, including Germany, and that his refusal to identify them will enable them to continue the war, blow up more buildings, kill more innocents—until American wakes up and uproots evil in our country. He did not name his accomplices."

Father Murphy stops abruptly. "Thank you for your hospitality, but I can't continue this conversation." When he stands, his left knee fails, and he falls back into the chair. "Must be the altitude," he says and laughs. "I'm sky-high."

"I'm sorry if I offended you," I say.

"Ma'am, your offense was to prick my conscience," he says. "That makes it difficult for me to remain in your company. It would have been better if you had asked about your relatives in Purgatory. Better for me, anyway. Pleasure. Good night."

As Father Murphy shuts the door behind him, Tom and I look at each other.

"I wonder what else he knows," I ask.

"We'll never know now."

"You should've poured the whiskey faster."

"Wouldn't have made a difference," Tom says. "You spooked him."

"I wonder if Father Murphy will sleep well tonight?"

"Probably not," Tom says. "If he broke the seal of the confession, he's probably afraid he'll be walking into Hell right behind McVeigh."

PART EIGHT

The Bombing Conspiracy: A Speculative Journey Toward the Truth

58

THE ARIZONA CONNECTION

The Fall of 1994
Only months before the bombing

"Author's Note"

"The following chapters contain my personal, speculative version of the events leading up to the bombing. I have invented meetings, dialogue, and activities that could have happened among the bombings participants, and among government agents. This is what I personally believe is likely to have occurred, because it fits many of the known facts. But I want to stress that this account is fiction—not fact—and is only presented for your consideration as a possible answer to many remaining questions."

Tim McVeigh, Terry Nichols, and Michael Fortier met in basic training at Fort Benning, Georgia, after joining the US Army. All three were assigned to the same company, which moved from Georgia to Fort Riley in Junction City, Kansas. After Fortier mustered out of the Army, he moved back to Kingman, Arizona, where he had lived since he was seven, and married Lori Hart. McVeigh was best man.

Once McVeigh left the Army, he visited Kingman frequently. The Fortiers and McVeigh shared groceries, dope, a love of guns, and a keen dislike of the federal government. When McVeigh returned from Waco after the ATF burned out the Branch Davidians, his dislike of the federal government had grown to hatred.

"If you're going to bring 'em down, you need to hook up with Colbern," Fortier told McVeigh, and that's just what McVeigh did.

The trio, Tim, Michael, and Lori, quickly became a quartet, with Stephen Colbern holding the fourth position. Colbern, 35, was a 1989 graduate of UCLA and had been working as a biochemist in a research institute at Cedars-Sinai Medical Center in Los Angeles until the previous fall. He had been arrested in August by police in Upland, California, charged with carrying a loaded weapon and possessing unregistered firearms, including a silencer and an illegal assault weapon. He was also charged with battery against a peace officer.

Jumping bail, Colbern fled to Oatman, Arizona, an old mining town where burros roam freely down the streets and walk down the sidewalks, sticking their heads into local businesses. He worked as a part-time dishwasher at the Oatman Mining Company restaurant, a twenty-minute drive from Kingman. Colbern made his home in an abandoned mine shaft, nothing more than a cave.

McVeigh, who had grown impatient for revenge after Waco, wrote a short note, placed it in an envelope, and tacked it to a utility pole at the head of the trail that led to Colbern's cave: "Colbern, looking for men who want to help straighten out the government and aren't afraid to act. If you want to help, tell Fortier." McVeigh signed the note using the name

Tim Tuttle, one of his many aliases. Colbern and Tuttle made a connection.

Ten days later, Tim Tuttle returns to Kingman, to the trailer park where the Fortiers live, and knocks. Lori, who had been taking a nap, rises from the tan Naugahyde sofa and walks to the door in a short, tight pair of running shorts. When she opens the door, McVeigh stands there holding a manual typewriter.

"Oh, you got it," she says. "You just missed Michael. He ran up to the Kwik Stop to buy beer and smokes; come on in."

McVeigh walks into the kitchen and sets the typewriter on the blue enamel-topped table with stainless-steel legs.

"Just in time, the driver's license kits got here this morning," she says. She sets up the typewriter, then rolls a fake driver's license onto the platen. "Name?" she asks.

"Um, Timothy Kling—no, Robert...Robert Kling."

"Robert Kling's date of birth?"

"How about April 19, 1972? That would make me exactly twenty-one years old the day of the Waco disaster."

"Okay, let me plug in the iron so I can laminate it," she tells him.

Finished with the license, McVeigh sets the typewriter on the floor. Lori sits on a metal folding chair and watches him.

"What are you doing?" she asks.

"I'm about to give you a basic bomb-making course. That Colbern knows his stuff."

Tim takes fifteen cans of Campbell's Soup out of the cabinet and sets them on the table.

"Each can of soup represents a 55-gallon drum," McVeigh tells her. Lori shuffles her bare legs and gives him a suggestive look.

"Cut it out, your old man's my best friend. I'm not going there."

"You're afraid of girls, aren't you Timmy? Mike told me you've never had a girlfriend, is that right?"

Her question angers McVeigh. "That's not true. I've had a girlfriend. I don't have time for women, I am on a mission."

Mike walks in, a cigarette dangling from his lips, carrying a twelve-pack of beer and two packs of smokes. "Hey, bud, what's going on?" he asks, taking in Lori's bare legs and the cans stacked on the table.

"Tim's showing me how to build a bomb."

Michael glares at McVeigh. "Whoa. Wait a minute, Bro. You gotta understand. Me and Lori, we don't leave Kingman. We're not putting fuel in barrels. We're not loading barrels on a truck. You really need to think again about blowing it up during business hours. Those people you're going to kill, they didn't burn down Waco."

"Doesn't matter, Mike. Doesn't matter. They represent the people who were there. The government didn't evacuate Branch Davidian before they sent in the tanks and the tear gas. We don't evacuate the Murrah. They struck in broad daylight. That's when we strike."

"There are kids in the daycare."

"Koresh had kids. That's war. Sometimes kids die. Sorry, but the kids will be collateral damage."

"Cold, man," Fortier says. "Cold."

"No, man. Janet Reno is cold. She picked this fight. This is not a first strike. This is a counterstrike. When the Arab slings a rocket into Jerusalem, that's a first strike. When the Jew fires back, that's a counterstrike."

"The deal was to blow up a building," Fortier says. "Not people. I got kids. I don't want to be on the ground when you do the deed."

"You can't back out now, Mike. You're in too deep. No one would take kindly to you jumping ship. If you love your family, you better stick to the plan."

59

THE PRACTICE RUN

The Fall of 1994
Only months before the bombing

Three days after McVeigh's visit to the Fortiers' home, McVeigh, Fortier, Nichols, and Colbern gather around an empty five-gallon lard bucket Stephen salvaged from a dumpster behind the restaurant. Now the bucket sits near the back porch of the vacant wood-frame house Colbern had chosen for the demonstration. The house sits at the end of a road just north of the old Route 66.

"First, we've got to pour in the ammonium nitrate pearls," he says to the men around the bucket. "Make sure the ammonium nitrate pearls are thoroughly mixed with the diesel fuel or it won't work." He stirs the mixture with a long broom handle. "Now make sure the bucket is under the porch.... Yes, like that. When you got the bucket right, flick your Bic, then run like hell is after you."

"Is this what they taught you at the University?" Tuttle asks.

"Yep, I got an A-plus in bomb-building."

"Why are you wasting your talents out here in the desert?"

"I like burros," Colbern says, laughing.

Tim tugs at a plastic sandwich bag in his jeans pocket. He pulls it free and holds it high so his companions can see the powder in the bottom. "A little nitrogen, fellows?" McVeigh asks. "I need to refuel. I'm too calm for my own good."

McVeigh pulls a small brass-and-steel pipe from his back pocket, takes a pinch of the meth, and loads his pipe. He hands a lighter to Fortier. "Flick my Bic, Bro," he said.

Fortier puts the flame to the meth and McVeigh drags hard. "You're going to set your lungs on fire," Nichols warns.

McVeigh refills the pipe and hands it to Nichols. "Ever smoke this stuff? Don't knock it until you've tried it."

"No, I haven't, and I'm not starting now. I'll pass."

"His mama don't want him smoking," Fortier says. Colbern and Fortier laugh. Nichols does not.

"As I was saying, now that we have the mix right, let's clamp down the lid. Let's run the fuse out here, and let's have a fireworks show. Nichols, I heard you were good with blasting caps. How about giving me a hand?"

"Why you asking me?"

"You're the stump-blower. Tim told me you and him used to blow them up all the time at your farm."

Colbern strings five feet of fuse from the bucket and lays it in the sand straight out from the house. He pushes the bucket beneath the porch.

"Put the flame right there, Terry," Colbern says, pointing to the end of the fuse. "Then run like your mama's going to switch you."

Terry takes the turquoise lighter from McVeigh.

"Wait till I tell you," Colbern says to Terry. Then he, McVeigh, and Fortier back away from the house. "Back, back," Colbern says. When the men are one hundred yards away, Colbern cups his hands and hollers to Nichols. "Flick your Bic, brother!" Then Colbern tells the others, "You're not going to believe the destructive force of a five-gallon bomb. If this is a tornado, it's an F-5."

Nichols leans toward the ground and tiptoes toward the fuse. "How long do I have before it explodes?" he yells.

"I bought the slow-burning fuse. You'll have enough time to run into town."

The men laugh. Nichols goes to his knees. Then the glint of flame. Fortier yells, "Run, Terry, run!" Nichols takes off running. Fifty yards from the barrel, the shock wave knocks him down. Pieces of debris are flying through the air like shrapnel. Black plumes of smoke billow skyward.

"Perfect!" Tim says. Then, "Guys, we better boogie. Someone will be calling the law."

The mission is a success. Thanks to Stephen Colbern, McVeigh now has the knowledge and expertise to blow up a building. Of course it will be on a much grander scale, but he knows exactly how many 55-gallon drums he will need and exactly how to arrange them in the back of a rented Ryder truck.

60

MCVEIGH AT DAYCARE

March 28, 1995
Twenty-two days before the bombing

Timothy McVeigh arrives at Elohim City from Decker, Michigan. Millar greets him like a favorite son, giving him a big hug. Soon they are joined by Strassmeir, Brescia, Mahon, and Guthrie.

Millar advises the group that it looks like the Murrah Federal Building in Oklahoma City is their best choice. After praising McVeigh for his bravery and dedication, he instructs him to visit Oklahoma City for a final inspection before driving to Arizona for final bomb training. Throughout the day, excitement about the big event has reached a fever pitch among the group and, in the evening, they top off their exuberance with drugs. Millar does not imbibe but enjoys watching his exuberant warriors.

The next morning Millar hands McVeigh an envelope stuffed with twenty-dollar bills, to fund his expenses, and McVeigh heads west in his old Pontiac station wagon. Arriving in the early afternoon, he finds the Murrah Building, locates a metered parking space down the street, and returns to the front entrance. He enters the lobby, checks the directory, enters the elevator, and pushes the 2 on the panel. When the door opens, he enters a large room full of children's toys and books with other rooms around the perimeter, where he can hear children's voices. He stands in the large room for a few minutes.

Then a pleasant-looking woman approaches and says, "Hello, I'm Danielle Hunt. May I help you?"

"Ah, yes" he says, "I am moving to Oklahoma City soon and I'm looking for a daycare for my two kids."

"How old are your children?" she says.

"Ah, four and two."

Danielle thinks it is a little strange that he was slow to remember his children's ages. "Great ages," she says. "So, what can I tell you about our wonderful program here?"

"How many kids to you have here?"

"Twenty-four right now, but we can handle up to forty, depending on ages."

He asks several more questions. "What kind of security do you provide? Do you have security cameras outside as well as inside the building? Do the kids stay here all day? What time to you open? Do all the kids have to be here by a certain time?"

Danielle answers the questions as best she can, but finds his questions extremely unusual.

That evening, over dinner, she tells her husband—who is head of security of the building—about the strange conversation. When the FBI questions her, she again describes the conversation as really strange.

MARCH 30, 1995—TWENTY DAYS BEFORE THE BOMBING

Edye and I are running late this morning. We usually park outside by the front of the building, but all the spots are taken.

Edye pulls into the parking garage underneath the Murrah. It is past rush hour, so the garage is dark and unoccupied except for three men hovering around a trash receptacle near the entry. They are dressed in jeans and very casual shirts, obviously not businessmen. The tallest is very animated, waving his hands and seeming to do all the talking. The garage is pretty dark, even in daylight, but we can see the tallest of the three has what we call a flat-top haircut. The other two are shorter—one average size, the other a stocky build. We pull up next to the glass door entryway, which is not a parking space but, as I tell Edye, we are late for work, and we are only going to leave the car there a few minutes.

When we step out of the car and open the back doors to take the boys, the men stop talking and all three turn to stare at us. We unstrap the boys, with our heads inside the car, and Edye says, "Well, this is creepy. What's up with them?"

Chase asks, "What's creepy?"

"Nothing, Chaser," I tell him. "Hop down and get out."

I'm holding Chase's hand and Edye is carrying Colton. We walk toward the entryway and, as we open the doors, we both look back and the men's eyes are still fixed on us. It was very awkward. Once inside the building I turn and look back through the glass doors. I can see clearly the men resume their huddle and talking.

"I wonder what that was all about," I say to Edye.

"I don't know, but I think they're up to something."

We drop the boys off at daycare on the second floor. We are dreading passing the men again in the dark, cavernous garage. But when we return to the garage, the men are gone.

After the bombing, we called the FBI to report the suspicious activity, but they are not interested in the information.

Later, by way of the media, I learn that two other people saw those men the same day.

Dr. Paul Heath, a public affairs officer for the Veterans Administration in the Murrah Building, hears the bell ring, indicating someone is entering the offices. Since the receptionist is on break, he walks to the front desk. A tall man is standing at the desk with two other men standing two or three feet behind him.

Dr. Heath greets the tall man. "Good morning. I am Dr. Heath, can I help you, sir?"

"Hope so," the tall man responds. "We're from out west, just arrived here. We're veterans looking for construction work."

"Oh, is that right? What is your name and what kind of construction work do you do?"

"McVeigh, Tim McVeigh," says the tall one.

"Oh, I know several McVays here in Oklahoma. You have kin here?"

"How do they spell it?"

"M-C-V-A-Y" says Dr. Heath.

"Not related to me, mine's spelled M-C-V-E-I-G-H, and I'm originally from New York."

"Oh, okay," says Dr. Heath. "But you know, sometimes people change the spelling to make it easier, so you just may have some kin down here. Tell you what, leave your phone number here and I'll see if anyone here can help with your job search."

"Don't have a phone," McVeigh says. "I'll just have to call you from time to time."

"Okay, here's my office number. Good luck to you fellows. I have great respect for you veterans."

Because the judge declared the jury hung during the sentencing phase of the trial Terry was no longer under the threat of the death penalty. Dr. Heath is briefly interviewed by the FBI a few days after the bombing, but that is the last he will hear from the agency.

On March 30, Jane Graham is parking her car on the second floor of the parking garage. She sees three men dressed in jeans and casual shirts standing near an old station wagon and looking at what she took to be a set of plans. At first, she thinks that they must be repair workers. But when they open the rear door of the station wagon, she doesn't think that repair people would be in that ratty old car. *Strange*, she thinks.

Jane also was interviewed once by the FBI, for about ten minutes.

61

LADY GODIVA'S

April 8, 1995
Eleven days before the bombing

Tim McVeigh pinches the hundred-dollar bill between the nail of his index finger and the fingerprint of his middle finger. Every time the stripper looks his way, he rubs the bill back and forth beneath his nose. She plays him for an hour. Then, at a quarter before nine, she walks to booth number 19. Michael Brescia and Dennis Mahon sit on one side, McVeigh alone across the table.

"Any plans for that money?" she asks.

"I was thinking of spending it on you."

"I'm off at midnight."

"Deal, I'll show you a good time."

"This may surprise you. I've heard that line before."

"I'm a very smart man."

"Every man in Lady Godiva's is a very smart man. Guess you could be smarter than most since you're flashing a hundred instead of a ten."

"It's about the cause, not the money."

"Where I come from," she says, "money is the cause."

"April 19 mean anything to you?"

Dennis Mahon is glugging Michelob from an icy mug when McVeigh says "April 19." Mahon can't believe what he hears and begins to choke. He drops the mug, and it spills on McVeigh. McVeigh glares but doesn't react.

"Glad I'm not wearing my good clothes," McVeigh says to the stripper. "I was about to tell you a secret. On April 19, you're going to remember me for the rest of your life."

"Kling," Brescia says, using McVeigh's most recent alias. "You're an idiot!"

The stripper asks, "Is that right?"

"What's your name?" Kling asks.

"Shawn Tea."

"Is that your real name?"

"It's my stage name."

On April 19, Shawn Tea remembers the conversation she had with the three men only days earlier. She discusses the conversation with her boss, and he pulls the security video from the camera in the dressing room. For April 8, the security camera shows three of the dancers chatting. The surveillance tape shows Shawn Tea, a busty brunette, walking into the dressing room. The clock on the wall shows the time is 9:00 p.m.

She begins talking with her stripper friend about a customer who had clearly made an impression on her.

Shawn Tea: "The smartest man in the world is waiting for you in Booth 19."

The stripper friend is called Candy Cane. "Good timing. I'm done for the night."

Shawn Tea: "He says he's gonna be famous, and that on April 19 I'm going to remember him for the rest of my life."

Candy Cane: "Weirdo. I don't care about famous. If he's got the money, he'll get the honey."

Shawn Tea laughs: "Okay, I'll hook you up."

Candy Cane pauses: “I’m pretty tired, but I’ve got to scam ’em somehow. I need the bucks.”

Shawn Tea: “He’s a weirdo.”

⌘

Twenty-seven minutes past 7:00 p.m. on April 22, 1995, three FBI agents—a woman and two men—no-knock their way into the dressing room at Lady Godiva’s. One of the men flashes a badge and shouts in a loud voice: “FBI!”

The four strippers on break jump. Shawn Tea stands up. She covers her breasts with a linen towel. The agent with the badge sits down on the sofa where Shawn Tea had been sitting. “Are you Elizabeth Teaberry?” he asks.

She hesitates. Then she says, “Yes, sir. My stage name is Shawn Tea.”

“I’m Agent Stowe. I went through the police academy with your dad before I went FBI. I talked to him this afternoon. He told me you work here. He thinks you may have met someone connected to the bombing.”

Shawn Tea’s dad had taught her never to trust anyone, especially in her line of work, a profession he thought was okay until his daughter joined it. “My dad’s embarrassed that I work here. He would never tell you I work here.”

Shawn Tea takes a quarter from her purse, which hangs in a locker with her jeans and turquoise pullover. She leaves the dressing room and walks to the pay phone next to the bar. In three minutes, she returns, tears in her eyes.

“You believe me now?” Agent Stowe asks.

“Okay. What do you want to know?”

Stowe sets a briefcase on his lap, flips the brass latches, pulls out a spiral notebook. "I'm gonna flip through these pages. Stop me if you recognize anyone." He turns the notebook upside down so the four women can see it.

On the fourth page, Shawn Tea points. "Him. He was in Booth 19, him and two other men."

"Did you get his name?"

"He hardly talked. He was throwing around hundred-dollar bills like they were Kleenex."

The agent takes a small pad and pen from his shirt pocket. "Did you get a name?"

"I don't remember. He told me on April nineteenth I was going to remember him the rest of my life. He said, 'I'm glad I didn't wear my church clothes' after his friend spilled beer on him. Then he looked real hard at the guy who dumped the beer on him. Told him I couldn't do the date, but I'd ask my friend if she wanted to go out with him. He said, 'Okay, doesn't matter to me. Any of you girls will do.'"

"Did she go with him?"

"Don't know. It was her last night."

⌘

Candy Jeffrey's parents hadn't spoken with her since Christmas. They know nothing. They tell an FBI field agent that they thought maybe she had plans to return to Ohio.

The agent presses: "We have reason to believe your daughter was involved with three men who bombed the Alfred Murrah Building. It is critical that we speak to everyone who may know anything. You are absolutely certain you haven't talked to her?"

"Nothing," the agent tells Stowe by telephone that night.

On the morning of April 24, Stowe takes three Tulsa police officers with him to Candy's apartment in Tulsa. The apartment manager opens Candy's door to the stench of a two-week-old body. The FBI medical examiner rules her death a suicide by heroin overdose and states the date of death as April 8 or 9.

62

THE PANCAKE HOUSE

April 9, 1995
Ten days before the bombing

The waitress at the Pancake House is pouring Richard Guthrie's fifth cup of coffee when the tinkly bell on the glass front door marks the arrival of Tim McVeigh and Dennis Mahon. Guthrie is sitting at a table in the back of the dining room. As McVeigh and Mahon approach, he asks, "You boys stop for brain surgery on the way over? You're two hours late."

"You said the joint with the rooster on the front," Mahon replies. "We went to Chicken in the Rough in Oklahoma City."

"I said the diner in Edmond with the chicken on the front," Guthrie says. "You dumb shit. You don't even know the difference between a chicken in Edmond and a rooster in Oklahoma City."

"Give me my seat," McVeigh says to Guthrie. McVeigh always faces the door.

Mahon starts to sit down by McVeigh. McVeigh glares and says, "I only share booth benches with bitches. Pull up a chair."

Mahon looks around; all the chairs are taken, so he slides in next to Guthrie. Guthrie grimaces but allows him to sit.

"So, Millar's filled you in on the change of plans, I take it?" McVeigh asks Guthrie.

"Yep," he replies. "Told me you'd go over the final details today."

"You ever been to the Murrah?" Mahon asks.

"Put a lid on it, Dennis," Guthrie replies.

"Me? I'm not the problem. Tim was passing out the blueprint to everyone within shouting distance at Lady Godiva's last night."

McVeigh gave Mahon the look, the same hard stare he'd turned on him at Lady Godiva's twelve hours earlier.

Guthrie interrupts. "Y'all went to Lady Godiva's? That's why you're late."

"Doesn't matter," McVeigh says. "Shut up and listen."

McVeigh pauses while the waitress sets two ceramic mugs on the table and pours coffee for him and Mahon.

"Today," McVeigh said, "we're going to map out several escape paths. We're going to take every possible route out of downtown. We are going to write down every stop sign, traffic light, yield sign, detour. At the moment, I'm thinking I'll leave town on I-35, and go to Perry. That's an hour.

"All the police officers will be heading south on the interstate. I'll have the road to myself. Richard, drive your truck and meet us at the warehouse at six in the morning. At 8:45 a.m. you drive to Fifth Street, park in the passenger loading zone—in front of the Murrah Building—to reserve our spot. When you see us coming, start the truck and ease out of the spot.

"It's critical we remain calm. Don't attract attention. Can't be burning any rubber. Brescia couldn't make it today, but he will be riding shotgun with me. We'll pull up in the Ryder truck and park under the awning. He'll exit the passenger side and head for the Mercury Marquis in the alley while I light the fuse. When the fuse is lit and everything is a go, I'll walk across the street to the *Journal Record* Building, where you'll be waiting.

"We'll follow Guthrie in his truck up I-35. We'll stop at the Perry city limits and you can get in the pickup with Stephen. We'll park it at the Kumback Café. That's something else we need to do—find a car to leave in Perry to switch into. We need something nicer than whatever we buy to get out of the city. It'll sit in the square overnight. We don't want a car that'll make the police officers suspicious.

"If this works for you all, it's a go. Ten days until we pull off the biggest fireworks show Oklahoma City has ever seen."

63

MCVEIGH AND FRIENDS IN KANSAS

April 14, 1995
Five days before the bombing

It's 7:45 a.m. on Saturday. Timothy McVeigh, Terry Nichols, and Michael Brescia arrive at the Santa Fe Diner in Herington, Kansas.

They have just completed intense days of learning how to make a big bomb. Chemist Stephen Colbern has carefully taught them how to make a simple but powerful bomb, with ammonium nitrate fertilizer, diesel fuel oil, and nitromethane. The final test was successful when they blew up a small building in a remote area near Kingman.

This training was so much better than what they learned from Dennis Mahon when he came to the Nichols farm in Michigan. Dennis was a highly respected white supremacist who was really good at motivating Nazi types in Germany, as well as the United States, and organizing terrorist activities. He was not so good at making bombs. They were fortunate they didn't blow themselves up while experimenting on the farm. Dennis was also a sometime FBI informant, which the three men entering the diner that morning did not know. He probably gave the feds just enough help to keep himself out of prison.

Barbara Whittenburg and her husband are owners of the diner. Barbara also is a cook and manager. This morning, her early-shift waitress is a no-show, so Barabara is waiting, cooking, serving, and dishwashing.

When the three men arrive, she notes that two of them get out of a Ryder rental truck and the third a blue SUV. Her son Charlie notices the car's Arizona license plate. She brings them fresh coffee and recognizes McVeigh and Nichols as customers who have been there several times. The third is a handsome, dark-complected man she has not seen before.

"Good morning, fellas. I see you have a rental truck. Somebody moving?" she asks.

"Yeah," McVeigh replies without looking up as he brings his cup to his lips.

"Moving here to Herington?" she asks.

"No, Oklahoma City," the darker man replies.

McVeigh, obviously startled by the response, turns aggressively to Brescia with a piercing stare. She feels buckets of ice poured over the conversation. She quickly asks, "Anyone for breakfast?" McVeigh shakes his head and gives her the same stare, which to her says, "Shut up and get the hell away from us." Barbara tops off the coffees and heads to another table.

Later, when Barbara is interviewed by the FBI, the agents insist she must have been mistaken because the Ryder truck was not rented until April 17. After that, when testifying before the grand jury, she tells them that despite the FBI's effort to persuade her otherwise, she knew what she saw and was telling the truth. For months, her account appeared in newspapers across the country until one day in 1996, when she was asked for an interview by a reporter and she said, "No more. I've been receiving all kinds of threats, including death threats. If the government doesn't believe me, then how can I count on them to protect me? No more interviews. Period."

When I visited Herington to check out Geary Lake and the Nichols home, I went to see Barbara. After I told her about my grandsons, she agreed to a discussion about that morning in April. She reiterated what she had been telling the FBI and the grand jury. I certainly believed her. I could see she was frightened and asked her who she was afraid of.

She said, "I don't know who it is, the bad guys or the good guys. Well, I guess that makes them both the bad guys, huh?"

As far as I know, she never mentioned it again, to anyone.

Following his stop at the Sante Fe Diner, just five days before the Oklahoma City blast. Timothy McVeigh shows up later that day at a Firestone tire store in Junction City, Kansas. White smoke pours from the blue-gray Pontiac station wagon he has driven for years. A head gasket has blown. A Firestone mechanic tells him the necessary repairs will cost several hundred dollars.

One store employee, Thomas Manning, whom McVeigh recognizes from his Army days, says he has a 1977 Mercury Marquis out back that "isn't a real pretty car" but "seems to run real good."

"How much do you want for it?"

"I'd take three hundred dollars as is, no guarantees."

"What about my car? It's got a blown gasket, but it's worth something."

Manning looks it over, reviews the repair cost, and says, "I'd junk it. Might bring seventy-five dollars, but I can only give you fifty. Might bring less than that."

"Deal," says McVeigh. "Give me fifty of that back."

McVeigh removes the Arizona license plate from the station wagon and puts it on the Mercury. One plate screw is missing, so he tightens the other as best he can. He leaves Firestone, stops at a pay phone booth, and places a call to Elliott's Body Shop. Using the alias Robert Kling, he asks about renting a Ryder truck. He reserves a twenty-foot truck for Monday, April 17.

He then drives a few blocks to the Dreamland motel. When he walks into the office, a cheerful lady is standing behind the counter.

"Can I help you?" she says with a thick German accent.

"Yeah, I need a single room for four nights, cheapest one you have."

"They're all the same" Lea replies. "Twenty-eight dollars a night. We change bedding and towels every night."

"Could you do it for twenty if I pay cash in advance?"

"I guess so. We're not full, so what the heck? Just don't tell the other guests, or anyone else."

He fills out a registration card under the name Bob Kling, then reconsiders, throws that registration card away, and fills out another card under his own name, giving his address as 3616 N. Van Dyke, Decker, Michigan—the Nichols family farm. He writes the plate number for his Mercury, but it is illegible. He peels off five twenty-dollar bills and lays them on the counter. She folds the bills over, slips them into her right pants pocket, and hands him the key to Room 25. As he exits the office and drives the Mercury around to the room, she notices the tag is lower on one side.

He opens the creaky door, tosses down his duffle bag, and within minutes hops back in the truck and is off to Geary Lake State Park, about halfway between Herington and Junction

City and only a twenty-minute drive from Terry Nichols's home in Herington.

When McVeigh arrives, Nichols is waiting in his blue pickup. Shortly, Michael Fortier pulls in driving the Ryder truck from Arizona.

The bombers would like to sleep. They drove straight through from Kingman, Arizona, the night before. They are exhausted but still cranked on adrenaline, and probably a line or two; but if they are going to have their surprise ready by April 19, the day Richard Snell is to be executed in Arkansas, they need to stay busy. They will just have to grab naps as they can.

For the past several months, Terry Nichols has been very busy buying the lethal fertilizer ammonium nitrate, as fast as possible without raising suspicion. At this time in Kansas there are no laws regarding the amount of this potentially lethal fertilizer that can be purchased, but dealers have been notified it can be used to make explosives. In any case, Nichols has convinced the co-op he is buying it for his farm, as well as for his neighbors who have hired him to fertilize their fields. In all he has purchased more than two tons. Meanwhile, McVeigh has been able to buy or steal 350 pounds of Tovex and a supply of Blastrite Gel (sausages) for ignition.

This afternoon the three are joined by Dennis Mahon and Richard Guthrie, and the five go to work. Inside the Ryder truck are thirteen barrels, which they remove. One by one they fill the barrels, nine with ammonium nitrate fertilizer and four with a mixture of fertilizer and diesel fuel. This is hard work that will take at least two days. In order to avoid detection, they will have to put everything in the truck at night. Then, according to the plan, they will have to move all of it to a different truck on Monday.

By night fall the phone in the small motel room rang once. McVeigh sat on the edge of the bed, fingers drumming on the battered desk beside him, watching the clock on the wall tick down the seconds. He knew what time it was. He wasn't sure who was calling, and he wasn't about to make the mistake of trusting anyone without getting the confirmation he needed.

He picked up the receiver, holding it to his ear, his voice low but steady. "McVeigh."

The voice on the other end was muffled at first, then came clear as day. A man McVeigh had never met, but whose name had been passed to him at Elohim City. "Tim? This is Louis. You got a minute?"

McVeigh's stomach tightened. Louis wasn't someone he had spoken to directly before, he didn't even know Louis's last name, but he knew that Louis was the man at the top, Millar and Butler revered him. Louis was the connection to a network of people who were as committed to the cause as McVeigh was.

"Go ahead," McVeigh said, his voice flat.

"Listen, I know you're getting into some deep waters, and it's important you know who you're working with," Louis continued. McVeigh could hear the low hum of background noise—a bar, a warehouse, something industrial. It made everything feel more distant, more dangerous.

"Louis said, "I have a man on the ground that I want you to work with, his name is Mitch."

"Yeah,who's this Mitch?" McVeigh asked, cutting straight to the point.

Louis's pause was brief but telling. McVeigh could practically hear him weighing his words. "Mitch is a solid guy Tim. You don't need to worry he's been with us since—"

"How long?" McVeigh interrupted, his eyes narrowing.

"Since '92," Louis said, the certainty in his tone making McVeigh's shoulders relax just a fraction. "He's been working with some of our people for a while now, running logistics. The man's sharp—keeps his head low, does the job without drawing attention. You know how we work."

McVeigh leaned back against the bed, taking in the words, trying to feel them out. "What's his game? What's he in for?"

Louis chuckled low, a knowing sound that didn't settle well with McVeigh. "What aren't we in for, Tim? Mitch has his reasons, like the rest of us. But he's no fool, this isn't some half-assed operation. You'll be working with someone who's committed, who knows what's at stake."

McVeigh rubbed his thumb along the edge of the receiver, thinking over Louis's words carefully. This wasn't just about buying a truck or making a delivery. This was bigger—much bigger. "Does Mitch have the right clearance for this?" McVeigh asked. "The right... motivation?"

The line crackled slightly. Louis's voice dropped to almost a whisper. "You don't get to where Mitch is without having skin in the game. And trust me, his motivations line up with yours. He'll get the job done, no questions asked."

There was a finality in Louis's words, a quiet confidence that McVeigh could feel.

McVeigh's gaze shifted to the window, where the pale morning light was filtering through the blinds. He had to make a decision, either he trusted Louis—and by extension,

Mitch—or he pulled back entirely. But backing out now wasn't an option.

"Alright," McVeigh said after a long beat, his voice cold but resolute. "I'll meet him, what's the plan?"

"On the 17th go to the McDonald's at the corner of I-70 and Washington Street. I'll have Mitch meet you there at 4:00 p.m. and the two of you can pick up the truck. Mitch will be driving a Jeep Grand Cherokee, you'll recognize him. He's a stocky guy in his late twenties. He has a big tattoo on his upper left arm that he's really proud of. And oh yeah, he'll be wearing a ball cap with flames on the side, can't miss him."

By now McVeigh is sold on the idea. "OK. Let's make this happen."

Louis's tone softened. "You're making the right call. Mitch knows how to handle his end. Don't worry about a thing. He'll help you get the truck, execute the mission, and you get out. That's how it goes."

There was a final click as the line went dead.

McVeigh placed the receiver back into its cradle, with his mind racing. He'd just made a deal with a shadow—the man, McVeigh believed to be the Godfather of the movement, Mitch was in.

64

MCVEIGH AND GUESTS AT THE DREAMLAND

April 15, 1995
Four days before the bombing

At 9:00 a.m., the maid at the Dreamland Motel unlocks the door to Room 25. She had seen McVeigh leave earlier that morning and thinks his room is unoccupied and ready to clean. As she starts to open the door, she is startled when a man appears. Towels are draped over his arms like he is hiding something.

"Sorry. I thought this room was empty," she says in her Cuban accent.

The man says, "Hold on." Then he hands her an armload of towels.

She goes back to the office to complain to her boss. "Look at all these dirty towels the man in Room 25 used. How could one man dirty this many towels?"

"What does he look like?" Lea McGown asks.

"He has brown hair, heavy build, not very tall."

"Hmmm. That's sure not the guy who registered. He's a big, tall, gangly kid."

Later that afternoon, diner owners Barbara Whittenberg and her husband stop at Geary Lake. It is a normal pit stop when they go to Junction City for restaurant supplies. There she sees the same Ryder truck and car she had seen yesterday at the diner.

"Wonder what those guys are up to?" Barbara comments. "I saw them in the diner yesterday. Sure weren't very friendly."

Her husband says, "Leave it alone. It's none of our affair. Just go in there and do your business. We're burning daylight."

When McVeigh realizes Barbara is watching them, he has Nichols move the truck behind a grove of trees, where it is less visible.

Retired Marine Sergeant James Sargent is celebrating his first day of retirement, fishing at Geary Lake. While he isn't catching many fish, he notices the activities around the Ryder truck parked near the lake. Although he can hear voices, he cannot make out what is being said. He can't imagine what the men are doing—not fishing, that's for sure.

Nichols notices the real-estate lady who sold him his house drive into the parking lot adjoining the pavilion. He tells Tim, "We need to get this done, too many eyes watching us. Maybe we should take the truck back to the motel tonight."

That evening, as Lea McGown is out front watering her flowers, McVeigh pulls into the parking lot in the Ryder truck. Obviously, an amateur truck driver is awkwardly trying to back the truck into a parking spot. McGown yells at him, "Be careful! You're going to smash my roof."

Lea goes back inside where a customer is waiting for her at the counter. Frustrated, McVeigh pulls the truck forward onto the grass by the swimming pool. McGown tells her son, Eric, to go tell him to park the truck in front of the motel, next to the sign.

With the truck moved, McVeigh flops on the bed, exhausted. Thirty minutes later a knock on the door awakens him. Pete Langan. and Guthrie arrive ten minutes later. The old, yellowed, laminated card next to the phone lists local restaurants. Langan calls a Chinese restaurant a few blocks away and places a large order of moo goo gai pan and egg rolls. McVeigh pulls a checklist from his left pocket and gives the group a progress report, noting they must stay on schedule. The food arrives. Later, the delivery boy says the man who answered the door and paid him was not McVeigh, and he could see a number of men in the room.

Earlier, as Eric exits the office, Lea turns back to the man at the counter. He is a six-footer, powerfully built, hair almost shoulder length with a US Navy tattoo on his left arm, a few inches above his thick wrist.

"Need a room?" she says with her customer smile.

"Sure do," he says, returning her smile with his well-trained one. "Just one night. On my way to Wichita and need to leave early in the morning. You do wake-up calls?"

"No wake-up calls here, but I can give you an alarm clock," Lea says.

"That'll do." He hands her a credit card with the name Harold Ferguson on the front as he fills out the registration form, steps outside to get the tag number from his '91 Ford pickup and returns to the desk, where she hands him back his card.

Harold climbs into the pickup and moves it to the room on his key tag, Room 24. The new Dreamland customer then removes the medium-size duffle bag and the McDonald's to-go from the passenger side of the pickup, unlocks the motel door, and enters the musty room. "Yuck," he says under his breath. But then thinks, *I've slept in worse places, like the jungles of Viet Nam.*

James L. "Rocky" Patterson was well trained to remember all the phony names he was required to use. He had never used Harold before, but it was as good as any. He had joined the FBI shortly after he left the Navy Seals, more than twenty years ago. Because of his special training and experience, he was hired specifically to perform the most dangerous and exotic assignments: gang infiltration, espionage, and drug rings, to name a few. This one did not seem too difficult. Working out of the Kansas City office, he was not told where the assignment came from, just that it was important. His boss had only told him to go to the Dreamland Motel in Junction City, look for a Ryder truck and install a transponder, without being detected. That seemed simple enough.

It is 7:30 p.m. While Rocky eats his bland meal in the dingy room, he hears men's voices from the next room. Wondering if these might be the truck guys, he removes his special listening device from the bag and places it against the wall. He can't make out everything but realizes quickly these definitely are the truck guys. One of them is obviously the leader, going over some kind of checklist about barrels and fuel. He hears one of them say, "Big as Waco?" "Bigger," the leader says in a loud voice.

After a while, the chatter grows sillier and Rocky thinks it sounds like drugs or alcohol talking. At 9:30 p.m. he hears footsteps outside. He pulls back the shabby drape just enough to see the lady from the front desk standing outside Room 25. After a few moments she moves on. By 11:00 p.m. Room 25 is quiet, and Rocky begins his work.

He is no stranger to transponders, or really most any other kind of detection device, having placed them on vehicles of all types, as well as headquarters of Mafia guys, the Viet Cong, and offshore rigs. He removes this one from the box and carefully inspects it, making sure it will be effective. He has a spare in case he finds a problem. By midnight he is satisfied with the device and ready. He decides to wait a bit to make sure all is quiet.

At 1:00 a.m., Rocky silently opens the door and slowly moves toward the front of Dreamland. All the rooms are dark, including the one next to the office where Lea lives. The only light is the one that shines on the sign. This is not good, because the Ryder truck is parked next to that sign. Rocky decides to circle the truck to the driver's side, which is away from the light. He will have to expose himself to light for a split second as he moves around the truck. He does that, then waits for three or four minutes to see if anyone notices. He finds what he knows is the perfect spot under the wheel well, mounts the device, checks the adhesive to make sure it is secure, and returns to his room by the same route. When he arrives there, he waits outside for five minutes to make sure that he was not noticed. He goes back into the room, sets his alarm for 5:00 a.m., and sleeps.

When Rocky leaves Dreamland at 5:30 a.m., there is no sign anyone else is up. Satisfied the job is done, he leaves the motel and heads out—not to Wichita, but back home to Kansas City.

I wonder what that's all about, he thinks as he enters I-70. *Oh well, like most my assignments, I'll probably never know.*

65

THE COUNTDOWN

April 16, Easter Sunday
Three days before the bombing

McVeigh drives the old Mercury to Oklahoma City and meets with Terry Nichols, who has his son, Josh, with him in his blue pickup.

At twelve years old, Josh is bigger than a lot of men. He usually lives with his mother in Las Vegas but came to Herington on spring break. He was aware that McVeigh, Fortier, and his dad were messing with explosives, but was not sure for what purpose. I now understand why Josh was so emotional when we visited the Memorial in Oklahoma City some years ago.

McVeigh parks the Mercury in an alley across the street from the Murrah. The lobby security camera in the nearby Regency Towers Apartments records images of Nichols's blue 1984 GMC pickup on that day. He leaves a note on the Mercury windshield that says, "Not abandoned. Please do not tow. Will move by April 19th. Needs battery and cable." Both men, along with Josh, squeeze into the cab of the pickup and return to Kansas.

Around 12:30 p.m., Herta King visits Room 24 at the Dreamland to see her son, David, who suffers from depression. As she approaches David's room with an Easter basket, she cannot see his car because a Ryder truck blocks the view.

When she returns to visit her son again around 7:00 or 8:00 p.m., the Ryder truck is gone.

McVeigh and Nichols moved the truck to back to Geary Lake. Nichols and Josh are headed for the Kansas City airport and McVeigh has returned to the motel. The bombers are now ready to rent the second Ryder truck and make final preparations.

Around nine o'clock that evening, Lea McGown walks the perimeter of the building to ensure that everything is secure before going to bed. When she walks by Room 25, she hears voices. She listens to determine if it's the television. She realizes it is not. It is live conversation involving several men, maybe four or five.

Timothy McVeigh, as lead bomber, has the bed to himself and the others find spots on the floor. A few joints ease the discomfort, and the self-styled patriots sleep like innocents.

When FBI agents interviewed Lea McGown, Herta King, her son David, and the delivery boy, they were told by each witness there were several men in Room 25 before the bombing. No attempt was made to identify those men. The FBI never identified the fingerprints in the room.

APRIL 17, TWO DAYS BEFORE THE BOMBING

Late Monday afternoon there are no vehicles parked at the Dreamland. Lea McGown watches as McVeigh leaves his room and walks down the hill to a convenience store, where he calls a taxi. The taxi drops him off at a McDonald's at the corner of I-70 and Washington Street.

At 3:57 p.m., according to McDonald's security cameras, McVeigh steps inside, walks to the counter, and buys a fruit pie. He walks out of McDonald's and looks around, no sign of Mitch who is supposed to be there at 4:00 p.m. McVeigh looks at his watch, it's 4:02 p.m. He starts walking up the hill to Elliott's Body Shop, where he has reserved a 20-foot rental Ryder truck. It is raining and McVeigh has no hat, no umbrella, no raincoat. Halfway up the hill, he sees a Jeep Grand Cherokee pulling up beside him. He knows it's Mitch because he sees the hat and the tattoo on his upper shoulder just like Louis had told him. Mitch comes to a quick stop and leans out the car window, "Hey Mac."

McVeigh is miffed. "You're late," he says, as he slams the door to the jeep as he climbs in.

"I'm sorry there was a speed trap, and I didn't want to run the risk of getting stopped." He looks at his watch, "What the heck! I'm only 4 minutes late."

"I was told you were a pro. Don't let it happen again or you're going to miss the fireworks."

There was no time to argue as they drove into Elliot's Body Shop. When they arrive the manager, Eldon Elliott, is in the shop, along with an employee, Vicki Beemer. Beemer asks McVeigh for his driver's license, and he gives her the fraudulent license that Lori Fortier made for him using the name Robert Kling. The license lists a home address of 428 Malt Drive, Redfield, South Dakota. The listed destination is 428 Maple Drive, Omaha, Nebraska. While McVeigh is waiting for the transaction to process, he makes small talk with Beemer about Easter and paying taxes. Beemer notices the birth date of April 19, 1972, on the Kling license. She tells him, "I've been married longer than you've been alive." McVeigh pays for the rental, plus a deposit in cash. Vickie hands the receipt to owner Eldon Elliott, who is not suspicious as a fair percentage of his rentals are cash.

Tommy Kessinger, a mechanic working in the body shop, is on break sitting in a chair eating popcorn when McVeigh walked in. Kessinger noticed Mitch entering behind McVeigh and later describe him to the FBI as a nice looking, dark-complected man, wearing a black T-shirt, with a tattoo visible below the sleeve on his left arm. He told the agents that the man accompanying Kling appeared younger and wore a ball cap with a blue-and-white zigzag pattern resembling flames. Kessinger described him as about 5'10", clean-shaven, muscular, with large arms, a broad chest, a smooth complexion, a thick neck, and a wide chin.

McVeigh asks for a dolly but the shop lacks one. Beemer calls Waters True Value Hardware and reserves a dolly for him. McVeigh steps into the Ryder truck and drives to the hardware store for the dolly. An employee notices McVeigh's attempts to avoid the focus of the security camera as he enters the store. He wheels the dolly out, again making a circle around the security camera, throws it in the truck, and drives off.

Later, when FBI agents interview Elliott, they try to convince him McVeigh was there alone and that what Elliott remembers is the two men who came in the *next* morning to rent a truck. Elliott said this could not be the case since he did not come to the shop the next day.

Monday afternoon, McVeigh returns to the Dreamland accompanied by Mitch in the new Ryder truck. The Dreamland's owner, Lea McGown, notices this Ryder truck is not the one she saw two days ago, the other was smaller and had a rounded cab. A few hours later McVeigh and Mitch leave in the truck, heading to Geary Lake. Now, with instructions from Elohim City, the five bombers unload the first Ryder and nail boards to the floor of the second Ryder, so the load cannot shift in transit. Then they begin loading the 13 barrels in a reverse "J formation," the fueled barrels closest to the ignition area behind the driver's seat.

McVeigh drills two holes under the seat and inserts the plastic tubes that will hold the fuses: one for a five-minute fuse, and the other for a two-minute fuse. He will also wear a shoulder holster for his Glock pistol, which he will use to ignite the blast if the fuses fail. They finish everything except the fuses and blasting caps, which they will prepare in the morning. At nightfall they head back to the Dreamland in the two sedans, leaving both trucks at Geary Lake. Richard Guthrie stays with the trucks to guard them until morning. He throws his sleeping bag in the first Ryder.

APRIL 18—ONE DAY BEFORE THE BOMBING.

At four o'clock the next morning, McVeigh and Mitch arrive at Geary Lake. Guthrie is already awake. McVeigh and Mitch enter the decoy truck and head out. Guthrie is following them in the Grand Cherokee. The trip to Oklahoma City is a trial run. Fortier will meet them in Oklahoma City to pick up his Jeep, and to help if needed.

The only interruption on this trip is a stop for gas and food. They arrive in downtown Oklahoma City a little after 9:00 a.m. McVeigh parks the decoy truck under the overhang, then he and Mitch step out and walk briskly toward the Kerr-McGee building. The security guard on duty in the lobby of the federal building sees the men leave. He waits a few minutes, then heads out the door to see what is happening. As he steps outside, he sees the men returning, but this time there are three of them. Richard Guthrie has joined them. They hop in the truck and depart before he has a chance to ask them any questions. Later he identifies McVeigh and Mitch from drawings and describes the third man as best he can remember. With the dry run completed, the three head back to Junction City, and Fortier departs for Kingman.

Tuesday afternoon the bombers gather at Geary Lake to put final touches on the bomb and prepare for the trip to Oklahoma City. By sundown all is ready, Tovex and Blastrite Gel in place, set to detonate.

66

THE SWITCH

April 18 and 19, 1995

By 8:00 p.m. on Tuesday, April 18, all are ready for the journey of 272 miles to Oklahoma City. Instructions from Elohim City order the departure of the decoy truck to leave at 10:00 p.m., followed by the bomb truck one hour later. The trip should only take about five hours, but they want to allow for changes in the plan or unforeseen delays.

Earlier that day, the feds are gathering at the Hilton Hotel West in Oklahoma City. Months of sorting evidence, evaluating tips and taps, and tracking the suspects are about to bear fruit. Special agents from the FBI and ATF and the top brass from state and local law enforcement agencies are assembled in the hotel conference room to complete plans.

Two days earlier, the special agent in charge in Dallas, the special agent in charge in Oklahoma City, and the ATF agent in charge of the Oklahoma operations participated in a conference call with superiors in Washington. What they likely discussed that day can be found in a document released by the FBI under the Freedom of Information Act. This document, a teletype from Director Louis Freeh, was sent to field offices and command posts in Omaha, Birmingham, Charlotte, Cincinnati, and Oklahoma City in January of 1996. The subject line includes OKBOMB and BOMBROB. These field offices, and investigations, have a common denominator. They were watching Richard Guthrie, Michael Brescia, and Pete Langan. The same memo makes references to an informant inside the compound working for the Southern Poverty Law Center, and Andreas Strassmeir's name and nickname "Andy the German" both fit perfectly within the redacted portions.

The CIA was intricately involved in activities at Elohim City, bolstered by the presence of spy satellites operated by the National Geospatial-Intelligence Agency. Elohim City was a focal point of an ongoing government initiative known as PATCON, short for Patriot Conspiracy. This program was conceived in 1991with the intent to infiltrate and monitor every militia group, neo-Nazi organization, and any collective critical of the US government. The strategy entailed placing informants within these groups, and Elohim City was a key target of these efforts.

Government operatives are aware of the impending Oklahoma City bombing and had prior knowledge of Timothy McVeigh's role in the attack. It's their conclusion that Butler and Millar are working together. The Butler connection goes all the way back to The Covenant, the Sword, and the Arm of the Lord, when they planned to blow up the Murrah Building back in '83. McVeigh and his band of bank robbers didn't mastermind anything like the Oklahoma City bombing. They needed a leader, and his name was Butler.

The taps from Robert Millar's phone detail the final plans for Oklahoma City. They listen to the recorded conversations with Strassmeir that describe the plan in minute detail. Early on there were four locations identified for bombing, all federal buildings: Dallas, Little Rock, Tulsa, and Oklahoma City.

It is only in the last few days Oklahoma City becomes the final choice.

Then, there was the bomb. Was it going to be placed in the parking garage, like in the World Trade Center attempt? Another consideration was a missile rocket, like the one aborted in 1983 when a test by the same perpetrators failed. Finally, only on Sunday this week did they learn from Strassmeir that it would be a truck bomb, most likely a rental truck. Then Monday, just before their meeting, they receive their last call from Strassmeir, saying a Ryder rental truck will arrive early Tuesday morning—the morning before Richard Snell's execution. They are now certain it is going to be the Murrah Building, but they do notify agents in the other locations to be on high alert on the morning of April 19. They do not notify the management or occupants of the Murrah, or the other federal buildings, to take precautions. They discuss the transponder, which the Kansas City office has confirmed was successfully placed on the Ryder truck. The plan is to intercept the truck just as it arrives at the Murrah Building. What they do not know, and Strassmeir does not know, is that there are two Ryder trucks, and the transponder is on the wrong one.

Still smarting from Waco and Ruby Ridge, the feds make sure there are plenty of agents at, or near, the Murrah Building, as well as other strategic locations in the area. The transponder reception equipment is in place and tested so that once the truck is within fifty miles of the city, they will track its every move. As midnight approaches, they do a final check and satisfy themselves that all is ready. Ralph Anderson, the special agent in charge of the operation, notifies headquarters in Washington that all is ready. He is reminded this must be a stunning success with no slip-ups, not even little ones.

Anderson assures the brass that he will make them proud. They even notify the press an important press conference might be quickly scheduled on Tuesday.

At Elohim City, Robert Millar is making his final plans. He wishes he could be there for the big event, but as commander in chief of the operation his job is to make sure everything proceeds as planned—as he planned. The design is brilliant, he is sure. He is convinced he has sucked the feds into a colossal, failed sting operation that will permanently destroy their reputations and initiate the final assault on the federal government. Andreas Strassmeir is the perfect patsy, really loyal to the German and US governments, successful at fooling everyone (except Millar) that he is a true terrorist, and really smart—just not as smart as Millar. Millar has been feeding him just what he wants the feds to know, then reinforcing it with information he knows has been tapped by the FBI.

Ironically, most of the information recorded by the FBI is true. That is why the feds ate it up. Only one detail is missing. Soon, but too late, they will discover it. Finally, Millar knows that when they realize how bad they failed, they will not be able to use the information from Elohim City because it will show they had prior knowledge and could have stopped the bombing—any time before April 19. *So, you want to wait till the last moment, ride in on your white horses and save the day? Well, let us see how that works for you.*

Millar smiles and looks at his watch. It will not be long now.

At exactly 4:45 a.m. on the nineteenth, the command center operator picks up a signal from the transponder on the truck. He pegs the distance at forty-six miles, the truck heading south on I-35, north of Guthrie. Minutes later a spotter at the Guthrie exit notifies the center that the Ryder truck is passing. Another forty-five minutes, and the blip steadily moves down the screen.

At 5:34 a.m., the Ryder crosses I-44 and enters the city, staying on I-35, bringing it east of downtown. Agents in plain cars, who have been stationed in the downtown area, prepare to move in if necessary. Unless they are notified otherwise, the plan is to swarm the truck just as it arrives at the Murrah. Special agents are stationed in hiding places surrounding the target. Also, there are bomb experts, in case the fuses are activated before they can reach the bombers. The truck exits on Reno Avenue and proceeds west, now twenty blocks from the Murrah.

At 5:50 a.m., the Ryder nears the intersection of Reno and Broadway, then pulls over fifty yards from the stop light. The transponder does not reveal whether the occupants step out, so there is concern the bomb may be activated there. A quick check tells the feds there are no federal targets near that area and none of their intel indicates another site in the city, so they decide to wait.

At 6:03 a.m., Andreas Strassmeir is sitting down to breakfast at a local diner in Vian, Oklahoma, not far from Elohim City. He places his order, then walks to a pay phone in a booth just outside the front door.

His government handler picks up on the first ring. “What’s up?”

“Special event has been aborted. Repeat, event aborted. Perps are onto the sting and are postponing the event. I’m not sure what the next move is but I will keep you posted as I hear. Got it?”

“Are you sure?” the handler says. “This is a big deal for the good guys.”

"Got word just twenty minutes ago from the man himself."

"Okay," the handler's voice says. "I'll relay up the line. Be sure to let me know when you hear anything at all."

"Will do." Strassmeir hangs up.

Anderson is visibly upset when the handler gives him the message. "Don't tell anyone else. Maybe the boss man gave our boy false information. We are not changing anything as long as that truck is in the area. In fact, if it doesn't go near the target in the next thirty minutes, we're going to take them, wherever they are."

At 6:15 a.m., the Ryder truck pulls away from the curb and heads toward the light. Instead of turning right, toward the Murrah Building, it turns left—headed south. The command center is confused, and the key leaders gather around Anderson. When the truck reaches I-40 it ascends the ramp and heads east on the interstate.

The Handler asks, "What now, boss? Should we go in now or wait?"

"Let me call headquarters," Anderson says, and dials the private-line number. A ten-minute discussion, then he hangs up the phone. "We think they might be headed for Little Rock. We're going to set up check points across I-40 and monitor the truck. Looks like our guy is right. You know he has worked for us and the German government for years and is considered totally reliable. They must have sniffed us out somehow. Let us hold everything for another hour, then shut down if the truck doesn't turn around. Tell the transponder boys to keep everything on until we are sure they are not coming back. And, just to make sure, have the OKC bomb squad sweep the building before the employees arrive."

At 7:10 a.m., the spotter in Shawnee reports the Ryder has just passed. The transponder receptor verifies. Some of the early-arrival employees see the bomb squad near the Murrah Building around 7:30 a.m.

"Wonder what that's about?" someone in the Social Security office says.

"Guess we'll find out when we read the paper in the morning," a co-worker responds.

67

HELL COMES TO OKLAHOMA CITY

April 19, 1995

On I-35, the real Ryder bomb truck follows the same route as the decoy, little more than an hour behind. The bomb truck, with Tim McVeigh and Mitch aboard, is followed closely by a pickup driven by Richard Guthrie. There is little conversation in the Ryder. The mood of the occupants is tense in both vehicles as each is lost in private thoughts. *Will we be caught before the bomb blows? Will it blow? If it does work, will we wind up in a shootout with the law?* It's hard to concentrate, but they know they must.

Without incident they reach downtown and proceed to an empty building in the old warehouse district, just east of the central business district. They selected this old building because it had not been used for some time, and because it had a steel door that could be secured with a padlock on the inside. It is now 6:15 a.m., and they are hoping the feds are busy with the decoy. Their hopes will be realized.

With both trucks inside, they close the rusty door and secure the lock. They synchronize their watches. McVeigh prepares the detonators and slides the fuse wires in place. All is ready. It is now a nerve-wracking wait until time to go.

AT 8:15 A.M.—FORTY-SEVEN MINUTES BEFORE THE BOMB EXPLODES

McVeigh drives the Ryder truck, with Mitch in the passenger seat, out of the warehouse. Guthrie is driving the brown pickup.

AT 8:40 A.M.—TWENTY-TWO MINUTES BEFORE THE BOMB EXPLODES

McVeigh pulls into Danny's Tires to kill a few minutes. When a man comes outside from the tire shop, McVeigh jumps from the truck to keep him from seeing the fuse that is strung from the cab to the cargo area. McVeigh then asks directions to Fifth and Harvey, though he knows the route well. After a couple of minutes, they go to the Regency Tower convenience store, across the street and down one block from the Murrah. McVeigh steps inside, leaving Mitch in the passenger side of the Ryder truck, and buys two Cokes and a pack of Marlboro Reds for Mitch.

AT 8:52 A.M.—TEN MINUTES BEFORE THE BOMBING

Guthrie pulls the brown pickup under the overhang directly in front of the entrance to the Murrah Building. Just above the overhang, on the second floor, the children in the daycare are lining up for their walk to the library. Guthrie is unaware of the nursery, but McVeigh knows the little ones are up there from his visit weeks earlier, when he cased the building.

AT 8:56 A.M.—SIX MINUTES BEFORE THE BOMBING

McVeigh pulls the Ryder Truck into the detonation position as Guthrie pulls away.

AT 9:00 A.M.—TWO MINUTES BEFORE THE BOMBING

McVeigh hands the key to the getaway car to Mitch, who is riding shotgun in the Ryder. Mitch jumps out, heading east before crossing the street, to make his way to the Mercury Marquis parked in the alley. McVeigh double-checks the setup and, satisfied that all is ready, activates the bomb. Thirty seconds later he reaches the Mercury, which is running with Mitch in the front passenger seat. They proceed north up Broadway to Fifteenth Street, where Richard Guthrie is waiting to pick up Mitch in the brown pickup.

AT 9:02 A.M.—HELL COMES TO OKLAHOMA CITY

As McVeigh reaches Twenty-third Street, eighteen blocks north of the Murrah Building, the Mercury is almost airborne from the shock of the huge blast. He does not turn around. He does not smile. He does not cry. He just heads north, as planned.

Eight blocks away, on the top level of St. Anthony Hospital's parking garage, Mahon and Langan have a clear view of the Murrah Building. The floor beneath them shakes violently as the powerful bomb blows the north face off the target, sending smoke and debris hurling through the clear April morning. As the smoke rises, they cheer as though their favorite player just hit a home run. Now blood-curdling screams are heard as torn bodies stagger through the dense smoke. Even at this distance they can see the human carnage. Stunned, they turn away. "Let's get the hell out of here," yells Mahon.

One hundred and sixty-eight innocents lost their lives. The Heartland is devastated. Hell has come to Oklahoma City.

THE END OF THE BEGINNING

10:00 A.M.—ONE HOUR AFTER THE BOMBING

"By God, he did it. Hallelujah, an eye for an eye!" screamed Richard Butler at the TV in his office.

Within minutes, the door swung open with a force that rattled the walls. Louis—tall, broad-shouldered, and imposing, his weathered face hardened by years of hate and militant rhetoric—stormed in. His eyes, cold and gleaming with a dangerous intensity, locked onto Butler as he spoke in his gravelly voice.

"Did you see that, Reverend? Never thought he had the guts, but he damn sure did."

His presence filled the room, even without words, his very being a symbol of the violent ideology he championed. The scar on his chin, the same one earned from a brutal scuffle years earlier, made his expression even more menacing. He was a leader, one of the most feared figures in the movement, a man whose name carried weight in the deepest, darkest corners of the nation.

Louis wasn't just a man; he was a symbol of chaos, a man who had long since discarded any pretense of civility. His reputation for ruthless tactics, his fiery speeches that could rally any disillusioned soul to his cause—these had earned him the respect of like-minded extremists and the terror of those who opposed him.

The word spread quickly throughout the compound, and cheers could be heard for miles as the team celebrated. They knew that Louis, like them, believed in violence as a tool for revolution. It was a world they inhabited together—a world of blood and vengeance, where loyalty to the cause was paramount, and the law was nothing more than a nuisance to be crushed beneath their boots.

Many miles and many hours away in southeastern Oklahoma, at Elohim City, similar cheers arise from the residents. In Reverend Millar's office, the "A-Team" are ecstatic. Reverend Millar himself is absent. Ironically, he is celebrating with Richard Snell, the radical who is to die later today for murdering a black Arkansas state trooper and a Jewish pawn shop worker.

As they high five, Snell wonders if Tim got away.

"They'll probably catch Tim and the others," he says.

"Do you think any of them will fold?"

"Let's say a prayer that they do not," Millar says with trepidation.

"What about Strassmeir and Howe?" says Snell.

Millar pauses for a bit and says, "My guess, they are as afraid of the feds as they are of us, and probably high-tailed it."

Across the country, in some of its most isolated areas, where militant radicals practice violent exercises on the weekends, they gather to celebrate the awesome news. To them, the bombing not only provides revenge for Waco but also signals the beginning of the second civil war, the first step toward an all-white America. They know not to contact Elohim City or Hayden Lake. Part of their training at those locations included a ban on any contact with leaders when these events occur. They must remember they are guerilla fighters, at least for now. Today the movement has taken a giant leap forward.

11:10 A.M.—TWO HOURS, EIGHT MINUTES AFTER THE BOMBING

All networks blast the news. "Timothy McVeigh, a radical from New York has been identified as a suspect in the Oklahoma City bombing. He is currently in jail in Perry, Oklahoma after being stopped by an Oklahoma trooper for a traffic violation and carrying a concealed weapon. An FBI spokesman says agents are on their way to Perry to pick him up. That is all we know at this time. We will break into our normal broadcast with further developments." Two days later the FBI will identify Terry Nichols and Michael Fortier as additional suspects. An eyewitness at the rental agency where the bomb truck was rented will identify a second suspect who was with Timothy McVeigh when he picked up the truck. The FBI has identified him only as John Doe 2."

1995—SOMETIME AFTER THE BOMBING

Robert Millar quickly "expels" Andreas Strassmeir from Elohim City, soon after he becomes aware that the FBI is looking at Strassmeir for possible ties to McVeigh and the bombing. CIA pilot Dave Holloway smuggles Andreas Strassmeir out of the United States by flying him to Mexico, where he gets a flight to Germany.

APRIL 1997—TWO YEARS AFTER THE BOMBING

McVeigh's trial is in its second week and recessed for lunch. Attorney Stephen Jones is meeting with Timothy McVeigh in his cell at the Reno, Oklahoma federal prison. He says, "Tim, we have now had a number of meetings. I have been involved in a number of criminal trials, and my experience tells me certain things about defendants. That experience and intuition tells me that you have been lying to me in saying that you are the lone bomber. It just doesn't ring true. Am I right? Can you tell me who the others are?"

Tim replies, "Would it make any difference for me?"

"Honestly, I don't think so," Jones says.

"Then I'm still the lone bomber—end of discussion."

JUNE 11, 2001—SIX YEARS AFTER THE BOMBING

Timothy McVeigh, the proud mass-murderer of scores of innocent people in Oklahoma City, is brought to the gurney that will be his death bed in a few minutes. He has just come from a meeting with a Catholic priest. We don't know if he went to confession, but he did meet with the cleric, so he might have. Now strapped to the gurney, the death drugs are released into his arm. He stares at the camera, which broadcasts the event to families of the victims and the press—a hard, vengeful stare—shudders and relaxes. He is examined and declared dead. It's over for him, his eternity settled.

NOVEMBER 9, 2006—TEN AND A HALF YEARS AFTER THE BOMBING

In the Ed Bradley studio at the CBS *60 Minutes* broadcast center on West Fifty-seventh Street in New York City, I am being fitted with equipment to accommodate my cell phone in preparation for a planned call with Terry Nichols, convicted participant in the Oklahoma City Bombing.

I've been communicating with Terry by phone and letter for the past ten years, and today, Terry is to call me and tell me the whole truth about the bombing—something I and the world have been waiting for all these years.

Ten a.m. comes and goes; he doesn't call…11, 12, 1, 2…I and the whole crew of *60 Minutes* staff waited. At two, the producer comes in and announces that Ed Bradley has succumbed to cancer just minutes ago. The staff is weeping openly. Tears form in my eyes, too, as I have been interviewed by Ed on several occasions and have great respect for him. The producer further advises that the legal department is talking to the prison in Colorado to find out what happened. At 4:30, I am told that the warden at the supermax facility cancelled my phone privileges before the call could be made, with no explanation.

My husband and I go back to the hotel, and we're devastated. I receive an unexpected call from Terry's mother. She says, "Come to my house next Sunday for my regular call with Terry. When it comes, I will hand the phone to you, and you can get your story." CBS is ecstatic. But I am not, because I believe that if that happens, Terry's mother will lose her privileges and I can't do that. CBS is upset with me, but I am at peace with myself.

The next morning, the sun comes up. In a few hours I will return to Arkansas. Life there is much quieter than in New York, but it is home and I have things to do.

I have people who love me, and life is good.

EPILOGUE

LOOKING BACK

April 19, 2025
Thirty years since the bombing

More than a quarter of a century has passed since justice denied me the privilege of aiding Mr. Timothy McVeigh on his one-way nonstop trip to hell. The day of the murders, I couldn't see beyond the sunset. I hurt so bad, I couldn't imagine living through the night. But I did, and I survived. I have lived through 10,950 nights, and now here I am, walking to the spot where the daycare once was.

I come to the memorial often, so often that most of the park rangers know me and my story.

Thirty years ago, the Murrah Building stood here, with only hours left. Thirty years ago, Edye and I were tucking the boys into their beds for the last time.

For the thirty years since the memorial opened, I have walked among the one hundred sixty-eight chairs that honor those who perished here. I walked here when the temperature was one hundred three, and when I had to brush a foot and a half of snow off the boys' chairs.

I come here every April 18, before sunset, so that I can be here at dusk when the photocells flip the switch that lights each chair. From the air, at night, the chairs look like the luminaria that line sidewalks and driveways at Christmas.

This year, I came a day early because there is something I want to do, I must do, and if I wait until tomorrow night, there will be too many people. Arriving just before dark, I start at the two eastern-most chairs. I read aloud the name inscribed in the glass base. I walk one chair to the west, call the name aloud, and move on. I work my way around the chairs, east to west, north to south. I walk the perimeter and work my way in, until, at the last, I stand in front of the chairs numbered 60 and 61, inscribed with the names of my grandsons, and say:

"Colton Wade Smith...Chase Dalton Smith."

I sit on each of the chairs for a few minutes, first on Colton's, then on Chase's. I talk to the little boys who once graced my life. I tell them about their mother, about their new brother and sister. I intentionally left behind anything that would mark the passing of time, no watch, and no phone. I sit first in one chair, then the other, frozen between nine-oh-one and nine-oh-three.

When the time is exactly right, I stand and kiss the back of Colton's chair, then the back of Chase's. I face the reflecting pool, knowing that I am standing almost exactly at the spot where the boys died. God is here now, as He was here that day too. It took me a long time to know that, and I still don't understand, but just knowing is enough.

At this spot, the boys exited that mystical door into the second most profound and mysterious moment of life, The Departure. I remove my shoes and put one on each chair. I recite my version of the Twenty-Third Psalm, which has evolved over the years.

The Lord is my shepherd; I lack nothing.

"He is with me in the face of evil and protects me from those who wish me harm.

He restores my soul and delivers me from the pit of despair.

Even though I walk through the darkest valley I will fear no evil: for the Lord is with me; he comforts me in the storm and protects me from all evil.

He prepares a table before me in the presence of my enemies: His anointing soothes my soul.

Surely goodness and mercy will follow me all the days of my life and I will dwell in the house of the Lord forever, with the two little boys lost so long ago.

This is my yearly ritual, and after I pray, I scan the sky for a sign that never comes.

I'm still, except for my red hair, which flutters across my face in the Oklahoma wind. I have somehow survived more than a quarter century. Thirty years have passed at a pace I wouldn't have predicted in those early days, when I was hoping that Tim McVeigh and I both would die. Now, I am not dead, and he is.

The first time I took this walk, which always ends at these two chairs, I didn't plan to make it annual. But 2001 came, then 2002, and I showed up, one year after another. On this thirtieth anniversary, as I sit on one chair and then the other, and the chilled wind raises small bumps on my skin, I think this may be the last year. Are thirty years enough? I will find out soon enough. Would this be the last act or the first act of a new ritual?

I leave the chairs and walk thirty steps to the edge of the reflecting pool.

I know this, on the thirtieth anniversary, I can't simply pray and walk away. Over these thirty years, I have lost any vestige of innocence about life on earth. I have learned that some people really are evil, and that even good people, including me, are capable of some awful things. For these thirty years, I have clawed at the veil that has hidden the truth, until the tattered shroud hung like a rotten curtain. It has allowed only enough light through for me to see the truth, at least a form of the truth, enough for me to persuade the right people that I was right, that Timothy McVeigh did not kill alone. So now, I wonder: can I move on?

The reflecting pool stretches east and west in exactly the place that once had been Northwest Fifth. The east-end gate reads 9:01 a.m., the minute before the bomb went off. The west-end gate reads 9:03 a.m.. The distance of the minute between them is one city block. Everything that happened in this one city block has changed my life and that of thousands of others. At this moment, I am standing on the very spot where Timothy McVeigh parked his truck and lit the fuse.

I walk the perimeter of the pool, which reflects the lights of the buildings that surround the memorial. I walk to the water's edge and put my right foot into the water, and it barely covers the top of my bare foot. I put in my left foot and stop. Then, taking small steps, I walk to the middle of the pool. I turn to my left, face west, and sit down, my arms wrapped around my knees. I then straighten my legs, lay them flat against the granite, and I lie down. The water soaks my shirt, and my hair floats like red moss in a stream, and I close my eyes. My shirt and pants wick the chilly water and I shiver.

The water, like my life, moves more quickly than I would have imagined, and I lie there with the cold water running past me until my clothes are drenched. I see the boys' faces and imagine that amazing moment at 9:02 a.m., April 19, 1995, when 168 souls, my boys among them, rose en masse from this spot.

As the last soul in my vision ascends, a park ranger kneels beside me, gently shaking my shoulder. I open my eyes to the illuminating lights in the chairs, the crescent moon still hanging in the sky.

"Mrs. Sanders, you need to leave now, before the news crews start arriving. I'm sure you don't want people seeing you like this."

I sit up, and the ranger stands alongside me, gently grasping my left elbow. I look into his face and point to the west gate.

"Yes, ma'am," he said, understanding that's where I want to go.

I walk west in the water, as if fording a shallow stream, the baptismal waters dripping from my hair and down my back, trailing into the pool.

I walk, not looking over my shoulder to the east, and step out of the pool and onto the dry sidewalk. I stop and lean back so that I can clearly see the numbers at the top of the west gate. Outside of this hallowed place, I have a new life; a loving husband, a large, blended family with new grandchildren; more happiness than I could ever hope for. But part of me will stay here always.

I look back one more time and then I continue into the cool night air.

APPENDICES

Jennifer McVeigh's signed confession to the FBI dated May 2, 1995

holding a garage sale at the residence. My brother and I had a conversation in the kitchen, as I believe there were other persons present at the residence in connection with the sale. At that time he advised me as follows:

He had been involved in a bank robbery but did not provide any further details concerning this robbery. He advised me that he had not actually participated in the robbery itself, but was somehow involved in the planning or setting up of this robbery. Although he did not identify the participants by name, he stated that "they" had committed the robbery. His purpose for relating this information to me was to request that I exchange some of my own money for what I recall to be approximately three (3) $100 bills. He explained that this money was from the bank robbery and he wished to circulate this money through me. To the best of my recollection, I then gave my brother what I recall to be approximately $300.00 of my personal cash, in exchange for three (3) $100 bills, which I deposited within the next several days in an account at the Unit #1 Federal Credit Union, Lockport, New York. I cannot recall if this money was deposited into a checking or savings account. I do recall that the deposit amount was for more than what had been provided to me by my brother. I believe the total deposit may have been for approximately $500.00.

I observed at that time that my brother had on his person an undetermined quantity of $100 bills, of which he

5

Jennifer McVeigh's signed confession to the FBI dated May 2, 1995, continued

JM provided me a small portion. I do not recall anything significant about the bills he provided to me. I cannot estimate the total amount or number of bills he had in his possession, but it is my recollection or opinion that these were all $100 bills. He retained the rest of the bills and I do not know the ultimate disposition of those bills.

It was my belief that this bank robbery had occurred within the recent past. I was not made aware of any of the details, or if there were additional robberies involving my brother or any of his associates. I do recall that my brother remarked that the money he had in his possession represented his share of the bank robbery proceeds.

The next matter my brother discussed with me occurred during this same time period. I recall that I was at my residence with my brother when I saw what I would best describe as a very angry look on his face. I had never seen such a look before, and asked him what was wrong. He was extremely angry and upset and told me to leave him alone. I did not pursue this matter at that time. I would better categorize his level of anger as "fuming."

A day or so later, my brother asked me to help move a bed from our grandfather's house to my residence. I met him at our grandfather's house and at that time he explained to me the reason for his anger during the previously described incident. He then informed me as follows: JM

6

May 4, 1995 FBI teletype which refers to the Midwest Bank Robbers/Aryan Republic Army as "McVeigh and His Associates"

174A-OC-56120 Lead Control #04467
TPR:tpr

The following investigation was conducted on May 4, 1995, at San Francisco, California, by Special Agent (SA) THOMAS P. RAVENELLE:

Reference Bureau teletypes to all field offices dated 4/27/95, and 5/1/95.

Referenced Bureau teletypes directed all field offices to review bank robbery files and compare methods of operations (mo's) to mo's outlined in the teletype dated 4/27/95, which are believed to have been used by subject MCVEIGH and his associates.

San Francisco reviewed bank robbery files dating back to 1/1/94, and only located five bank robberies wherein a hoax explosive device was used and all five of these bank robberies occurred between September and December of 1994. PAUL ROBERT FRANKS was arrested for the five robberies, and during the subsequent interview he admitted to acting alone. FRANKS advised that his robberies only began after his wife left him for her lesbian lover. FRANKS has been convicted and is to be sentenced soon. He received approximately sixty to seventy thousand dollars as a result of these robberies.

The San Francisco case agent for these five bank robberies was involved in the interview of FRANKS and that agent is confident that FRANKS acted alone and is in no way connected to the subjects of the Oklahoma City bombing or any militia group. FRANKS' bank robberies occurred in and around Santa Cruz and San Jose, California, and he has been a long time resident of Santa Cruz.

San Francisco was unable to find any other bank robberies with a similar mo as described in the referenced teletype.

E-4206

174A-OC-56120-E-4206

FBI report showing that the FBI crime lab compared the BOMBROB bank robbery fingerprints to Timothy McVeigh's fingerprints on May 4, 1995

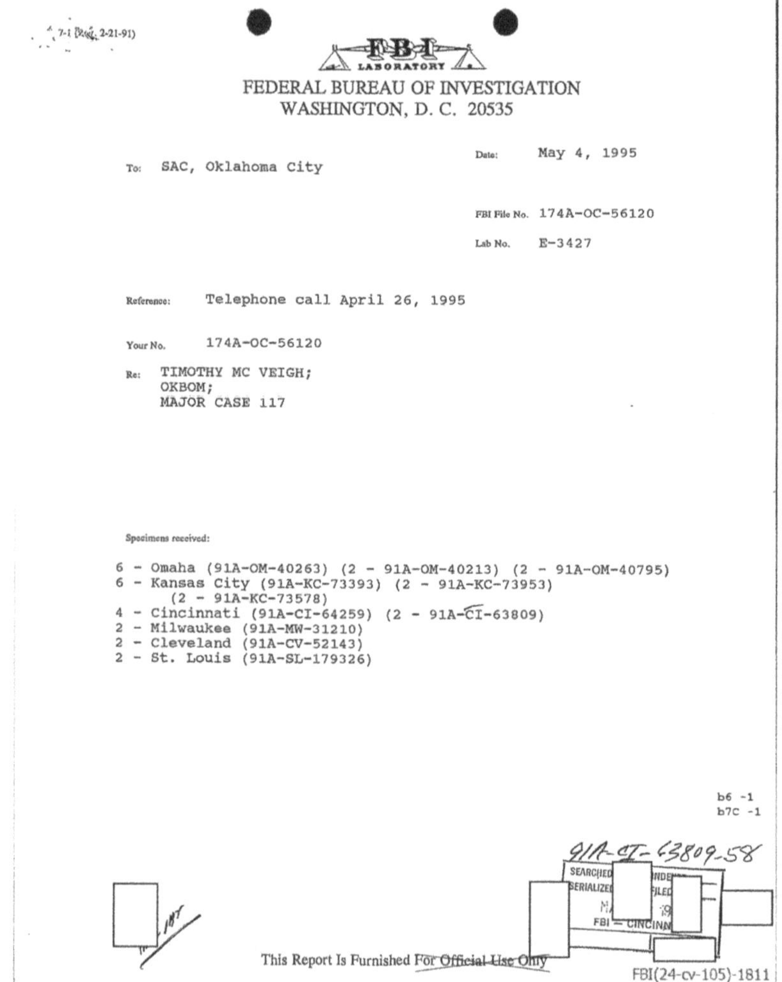

7-1 (Rev. 2-21-91)

FBI LABORATORY

FEDERAL BUREAU OF INVESTIGATION
WASHINGTON, D. C. 20535

To: SAC, Oklahoma City

Date: May 4, 1995

FBI File No. 174A-OC-56120

Lab No. E-3427

Reference: Telephone call April 26, 1995

Your No. 174A-OC-56120

Re: TIMOTHY MC VEIGH;
OKBOM;
MAJOR CASE 117

Specimens received:

6 - Omaha (91A-OM-40263) (2 - 91A-OM-40213) (2 - 91A-OM-40795)
6 - Kansas City (91A-KC-73393) (2 - 91A-KC-73953) (2 - 91A-KC-73578)
4 - Cincinnati (91A-CI-64259) (2 - 91A-CI-63809)
2 - Milwaukee (91A-MW-31210)
2 - Cleveland (91A-CV-52143)
2 - St. Louis (91A-SL-179326)

b6 -1
b7C -1

91A-CI-63809-58

SEARCHED INDEXED
SERIALIZED FILED
FBI — CINCINNATI

This Report Is Furnished ~~For Official Use Only~~

FBI(24-cv-105)-1811

FBI report showing that the FBI crime lab compared the BOMBROB bank robbery fingerprints to Timothy McVeigh's fingerprints on May 4, 1995

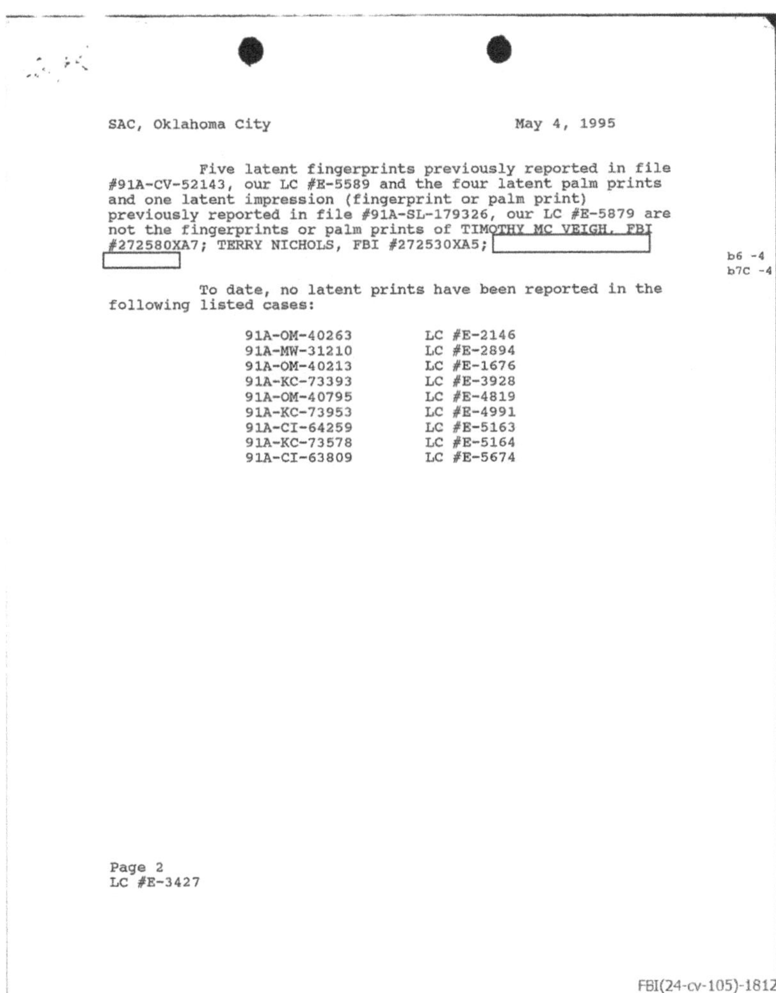

SAC, Oklahoma City May 4, 1995

Five latent fingerprints previously reported in file #91A-CV-52143, our LC #E-5589 and the four latent palm prints and one latent impression (fingerprint or palm print) previously reported in file #91A-SL-179326, our LC #E-5879 are not the fingerprints or palm prints of TIMOTHY MC VEIGH, FBI #272580XA7; TERRY NICHOLS, FBI #272530XA5; [redacted] [redacted]

b6 -4
b7C -4

To date, no latent prints have been reported in the following listed cases:

91A-OM-40263	LC #E-2146
91A-MW-31210	LC #E-2894
91A-OM-40213	LC #E-1676
91A-KC-73393	LC #E-3928
91A-OM-40795	LC #E-4819
91A-KC-73953	LC #E-4991
91A-CI-64259	LC #E-5163
91A-KC-73578	LC #E-5164
91A-CI-63809	LC #E-5674

Page 2
LC #E-3427

FBI(24-cv-105)-1812

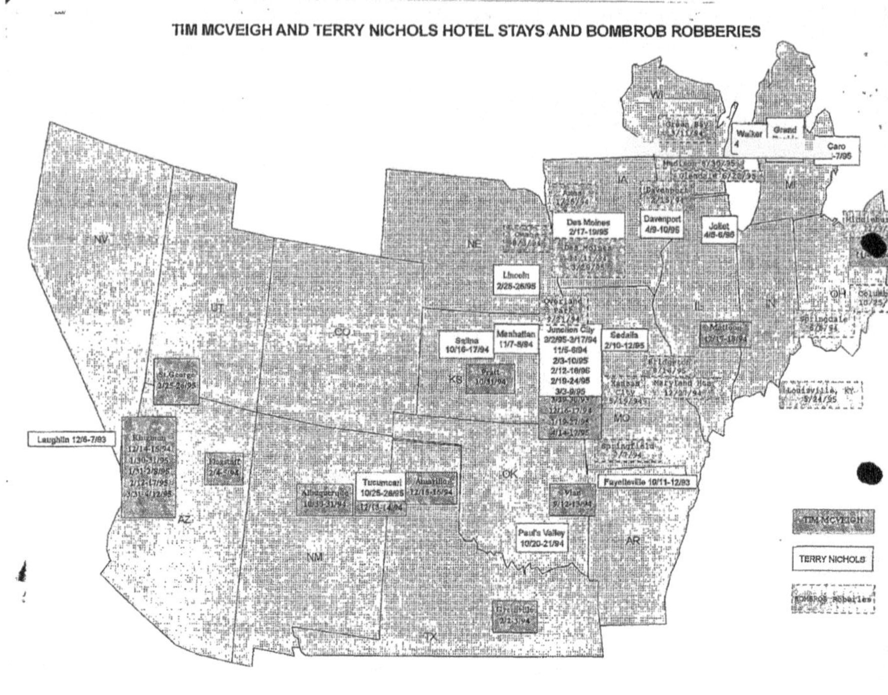
TIM MCVEIGH AND TERRY NICHOLS HOTEL STAYS AND BOMBROB ROBBERIES
NV
UT
CO
NE
KS
IA
WI
MI
IL
IN
OH
MO
OK
AR
AZ
NM
TX
St George 2/25-26/95
Laughlin 12/6-7/93
Kingman 12/14-15/94 1/30-31/95 1/31-2/8/95 2/12-17/95 3/31-4/12/95
Flagstaff 2/4-5/94
Albuquerque 10/30-31/94
Tucumcari 10/25-26/95 12/13-14/94
Amarillo 12/15-16/94
Green Bay
Walker
Grand
Caro
Des Moines 2/17-19/95
Davenport 4/9-10/95
Joliet 4/5-6/95
Lincoln 2/25-26/95
Overland Park 9/21/94
Salina 10/16-17/94
Manhattan 11/7-8/94
Junction City 3/2/95-3/17/94 11/5-6/94 2/3-10/95 2/12-16/95 2/19-24/95 3/3-9/95
Sedalia 2/10-12/95
Pratt 10/31/94
Mattoon
Louisville, KY 5/24/95
Fayetteville 10/11-12/93
Paul's Valley 10/20-21/94
TIM MCVEIGH
TERRY NICHOLS

On January 4, 1996, FBI Director Louis Freeh sent a four-page teletype to the OKBOMB command post in Oklahoma City and copied FBI field offices participating in the BOMBROB (bank robbery) investigation

This teletype is significant because it reveals the Southern Poverty Law Center had an informant at Elohim City and that Timothy McVeigh placed phone calls to Elohim City on April 5th and April 17th to a recipient who was later confirmed by Robert Millar to be Andreas Strassmeir. The memo says this person "allegedly has had a lengthy relationship with Timothy McVeigh."

Additional contextual clues in the document make it easy to discern that the redacted name must be Andreas Strassmeir.

Reproduced below are pages four and five of the teletype as they appear in the redacted copy.

The following page shows what the redacted portions may be, based on an analysis of the monospace font used and the contextual clues.

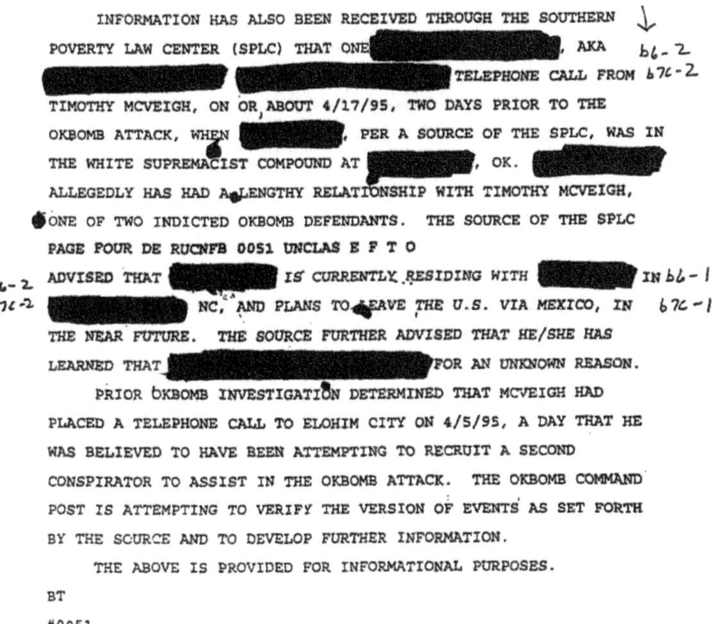

INFORMATION HAS ALSO BEEN RECEIVED THROUGH THE SOUTHERN POVERTY LAW CENTER (SPLC) THAT ONE , AKA TELEPHONE CALL FROM TIMOTHY MCVEIGH, ON OR ABOUT 4/17/95, TWO DAYS PRIOR TO THE OKBOMB ATTACK, WHEN , PER A SOURCE OF THE SPLC, WAS IN THE WHITE SUPREMACIST COMPOUND AT , OK. ALLEGEDLY HAS HAD A LENGTHY RELATIONSHIP WITH TIMOTHY MCVEIGH, ONE OF TWO INDICTED OKBOMB DEFENDANTS. THE SOURCE OF THE SPLC

PAGE FOUR DE RUCNFB 0051 UNCLAS E F T O

ADVISED THAT IS CURRENTLY RESIDING WITH IN NC, AND PLANS TO LEAVE THE U.S. VIA MEXICO, IN THE NEAR FUTURE. THE SOURCE FURTHER ADVISED THAT HE/SHE HAS LEARNED THAT FOR AN UNKNOWN REASON.

PRIOR OKBOMB INVESTIGATION DETERMINED THAT MCVEIGH HAD PLACED A TELEPHONE CALL TO ELOHIM CITY ON 4/5/95, A DAY THAT HE WAS BELIEVED TO HAVE BEEN ATTEMPTING TO RECRUIT A SECOND CONSPIRATOR TO ASSIST IN THE OKBOMB ATTACK. THE OKBOMB COMMAND POST IS ATTEMPTING TO VERIFY THE VERSION OF EVENTS AS SET FORTH BY THE SOURCE AND TO DEVELOP FURTHER INFORMATION.

THE ABOVE IS PROVIDED FOR INFORMATIONAL PURPOSES.

BT

#0051

INFORMATION HAS ALSO BEEN RECEIVED THROUGH THE SOUTHERN POVERTY LAW CENTER (SPLC) THAT ONE ANDREAS STRASSMEIR, AKA "ANDI THE GERMAN" [redacted] TELEPHONE CALL FROM TIMOTHY MCVEIGH, ON OR ABOUT 4/17/95, TWO DAYS PRIOR TO THE OKBOMB ATTACK, WHEN STRASSMEIR, PER A SOURCE OF THE SPLC, WAS IN THE WHITE SUPREMACIST COMPOUND AT ELOHIM CITY, OK. STRASSMEIR ALLEGEDLY HAS HAD A LENGTHY RELATIONSHIP WITH TIMOTHY MCVEIGH, ONE OF TWO INDICTED OKBOMB DEFENDANTS. THE SOURCE OF THE SPLC

PAGE FOUR DE RUCNFB 0051 UNCLAS E F T O

ADVISED THAT STRASSMEIR IS CURRENTLY RESIDING WITH KIRK LYONS IN BLACK MOUNTAIN NC, AND PLANS TO LEAVE THE U.S. VIA MEXICO, IN THE NEAR FUTURE. THE SOURCE FURTHER ADVISED THAT HE/SHE HAS LEARNED THAT STRASSMEIR LEFT ELOHIM CITY FOR AN UNKNOWN REASON.

PRIOR OKBOMB INVESTIGATION DETERMINED THAT MCVEIGH HAD PLACED A TELEPHONE CALL TO ELOHIM CITY ON 4/5/95, A DAY THAT HE WAS BELIEVED TO HAVE BEEN ATTEMPTING TO RECRUIT A SECOND CONSPIRATOR TO ASSIST IN THE OKBOMB ATTACK. THE OKBOMB COMMAND POST IS ATTEMPTING TO VERIFY THE VERSION OF EVENTS AS SET FORTH BY THE SOURCE AND TO DEVELOP FURTHER INFORMATION.

THE ABOVE IS PROVIDED FOR INFORMATIONAL PURPOSES.

BT

#0051

Excerpt from an ATF document—dated before the bombing—which says Andreas Strassmeir "plans to act to destroy the US government with direct actions and operations such as assassinations, bombings, and mass shootings"

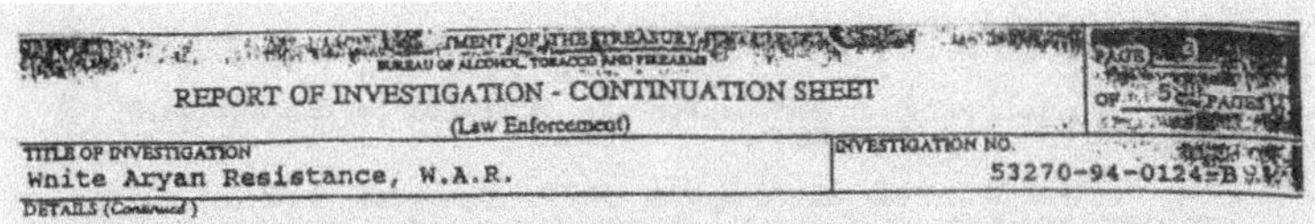

...MENT OF THE TREASURY
BUREAU OF ALCOHOL, TOBACCO AND FIREARMS
REPORT OF INVESTIGATION - CONTINUATION SHEET
(Law Enforcement)

PAGE ... OF 5 PAGES

TITLE OF INVESTIGATION
White Aryan Resistance, W.A.R.

INVESTIGATION NO.
53270-94-0124-B...

DETAILS (Continued)

could convert an SKS to full auto using a piece from a food can. Andy leads the young adults in guerrilla warfare and tactical maneuvers training on Sunday afternoons. This training is done discreetly and CI-183 is excluded from participating. Andy said that he spends 96% of his money on weapons and military supplies. He helps to outfit others with firearms and equipment.

The security uniforms are a dark blue t-shirt with "SECURITY OFFICER" in yellow on the back and a shield or badge on the left breast. They also wear black jeans or fatigues and combat boots.

Andy stated that he was involved with CSA, the Covenant, Sword and Arm of the Lord. He was born in 1959 and served in the West German military starting in 1979. He was an infantry officer. His plans are to forcibly act to destroy the U.S. Government with direct actions and operations such as assassinations, bombings and mass shootings. He believes the biggest enemy to be the United States Government (ZOG).

Andy stated that when someone comes to EC and does not work out, fit in or is found to be a snitch, he and his security team have the capability of making their lives hell on the outside. They will beat people, sabotage them financially, ruin their reputation or do whatever they can unless they get the word from Millar to cease action.

Andy stated that he is in charge of all applicant background checks and has connections all over the world. He would not check 183 due to the fact that he/she had already been screened by Mahon.

Most of the weapons are stored at Andy's house. There are approximately 25-30 ammo cans full of ammo and grenade casings on shelves. It is not known the type of ammunition or if the grenades are destructive devices.

Every Saturday is the "Sabbath" and the people have worship for approximately four hours. During this time, Andy walks in and out of the church building searching for people who have left the meeting then he brings them back to the meeting.

There is a curfew every night at 9:00p.m. for all the people in school and 10:00p.m. for everyone else. The curfew is enforced and people must be in their homes by this time. This is the time that Andy closes and locks the gates. Around 12:00a.m. he and the other security officers patrol the perimeter.

People arise each day, except Saturday around 4:00a.m.. Men begin working around 6:00a.m. and children start school at 5:45a.m.. School ends at 4:30p.m.. Everyday the people have a meeting and worship at 11:30am and it lasts from one hour and a half to two hours. Most people attend the meeting, even if they work away from EC.

Undated May 1995 FBI Memo Discloses FBI Command Post Has Stopped Accepting John Doe #2 Leads

174A-OC-56120
TPR:tpr

The following investigation was conducted by Special Agent (SA) THOMAS P. RAVENELLE:

Columbia airtel dated May 3, 1995, identified RICHARD DEHART, DOB 6/21/65, as a Phoenix resident and a possible look-alike for unsub #2 regarding captioned matter.

Phoenix determined a recent address for DEHART, but could not locate him. Phoenix directed San Francisco to attempt to contact the landlord for DEHART'S apartment to determine his whereabouts.

San Francisco made numerous attempts to locate the landlord, ERNEST C. RENO, with negative results.

In view of the fact that the Oklahoma Command Post has directed all offices to hold unsub #2 leads in abeyance, San Francisco will conduct no further investigation regarding this lead.

Reference lead #10,220:

Referenced lead #10,220, San Francisco was directed to locate and interview LESTER SCANLON concerning his knowledge of STEVEN COLBERN. In view of the fact that COLBERN has been eliminated as a suspect in this matter, San Francisco will conduct no further investigation concerning lead #10,220.

E-4153

174A-OC-56120.

McVeigh traffic ticket, issued just months before the Oklahoma City bombing, raises chilling questions: what was a man from New York doing deep in the remote hills of southeastern Oklahoma only a few miles from Elohim City?

UNIFORM TRAFFIC TICKET AND COMPLAINT

PAGE No.

CASE No. DOCKET No.

ARKANSAS STATE POLICE

No. F 735922

COUNTY OF

COMPLAINT AFFIDAVIT

CITY OF

THE UNDERSIGNED, BEING DULY SWORN, UPON HIS OATH DEPOSES AND SAYS

ON THE DAY OF 19 AT A.M. P.M.

NAME (PLEASE PRINT) FIRST INITIAL

STREET

CITY - STATE

AGE BIRTH DATE RACE SEX HT. WT.

DRIV. LIC. No. DID UNLAWFULLY (PARK) (OPERATE)

VEH. LIC. No. NUMBER STATE YR. MAKE

UPON A PUBLIC HIGHWAY, NAMELY AT (LOCATION)

EMPLOYED BY

Leading Causes of Accidents

SPEEDING (over limit) (m.p.h. in m.p.h. zone) — 5 - 10 m.p.h. — 11 - 15 m.p.h. — over 15 m.p.h.

Improper LEFT TURN — No signal — Cut corner — From wrong lane

Improper RIGHT TURN — No signal — Into wrong lane — From wrong lane

Disobeyed TRAFFIC SIGNAL (When light turned red) — Past middle intersection — Middle of Intersection — Not reached intersection — Radar

Disobeyed STOP SIGN — Wrong place — Walk speed — Faster

Improper PASSING AND LANE USAGE — At intersection — Cut in — Wrong Side of pavement — Between Traffic — On right — On hill — Lane Straddling — Wrong lane — On curve

OTHER VIOLATIONS

IN VIOLATION OF SEC.

Conditions that Increased Seriousness of Violation

SLIPPERY PAVEMENT — Rain — Snow — Ice

CAUSED PERSON TO DODGE — Pedestrian — Driver

TYPE ACCIDENT — PD — PI — FATAL — Ped — Vehicle — Hit Fixed Object — Right Angle — Head on — Sideswipe — Rear end — Ran off Roadway — Intersection

DARKNESS — Night — Fog — Snow

JUST MISSED ACCIDENT

OTHER TRAFFIC PRESENT — Cross — Oncoming — Pedestrian — Same direction

AREA: — Business — Industrial — School — Residential — Rural

HIGHWAY TYPE — 2 lane — 3 lane — 4 lane — 4 lane divided

NAME LAST FIRST INITIAL

DO NOT WRITE IN THIS SPACE

"You may present this ticket to the ______ any time before the court appearance date and time shown below."

COURT APPEARANCE DAY OF 19 AT M.

ADDRESS OF COURT

I PROMISE TO APPEAR IN SAID COURT OR BUREAU AT SAID TIME AND PLACE

SIGNATURE

The undersigned further states that he has just and reasonable grounds to believe, and does believe, that the person named above committed the offense herein set forth, contrary to law.

SWORN TO AND SUBSCRIBED BEFORE ME

THIS DAY OF

(Signature and identification of officer or other complainant)

(Badge No.)

(Name and title)

F 735922

ACKNOWLEDGMENTS

A special thanks to my friends Jay Grelen and Cindy Norlin for making this book possible.

ABOUT THE AUTHOR

Kathy Sanders's life was forever changed on April 19, 1995, when a bomb destroyed the Alfred P. Murrah Federal Building, killing her two young grandsons and 166 others. Devastated, Kathy embarked on a courageous search for answers, determined to understand why this tragedy happened. Refusing to accept official explanations alone, she launched her own investigation, appearing in national media to demand answers and uncovering key details through independent research.

Her pursuit even led her to connect with the families of the convicted bombers, Timothy McVeigh and Terry Nichols, ultimately meeting Nichols himself. Kathy's journey to find the truth brought her national attention on programs like *Good Morning America*, *Dateline NBC*, and *20/20*. Her story is a powerful testament to resilience, showing how a relentless search for truth can bring understanding, even in the face of unimaginable loss.

In 2003, Kathy remarried and began a new chapter of life with her husband, Tom, on the shores of a serene and beautiful lake. Together, they share a loving, blended family of six children and thirteen cherished grandchildren, with two precious little ones waiting for them in heaven.

Kathy is a woman of many talents and passions. An accomplished artist, her works reflect the depth of her creativity and love for beauty. As a sought-after public speaker, she inspires audiences with her warmth, wisdom, and life experiences. In the kitchen, she is a true gourmet, delighting family and friends with her culinary masterpieces.

Through her art, her words, and her cooking, Kathy celebrates the richness of life, family, and faith.

www.ingramcontent.com/pod-product-compliance
Ingram Content Group UK Ltd.
Pitfield, Milton Keynes, MK11 3LW, UK
UKHW021651190726
13853UKWH00001B/205